"God has been speaking through dreams and visions for generations and promises to pour out His Spirit in the Last Days. What will that look like? How can we know? Laura Harris Smith has done our homework for us. This book is a must-read for the hour we live in!"

Terry Meeuwsen, co-host, *The 700 Club*

"I am so glad that my friend Laura has written this eye-opening book about a subject that intrigues me and that the Church should not ignore."

Mac Powell, lead singer, Third Day

"Laura has a passion to pray, communicate, converse and simply listen with expectancy. Her gentle spirit is evident, and I'm a blessed man to have seen and experienced God's heart in a very practical and biblical way in Laura—with passion."

Kerry Woo, former regional director, Promise Keepers

"Laura's character is defined by integrity, commitment, consistency and quality; she's a gifted writer and talent. Laura has touched so many lives, and I highly recommend this book for anyone seeking an authentic relationship with God."

John Niec, producer, JTV; former producer, Shop at Home TV, HSN and QVC

"This book is a unique treasure. *Seeing the Voice of God* reveals how to unlock the answers you've needed to life's most pressing issues even while you sleep! Just think, all that time at night that you thought was only good to rest your body is actually His gift to you to reveal mysteries. It is well-researched and deeply scriptural. You can use it both in your personal life and as a manual to teach and train. I love this book!"

Cindy Jacobs, Generals International

SEEING
THE VOICE
OF GOD

SEEING THE VOICE OF GOD

*What God Is Telling You
through Dreams and Visions*

LAURA HARRIS SMITH

Chosen

a division of Baker Publishing Group
Minneapolis, Minnesota

© 2014 by Laura Harris Smith

Published by Chosen Books
11400 Hampshire Avenue South
Bloomington, Minnesota 55438
www.chosenbooks.com

Chosen Books is a division of
Baker Publishing Group, Grand Rapids, Michigan

Printed in the United States of America

Library of Congress Cataloging-in-Publication Data
Smith, Laura Harris.
    Seeing the voice of God : what God is telling you through dreams and visions / Laura Harris Smith ; foreword by James W. Goll.
        pages cm
    Includes bibliographical references.
    Summary: "Discover what your dreams are telling you with this personal guide to hearing God through dreams and visions from prophetic leader Laura Harris Smith"—Provided by publisher.
    ISBN 978-0-8007-9568-9 (pbk. : alk. paper)
    1. Dreams—Religious aspects—Christianity. 2. Visions. I. Title.
BR115.D74S58 2014
248.2′9—dc23   2013032768

Cover design by Lookout Design, Inc.

14 15 16 17 18 19 20   7 6 5 4

For Sheila, who smiled and listened
to everything I first saw.

Contents

Eye-Yai-Yai
What Say You?

Foreword

I am constantly on the search for next-generation voices that carry content full of the Word of God, walk in the present-day anointing of the Holy Spirit and have character to carry the gift. One of these leaders is Laura Harris Smith. She is a godly woman with her priorities straight.

Living in the Nashville region now for the past several years, I have become a friend and adviser to Eastgate Creative Christian Fellowship, which Chris and Laura Smith co-lead. It is a passionate, Spirit-filled church cultivating the arts as an expression of the faith. I shout a loud AMEN to that!

Balance with an Edge

Seeing the Voice of God is a prophetic, progressive book with a cutting edge of truth, yet filled with so much Scripture and life experience that it is uniquely balanced as well. So I call this book "balance with an edge."

Looking for a source that is biblically centered? Looking for an author who lives her message? Looking to be stretched out of your present comfort zone into new light of the Holy Spirit?

Then look no further. You are holding a balanced book with a sharp edge.

Impartation

If you want to grow in the area of dreams and visions, the gifts of the Holy Spirit and especially discerning of spirits, then your wait is over. Listening, waiting and watching are keys to growth in the things of the Holy Spirit.

The following Scripture exemplifies the content in this book:

> For from days of old they *have not heard* or perceived by ear, nor has the eye seen a God besides You, who acts in behalf of the one who waits for Him.
>
> Isaiah 64:4 NASB,
> emphasis added

Notice the emphasis in this great Word. Eyes . . . ears . . . are all filled with the revelation of the Holy Spirit. After all, God acts on behalf of the one who waits for Him! Impartation happens when we cooperate with His ways! God acts on behalf of the one. . . . Who is that one?

God is an equal opportunity employer. That one He acts on behalf of can be you. Yes, you can come into a new level of activity of the Holy Spirit!

Fruit That Remains!

The thing I know for sure is that Laura Harris Smith wants to see fruit that remains to the glory of God! Learn the hindrances and move forward with keys to greater growth.

From a deep place of esteem, it is my great honor to commend to you the life, ministry and now writings of Laura Harris

Smith. May your eyes see and may your ears hear the Word of the Lord for such a time as this.

Dr. James W. Goll, director,
Encounters Network and Prayer Storm;
author, *The Seer*, *Dream Language*, *The Lifestyle of a Prophet*,
The Coming Israel Awakening and many others

1

Is God Ever Silent?

It was early 1997, and I had a choice to make and about ten seconds in which to make it. I was in North Carolina at Chimney Rock State Park near Asheville, and my hike up to the top of Hickory Nut Falls had temporarily separated me from the rest of the pack when I had decided to dart into a small, recessed, craggy cave. But it was not just any cave. It was the famous cave behind the 404-foot waterfall featured in the final minutes of the 1992 epic film *The Last of the Mohicans*, the cave that the entire all-star cast filed into to hide, resulting in a heart-stopping escape that required jumping through the falls from the backside and plummeting into the river below.

I stood there looking at the backside of the waterfall, which was about 15 feet in front of me, and within seconds I was damp from the deafening mist. There was no guard rail, no attendant and most dangerously, none of my family standing there telling me not to go for it (the way they do when I express my desire to go skydiving). I could not believe the peace and fearlessness I felt. It was not as if I did not know where

I would land, because just before heading up the mountain, I passed right by it.

All of a sudden, it was not 404 feet in my mind, but just 5 seconds. Tops. So that I could get a running start, I backed up a few feet, and without a moment's hesitation, I was off. I do not even remember hitting the wall of water. Just the fall. Arms and legs flailing, it felt like 5 minutes of free fall, not 5 seconds, but the rush was indescribable! And then it happened. What I wish had not. I woke up.

But just before I did, on the way down in the dream, I had heard a booming voice say, "You are going to have a great fall." It is actually what jolted me awake, not the cold river itself, which I never reached. I sat up in bed with a gasp and immediately shook Chris, my levelheaded husband. Foregoing the cinematic details, I told him about the booming voice in the waterfall, which gave new meaning to John the Revelator's words, "His voice was like the sound of many waters" (Revelation 1:15 NASB). Fearfully, I repeated what I had heard: "You are going to have a great fall."

Without even opening his eyes, Chris calmly said, "Autumn, Laura. You're going to have a great autumn." Then he rolled over and went back to sleep. That precise interpretation instantly took me back to the misty peace and fearlessness I had felt just before my leap of faith about 5 seconds and 404 feet before.

It was indeed a great fall that year, and knowing it was coming made the hard summer more tolerable as autumn began to unfold play-by-play following that riveting dream. The adrenalized leap of faith I had experienced at the waterfall (which I later discovered integrated a man-made set in the movie for internal cutaway shots to the cave scenes) perfectly mirrored the plunge we had taken about a month before the dream, when Chris had made the decision to leave his corporate job after a successful, nearly two-decade music career in the Christian record industry. The emotions of the jump were the same as in the dream: peace and fearlessness on the front end and giddy terror immediately following. God had told us to trust Him and jump, but counting all the additional perks and public opportunities (like TV appearances) that came with his job, it meant going from a six-digit income to zero overnight.

Not to mention that we had five children, the sixth being born during our free fall.

I start with that waterfall dream because it is a classic prophetic dream. Vivid during, stirring afterward and just plain ole pesky. Whether it is an encouragement, a warning, apocalyptic in nature or just giving practical life direction, a prophetic dream has a "gnawing drawing." You cannot shake it. We will discuss the various types of prophetic dreams in chapters 2 and 3, but the most important thing to remember is that they are invitations. The Holy Spirit Himself is handing you a written invitation to seek Him. For interpretation. For application. For motivation.

> Just as light can eventually produce sound, a true prophetic illumination during the night will talk to you all day long.

Just as light can eventually produce sound,[1] a true prophetic illumination during the night will talk to you all day long.

I call my waterfall dream a prophetic dream, but before we delve further into exactly what that means, let me just say this about personal dreaming: One of the standard definitions when discussing prophecy or prophets in the Hebrew language is the word *nabi*, whose Arabic root word, *naba*, means "to announce." Thus, a personal prophetic dream is merely God announcing something He is hoping to do through, for or to you.

After trudging through a financially trying summer, I decided to start my "great fall" (the autumn of 1997) off right in anticipation of God's promise in my waterfall dream. We felt He had directed us to start a Christian management company with a vast artisan roster. Not just musicians, but also actors, artists, dancers and more, and while we already had one solid artist generating revenue, it was not enough to feed our huge family. We wondered why God was not speaking and telling us what else to do. Were our ears clogged? Was He playing hide-and-seek?

I started noticing swarms of Christian books being published on what to do when God is silent. It really started the wheels turning in my head. Was God truly ever silent? Who wants to serve a God who will not talk to them? Did He really see me down here begging for answers and just turn His head and ignore me? If so, I had to figure out why. If not, then all these books on a muted God had to deeply sadden Him. I had to know.

Five Days

More than 5 percent of the world's population is deaf or has disabling hearing loss—an estimated 360 million people.[2] But ask any Christian, and 100 percent of us will admit to experiencing disabling spiritual deafness, a much more startling figure. Undoubtedly, you have experienced seasons when the heavens were bronze and God seemed silent. These seasons are dangerous to the heart because they can cause it to wander and waver. That is exactly where I was headed. Proverbs 13:12 (NIV) says it best: "Hope deferred makes the heart sick, but a longing fulfilled is a tree of life." Finally, while praying one day, I heard God's voice! But He spoke the most random phrase that had nothing to do with the answers I needed. I heard, "Five days."

All at once—and I do mean all at once—this plan just laid itself out in front of me, accompanying the random phrase. I felt God saying that I was somehow going to read the Bible in five days, and that I was going to do it with one question in mind: "Is God ever silent?" I would do it not to study any doctrinal or historical context along the way, but just to see if God ever took an uncommunicative posture with mankind. It was as though He was going to settle this in my mind once and for all by taking me through the totality of Scripture to see how He interacted with every now-famous Bible character. When the answers you need are big, no self-help book will do. You have to go to the Author of authors.

But aside from wondering how on earth a mom of then five could steal away for that long, and aside from wondering how on earth a person could read the Bible in five days, there was the other question of where I could go to do this. For free. My father had just built a tiny prayer cabin in the woods on his 250-acre farm, and he agreed that I could be his first guest.

Before leaving for the farm, I did an experiment and timed myself by reading one average-sized Bible chapter to see if this goal was even feasible, because it sure seemed impossible to me. It took a little over two minutes for one chapter. Of course, some chapters are longer, but others are shorter, like Psalm 117, which is 2 verses long and contains fewer than 30 words. I then multiplied that 2¼ minutes by 1,189—the number of chapters within the 66 Bible books. The time came out to only 44¾ hours. That meant only a 9-hour reading day over 5 days, which was really no different from working a 40-hour workweek! I was thrilled at this attainable goal. Here was how it panned out in the end:

Day 1: Read Genesis through Numbers, 153 chapters @ approximately 2¼ minutes each = 5¾ hours.

Day 2: Read Deuteronomy through Esther, 283 chapters @ approximately 2¼ minutes each = 10½ hours.

Day 3: Read Job through Ezekiel, 414 chapters @ approximately 2¼ minutes each = 15½ hours.

Day 4: Read Daniel through Acts, 196 chapters @ approximately 2¼ minutes each = 7½ hours.

Day 5: Read Romans through Revelation, 143 chapters @ approximately 2¼ minutes each = 5½ hours

Total: 66 books (1,189 chapters) in 44¾ hours within 5 days.

I did not "chew" on each verse, but read continuously, stopping only to write in a journal about any passages related to God's mouth or man's ears. God had given me this insatiable desire to read through the Bible with one question in mind: "Is God ever silent?" The books dealing with this topic were selling like hotcakes, and it seemed to me that they were putting words in God's mouth out of desperation in a hearing drought. I wondered if God was frustrated at the assumption that He would zip His lip and withhold direction from us. I found that contradictory to His benevolent nature. My hopeful hunch was that these authors were using such titles as a tease, and then leading their readers through steps on rest and perhaps repentance that would unclog their ears.

> Surely no author would waste two hundred pages defending the argument that God has a mute button.

Surely no author would waste two hundred pages defending the argument that God has a mute button.

Those five days changed my life. In a prayer cabin with only a wood stove, chopped wood and an oil lamp, I read through the entire Bible and answered my question without a doubt: "No—God is *never* silent." I found plenty of verses that put the burden back on the shoulders of mankind, such as, "If I regard iniquity in my heart, the LORD will not hear me" (Psalm 66:18 KJV). But I found nothing to imply that God becomes deaf and mute and withholds His counsel when we are walking uprightly in Him. Psalm 50:3 (NIV) even says, "Our God comes and will not be silent." That was answer enough for me. God will *not* be silent.

There was a period referred to as the "400 years of silence" that took place between Malachi (the very last of the Old Testament prophets) and Jesus' birth. But both Jews and many Christian groups view this period as one in which the prophets were silent nationally, but not as a time when God Himself was silent. Luke 2:36 mentions that the prophetess Anna was very old at the time of Jesus' birth, so clearly God was still speaking and prophets and prophetesses were still prophesying during those 400 years. God did not speak Scripture during this time, but He spoke individually and congregationally. Likewise, God did not speak Scripture during the time humankind was in the Garden of Eden, but He was still speaking. In fact, He has not spoken Scripture for more than nineteen centuries, but He has still been speaking. He will not be silent.

So then, if God is never silent, why did it seem as though God was not speaking to my family and me lately? We had scraped the sides of our hearts clean a hundred times, humbly seeking Him. And then it hit me. If you have done the last thing God told you to do and are hearing nothing new, then you are perfectly within His will and can relax until the next step comes. We had, and we did.

To this day I hold that cabin journal in my hands and marvel at what God did during that "great fall." A quote from my journal says, "I believe these five days in God's Word are key days in this fall saga. I am expectant at what God will do during this season, at who He will be for me for the first time and who I will become in Him that will affect my lifetime." That woman was right. Through a dream, He had used her eyes to open her ears.

He wants to do the same for you.

Four Eyes and Four Ears

Every Christian has four eyes and four ears. You are given one set when you are born and another set when you are born again. Through prophetic dreaming, God can communicate direction to you that perhaps you would not be able to hear while awake in your distracting environment. This is the entire basis behind the idea of this book about *seeing* the voice of God, because it involves communication without speech. We all know it is possible to communicate without words. Baseball players do it. Participants in a game of charades do it. Animals do it. Even babies do it.

Why, then, should God be limited to using only our ears to communicate with us? Did He not also give us four other senses with which to experience Him? He can speak to us through touch, taste, smell and, most certainly, sight. He created them all, and everything He created is intended to help us comprehend Him. And besides, just as in my waterfall dream, oftentimes dreams do contain spoken words, so the spiritual ears are engaged. It is as if through dreams, the person who claims to have a hard time hearing God's voice suddenly hears with undistracted precision. Job 33:14–18 confirms this:

> For God may speak in one way, or in another,
> Yet man does not perceive it.
> In a dream, in a vision of the night,
> When deep sleep falls upon men,
> While slumbering on their beds,
> Then He opens the ears of men,
> And seals their instruction.
> In order to turn man from his deed,
> And conceal pride from man,
> He keeps back his soul from the Pit,
> And his life from perishing by the sword.

"In a dream . . . He opens the ears. . . ." There you have it. We can hear with our eyes! Thus, dreams are an essential tool for people who question their ability to hear the voice of God. Visions, too. I often find that when people say they cannot hear God's voice, they are actually seers in training and do not know it. It is as though God is bypassing their ears and going straight to their eyes, which may become their strongest line of communication with Him. They have an enhanced prophetic eye through dreams and visions, and God wants to grow them in that.

As you can tell by now, I believe that God wants to speak to you at night. (If you are someone who works at night and sleeps by day, these promises are still just as much yours.) If we spend a third of our day in bed, and thus a third of our life in bed, then that means a 60-year-old woman has been asleep for 20 years of her life. With this math, it means that you yourself are asleep about 122 days out of every year. Why would God waste so much of your lifetime by being out of touch with you during those precious hours?

If God wants to speak with you during the day, then of course He wants to speak with you at night.

Does God sleep at night? No. Psalm 121:3 (NIV) says, "He who watches over you will not slumber." And the first chapter of Genesis records God saying, "Let us make mankind in our image, in our likeness" (verse 26 NIV). Notice the wording: *our* image and *our* likeness. He is already referring to the Trinity in the first chapter of the Bible. We see that just as God is made up of three parts, then we, being made in His image, are, too. We have a body and a mind, and they both slow down at night and rest. But we also have a spirit, and it never sleeps. It is the part of us that is like the One who, as we established, "will not slumber." Our spirit is awake all night, longing to convene with God.

> If we spend a third of our day in bed, and thus a third of our life in bed, then that means a 60-year-old woman has been asleep for 20 years of her life.

I like to think of it like a fulfillment of Song of Solomon 5:2 (KJV), "I sleep, but my heart waketh: it is the voice of my beloved that knocketh, saying, 'Open to me.'" I often pray that verse over myself when I go to bed: "Lord, You are my Beloved. I am going to sleep, but my heart is awake, listening for Your voice." I expect God to speak and minister to my spirit each and every night in some creative way. Why would He just tuck you in at bedtime and move on to ministering to people who are awake in other time zones? Deuteronomy 31:8 (NIV) says, "He will never leave you nor forsake you." Doesn't that pretty much mean "never"? Not even when you sleep? On the fourth day of creation, why didn't He just skip over the invention of nighttime and never make a moon? Or stars?

I tell you, nighttime is God's idea. It belongs to Him, and He is busy during it. The problem may be that many of us are dismissing our dreams, in which case the dreams will begin to cease coming. But look at the first part of the Job 33 passage again: "For God may speak in one way, or in another, yet man does not perceive it" (verse 14). We see here that God does speak through dreams and visions, but many people do not perceive it.

Perceive is a verb that means "discern, appreciate, consider, realize, recognize, become aware of, see, distinguish, grasp, understand, take in, make out, find, comprehend, apprehend, sense, figure out; regard, view."[3] Let it never be said of you that God speaks but that you do not discern, appreciate, consider or realize it! What a shame that would be for the Creator of the universe to have something to say to you and say it, only to have you disregard it as a "pizza dream." With that mindset, the entire mysterious book of Ezekiel and all of its illogical, disorderly symbols could easily have been attributed to too much pizza. The Lord often chooses to speak obscurely, with seemingly unintelligible symbols, so that we must seek Him for interpretation. (We will discuss that further in chapter 7.)

Two Streams

Bestselling author James Goll makes a brilliant comparison between the Nile River and the prophetic flow of God on earth in his book *The Seer: The Prophetic Power of Visions, Dreams, and Open Heavens*. Although the mighty Nile is the longest river in the world at about 4,100 miles long, it begins its life as two separate rivers: the White Nile, which flows from Tanzania, and the Blue Nile, which springs from Ethiopia. Goll likens this to how God's prophetic ministry overall on earth is fueled by two streams: the stream of the prophet and the stream of the seer.

What is the difference? In a multifaceted answer, Goll writes, "All true seers are prophets but not all prophets are seers."[4] He adds, "When it comes to prophetic revelation, a prophet is primarily an inspired hearer and then speaker while a seer is primarily visual. In other words, the prophet is the *communicative* dimension and the seer is the *receptive* dimension."[5]

Hence, one stream involves the ears, and the other the eyes. I include Goll's river parallel here because it undergirds my sole ambition for this book, *Seeing the Voice of God*. His analogy applies to the offices and ministries of prophet and seer church-wide, however, whereas my points are more applicable to your individual life. You have the ability to both see and hear spiritually. Those are two streams flowing back and forth between your spirit man and God. But in seasons when we feel God is silent, or we are in geographical regions where hearing God's voice is difficult due to territorial strongholds of evil that seek to hinder His full reign, we can still *see* the voice of God through dreams and visions. We all sleep. We all dream. Science proves this, and we will explore medically in chapters 4 and 5 how to improve our dream recall so that we can better steward what God might be trying to communicate to us.

When your ears fail you, the eyes have it. When one stream temporarily dries up, the other still flows—and oftentimes floods. This is my personal testimony. When I found myself in the greatest hearing war of my life by day, my eyes opened at night through dreams, so much so that I began to "see" not only for myself but for other people, and then ministry was birthed.

While God was healing the dry spell in my other stream, my seeing stream began to gush. Even the physically hearing impaired will tell you that their eyesight becomes sharper to compensate for their deafness. Not that they have better vision than hearing people per se, but they learn to use and rely on their other senses better to compensate.

> Even the physically hearing impaired will tell you that their eyesight becomes sharper to compensate for their deafness.

Likewise, a hearing drought is the perfect time to ask God to open your eyes. Many times, those dreams and visions that come forth lead right back to open ears. Remember Job 33:15–16: "In a dream, in a vision of the night, when deep sleep falls upon men, while slumbering on their beds, then He opens the ears of men."

The Sixth Sense?

The *New Oxford American Dictionary* defines *sixth sense* as "a power of perception like but not one of the five senses: a keen intuitive power."[6] I guess I disagree that we even need a sixth sense. Are not the five senses that God gave us amazing enough? Can we not use them for constant communication with Him if we are seeking Him? In chapter 10, we will explore how God sharpens these senses further with the gifts of His Holy Spirit as we mature in Him. But even now, as that maturity is in the process of developing, your natural five senses are longing to experience Him. What are you waiting for?

Here are some examples of God Himself using these remarkable five senses in His relationship with humankind (the italics are mine):

Sight: "*God saw* all that He had made, and behold, it was very good" (Genesis 1:31 NASB).

Sound: "*God heard* their groaning and he remembered his covenant with Abraham, with Isaac and with Jacob" (Exodus 2:24 NIV).

Smell: "*The Lord smelled* the soothing aroma" (Genesis 8:21 NASB).

Taste: "When *Jesus had tasted* it [the vinegar], he said, 'It is finished!'" (John 19:30 NLT).

Touch: "*God touched* the hearts of certain brave men who went along with him" (1 Samuel 10:26 NCV).

Here are some examples of humankind using these five senses in relationship with God (again, the italics are mine):

Sight: "Blessed are the pure in heart, for *they will see* God" (Matthew 5:8 NIV).

Sound: "*My sheep hear* My voice, and I know them, and they follow Me" (John 10:27).

Smell: "But thanks be to God, who always leads us in triumph in Christ, and manifests *through us the sweet aroma* of the knowledge of Him in every place" (2 Corinthians 2:14 NASB).

Taste: "*Taste* and see that the Lord is good" (Psalm 34:8 NLT).

Touch: "And all the *people were trying to touch* Him, for power was coming from Him and healing them all" (Luke 6:19 NASB).

I do not think we need a "sixth sense" as the world defines it. I think the Holy Spirit can make our five senses naturally supernatural all day long and communicate with us enough to draw us to Himself. Of course, we not only want to communicate with Him, but *for* Him, and that is where our spiritual senses come into play, which we will discuss in chapter 10 (prophecy, words of knowledge, words of wisdom and others). But even when we are walking in the Spirit and fully employing those spiritual senses, God still can use the five natural senses He has given us, with which we experience Him.

One Angle

I have no idea where you are in your walk with God, or if you even believe in Him. I have no way of knowing if you eagerly bought this book or if an insightful friend gave it to you. When authors write, they first establish an audience in their heads that they then easily speak to—a specific population of people they have in mind. But in this case, even after writing a full chapter, I still cannot discern who that demographic is for this book. It is as if I cannot narrow it down. I see the faces of some of you who have spent a lifetime loving God, yet I see others who revere Him at a distance but need persuading that He really wants to say anything specific to them—or they are scared that He might. Then I see even others who are intrigued by the theme but put off by all the Scripture.

What we all have in common—and therefore, the angle from which I will write—is that we all want to know and be known. And whether this book is too churchy for you or not churchy enough is secondary to what we might accomplish together by the end of it.

I find myself in a risky position writing this book, because while I know that it is going to bring purpose and revelation to countless fledgling seers all over the world, I also run the risk of being crucified by all those whose eyes are shut. I am in danger of upsetting any Christians who do not believe that seers still exist, and in danger of upsetting the lost who do not believe that Christ exists. It is my prayer that both camps will listen and learn, because by the end of this book, I believe they both will see undeniably that not only is Christ still alive, and not only is He desiring to communicate with us, but that He is raising up a generation of sharp-eyed seers in a spiritually deaf world.

The prophet Joel foresaw this generation, prophesying,

"And it shall come to pass in the last days," says God,
"That I will pour out of My Spirit on all flesh;
Your sons and your daughters shall prophesy,
Your young men shall see visions,
Your old men shall dream dreams.
And on My menservants and on My maidservants
I will pour out My Spirit in those days;
And they shall prophesy."

Acts 2:17–18 (see also Joel 2:28–29)

The apostle Peter, familiar with Joel's prophecy, reiterated it as he saw its budding fulfillment in Jerusalem almost two thousand years ago.

The pouring out has begun. The stewardship of it has not begun in full, although some in the prophetic community are doing a great job of teaching their hearts out in an attempt to see the outpouring governed well. If overmanaged by those who view dreams and visions as a messy threat to a tidy gospel, the outpouring is quenched. But if undermanaged by sloppy, self-appointed prophets, dreams and visions are left up to the seer's own interpretation and quickly become confusing, un-edifying and even psychic in nature.

Let me state forthrightly that you do not need a dream or a vision to believe the Bible. If you feel you do, something is missing in your heart toward God, and it might just be His Son. If Jesus *is* in your heart as a result of a definitive invitation to Him, but you still feel the Word of God is not illuminated when you read it, then your issue is not with Christ but with the Holy Spirit. The Holy Spirit does not just seal you on the day of your salvation and retire. He wants constant communication with you. That includes dreams and visions, yes, but should the content of one ever stray from what God's Word teaches, it is not from Him.

You were made in the image and likeness of God—the all-powerful One and Creator of all things supernatural—so it is perfectly normal for you to desire powerful, supernatural encounters. Sadly, though, people equate communication with God as a supernatural encounter, when really it is just your birthright as His child. As we move forward, please lay aside all preconceived mysticism relating to dreams and visions. Also lay aside any critical thoughts suggesting that teaching such as you will find in these pages seeks to replace God's Word with supernatural encounters. Encounters like dreams and visions do not compete with God's Word; they complement it.

In this book you will find biblical teaching on how to hear God's voice, and also on how to *see* God's voice through dreams and visions—which comes in particularly handy when you feel your spiritual ears are failing you. You will read information from doctors about sleep and dream cycles, and also learn which vitamins and minerals are beneficial for improving your dream recall. You will learn what a prophetic dream is and what it is not, as well as how to classify it from one of ten biblical categories so that you know what to do with one when it comes. You will study dozens of dreams in Scripture and hear modern testimonies of vivid dreams that were fulfilled with utmost accuracy. You will get to scan a dream dictionary that will help make sense of the symbols in your visions and dreams, since revelation without interpretation hinders application.

You will learn how the life of every believer in Jesus must include a hunger for the constant filling of the Holy Spirit in order to accomplish holiness, without which no one will see the Lord. (This applies to seeing in dreams and visions, too.) You will also discover how that environment of hunger opens the communication lines between you and heaven, resulting in "20/20 hearing" and even fostering angelic visitations. But remember, seek the Giver and not the gifts, for if you seek the gifts themselves, the enemy will make sure to hand-deliver to you every counterfeit he can conjure. You will hear in chapter 10 from a former psychic who will describe his experiences in that lifestyle. He will explain what the prophetic flow of revelation feels like in comparison to the psychic flow and describe how the successes he had in spell-casting brought him a revelation of the power in his words—a biblical truth that remains with him today as he serves God and seeks to be His voice to the lost and dying.

As you read the words of this book, I pray the prayer of Elisha over you from 2 Kings 6:16–17 (NIV):

> "Don't be afraid," the prophet answered. "Those who are with us are more than those who are with them."
> And Elisha prayed, "Open his eyes, LORD, so that he may see." Then the LORD opened the servant's eyes, and he looked and saw the hills full of horses and chariots of fire all around Elisha.

Life gets tough, but when God opens your eyes to the spirit realm it changes everything. Your courage in fearful situations increases, your ability to make wise choices increases, your tolerance of hard-to-get-along-with people increases and your ability to trust God and discern the spirits that oppose Him increases. And as these eye-opening experiences heighten with your reading of this book—including having more dreams and visions—I urge you to begin keeping a Lookbook, which is a journal of all your seeing encounters, both sleeping and waking.

Finally, if this book is in your hands, it is not by chance. I have been praying for you and probably even did so this very morning. Yes, it is full of Scripture, because in the end, God's words will do more for you than my words. He is the Author of authors, so in my book, His book has final authority.

How did people in the Bible interpret their dreams without a Bible to guide them? In the end, it all came down to relationship. They knew and were known by the living God, with whom they had a relationship. They learned to hear and see His voice with the Holy Spirit's help. And most important, they applied faith to what they heard and saw and let it interrupt their lives. You will have to do the same when reading this book.

It is so very simple. God loves you. He is intimately concerned with the details of your life. If you will let Him, He wants to help you navigate through life and dodge the detours. When dodging a detour is impossible (due to the will of another person whose disobedience to God is affecting you adversely), He wants to help you navigate through the emotions of that situation and get back on course.

But it all begins with a relationship with Him. If you have wholeheartedly come to the Father through His Son, Jesus, you should expect to communicate with Him daily. And nightly. You should be hearing Him with your ears during the day and with your eyes at night. If you are not, then I truly believe that this book will provide both the diagnosis and the cure for your spiritual deafness and blindness, because within its pages are enough Scriptures and testimonies to convince even the greatest skeptics that God is never silent and that He is, in fact, unceasingly trying to communicate with us.

> If you have wholeheartedly come to the Father through His Son, Jesus, you should expect to communicate with Him daily. And nightly.

"Common Senses"

You came into my heart that day, I knew it in my head
But now mere knowledge will not do, I need Your touch
   instead

I want to see Your voice at night and hear it in the day
I want my feet to not retreat, but briskly to obey

I want to feel Your gentle touch; I want You to feel mine
I want Your personality to cause my face to shine

I want to see Your smiling face each time my faith's
   been great
And taste and see how good You are whenever it's been
   late

Where once I gave my heart to you and felt it come alive
Today I dedicate to You my senses, Lord, all five.

© Laura Harris Smith, July 23, 2012

PRAYER

Let's pray out loud together:

God, thank You for wanting to communicate with me. I want a deeper relationship with You, and I invite You into my heart for a 24/7 experience that allows me to hear Your voice by day and see it by night. Jesus, You say in John 10:27 that Your sheep know Your voice and follow You, so today I call myself Your sheep and call You my Shepherd. I vow to follow You whether waking or asleep. Lord, thank You for my four eyes and four ears, and for how You have equipped me to comprehend Your will for my life with all of the five senses You have given me. O God, open the eyes of my heart! Open the ears of my heart! Use both streams flowing from Your throne to hone my senses. Forgive me for where I have not perceived that You were speaking—especially in dreams and visions. I vow no longer to dismiss, despise or dread the prophetic gift. Ground me in

Your Word, Lord. I vow to also use my eyes to study it more. In Jesus' name, Amen.

IMPARTATION

Right now, I release and impart to you the ability to perceive when God is communicating to you and the desire to seek Him quickly. (Now open your hands, shut your eyes and receive it.)

2

When Your Dreams Are for Now

Five Types of Prophetic Dreams for the Present

Now that hopefully I have convinced you that God is never silent and that you can hear Him with your eyes, let's discuss the various types of dreams He will give you. If you already have a journal full of dreams, now you will know how to classify them so you can determine what to do with them. If prophecy "announces" something, then a prophetic dream is merely one where God is announcing something to the dreamer.

Over the years, I have found biblical support for ten distinct categories of prophetic dreams, but I have found that some of these nocturnal announcements are for immediate application, while others need to be marinated in prayer and patience. In this chapter we will discuss five types of the former, and then in chapter 3 we will look at five types of the latter. At the end of each of these chapters, we will pray together for such dreams to come more often. It is also important to explore the physical obstacles that could prevent them from coming at all, and we will do that in chapters 4 and 5. For each prophetic dream type I will give a biblical example, but I will also give some personal dream examples along the way, helping us take this from mystical to practical.

Are you ready? Let's take a look at the five categories of prophetic dreams that are for immediate application.

1. Waking Dreams

If waking dreams were punctuation, they would be an <u>underscore</u> because they are very significant and stress importance.

I absolutely love waking dreams. There is no escaping their imprint on your day. While the categories that follow are "types," waking dreams are more about timing. They occur just as you awaken for your day. These are not dreams that wake you up in the middle of the night, after which you return to sleep. These dreams happen after the night's rest. They are your first impression of the new day, which is why I usually say they require action.

The purpose of waking dreams is to show you something that stays with you and is not forgotten when you wake up. We all know it is possible to dream in the night and not remember it, but it is next to impossible to forget a waking dream. I often find that when God awakens me with a dream in the morning, I am to take action soberly. Sometimes to pray patiently, and sometimes to apply it to my life immediately (or to someone else if it is for another person). The bottom line is that you cannot shake the feeling that a waking dream is an immediate assignment.

Genesis 41:1–7 describes Pharaoh's two compelling and abstract dreams that saved a nation and preserved God's chosen people through Joseph, the obedient dreamer and dream interpreter. Verses 7–8 describe a waking dream perfectly: "Then

Pharaoh woke up; it had been a dream. In the morning his mind was troubled. . . ." The first dream was not a waking dream, and no emotion was recorded. The second dream, however, left Pharaoh troubled. Dreams you have just before you wake up leave you feeling definite emotion. They will either trouble you into action or encourage you into peace. Pharaoh was troubled, but not for long, because Joseph's interpretation brought peace. Seven bad economic years were on their way, but seven plentiful ones would precede them so the nation could store up and prepare. Pharaoh's first dream, followed by the second, a waking dream, drove home the point, and fourteen years later the nation was back on track.

> You cannot shake the feeling that a waking dream is an immediate assignment.

Although I have waking dreams weekly or even more often, God is bringing to mind two in particular. One time I had delayed returning a friend's call because I was frustrated with her. The longer I put off the call, the harder it was to make, not to mention that she was sitting over there worried sick about our relationship. Finally, one morning I awoke to a dream that I walked out of my bedroom and she was sitting right outside my door, waiting patiently. No escaping her now! I knew God was saying to call her first thing.

I am so glad I acted on that dream, because during our call my friend described a vision God had given her that I really needed to hear. In it she saw me in new glasses, and I was ministering on television to a large audience. (And I had indeed bought new glasses since seeing her.) What minister would not be happy about that vision? That is one example about how a waking dream can be both a sign and an assignment, and I am so thankful I obeyed.

Another example was when I was executive producer and senior editor of our church's weekly television show. Each Tuesday, our drop-off deadline at the station loomed over my head like a gauntlet. If I went to bed at all on Monday nights, it was late. This particular Monday night, I had finished editing just before midnight (which was early), pressed "export" and gone to bed, knowing that the typical multihour process would be completed as I slept and that I would awaken to the finished high-res mega file.

I rolled into bed exhausted and looking forward to a full night's sleep, only to be awakened the next morning by a dream a full hour before the alarm clock was set to go off. In the dream, my longtime friend Susan was standing at my bedroom door. "Laura, wake up. Wake up, Laura. Wake up right now," she said softly.

When I opened my eyes, I knew immediately that something had not gone as planned and that God was awakening me so that we would not miss our deadline. Sure enough, I went to my computer and saw that the application the project was being created in had frozen during export. I got busy and finished within fifteen minutes of our deadline, and the television studio was fifteen minutes away. We made it under the wire, and I laughed at how God had let me sleep until the last possible moment, proving that He cares about my rest. Why did He choose this particular friend for the dream? She is perhaps the most punctual person I know on the planet. Punctual and precise and calm. Her unemotional face and relaxed tone set the mood for the morning, and through a waking dream, gave the emergency a happy ending.

2. Decision Dreams

If decision dreams were punctuation, they would be a question mark. Why?

Because a decision dream is where you are asked a question or given options, and you watch yourself provide an answer or make a choice. To me, this is the greatest proof we have that we are made up of three parts. Your mind is turned off at night as your body rests, and neither can help you make a decision in your dream, but your spirit can. Your spirit does. Watch carefully the choices you see yourself make in your dreams, for they are very telling when it comes to what is going on in your spirit, good and bad.

Biblically, we see this in the famous story of Solomon in 1 Kings 3. We credit Solomon with being the wisest man in the world, all because when given one wish, he asked for wisdom and made the right decision. But did you know he was asleep when he made it? It was a dream: "At Gibeon the LORD appeared to Solomon in a dream by night; and God said, 'Ask! What shall I give you?'" (verse 5). Solomon's spirit chose correctly, and he asked for wisdom to lead God's people. I have no doubt that since that same spirit remained in him while he was awake, he would have given the same answer any time of day.

> Watch carefully the choices you see yourself make in your dreams, for they are very telling when it comes to what is going on in your spirit, good and bad.

Perhaps the most compelling decision dream I have ever had was when I, too, was faced with a sobering question and saw myself answer it. I was standing in a dark room, almost an underground, cavelike space, and the prophet Elisha walked around the corner toward me. I somehow knew that the cloak he was wearing was the one Elijah had thrown down when he left this world in that now-famous chariot of fire. It was his sign to Elisha that he was leaving a double portion of his spirit to him. As Elisha approached me, I stood very still, until finally, we were standing face-to-face about two feet apart. He looked about half a foot taller than my height of five foot two. Then he asked me a point-blank question: "Will you take a vow to pray for America?"

Without hesitation I answered yes, and with that, he said to kneel in front of him. Taking his staff—the same miracle-working staff he had sent with Gehazi to raise the little boy from the dead—he placed it on my shoulder, almost as if he were knighting me. There were no words. Only the anointing. I never saw myself get up off my knees before I awoke, which probably symbolized my vow to pray without ceasing. I was shocked on many levels. I also had many questions. *Why me? Why Elisha? Why not Jesus? Why the shoulders?*

My investigation began in Scripture with Elisha. He was a prophet, and I had always identified with the lifestyles, instincts and reactions of the biblical prophets. Secondly, he had asked for a double portion, and in 1997—a couple of years before this dream—double portion had been prophesied over our family. *Twins* became the recurring prophetic word spoken over us by visiting ministers and even by total strangers, and I eventually stockpiled more than forty prophetic words about *double portion* and *twins*.

It became hilarious to our friends when these ministers would come to speak and we would get called out of a crowd for prayer, and at some point the words *double* or *twins* would come out. One time, Jill Austin, a Kansas City prophetess whom God used as a mouthpiece all over the world, said it in front of the whole congregation. Then she paused and added, "No. It's a double double. Quadruplets!"

The promise for double portion was so strong in our spirits that it was doubling itself! We just knew we were going to have twins physically, and we already had five children. When I became pregnant the sixth time, we were shocked that I did not deliver twins. But then, ten years later, our oldest married daughter made us grandparents of—you guessed it—twins, Avery and Ezra. Those precious bundles of blue became a symbol for our whole family that the double-portion promise was for our legacy, too, not just for Mom and Dad. Our lives were and still are defined by double blessing, double productivity and double portion. We even see it already in various packages in the homes of each of our married children.

While I would have loved to be standing face-to-face with Jesus in my dream, I knew exactly what Elisha represented, and the fact that he was already wearing Elijah's cloak symbolized that he had inherited the double-portion mantle and was able to impart it to me. As for the shoulders, they represent a sense of responsibility or a burden to carry (see Psalm 81:6). Shoulders also can indicate rulership or authority, or symbolize government. Isaiah 9:6 prophesies that the government will be on the Messiah's shoulders. I knew, therefore, that the call to pray for America in the dream included praying for our government officials, so I do to this day.

3. Encouraging Dreams

If encouraging dreams were punctuation, they would be a smiley face emoticon :-).

There is nothing like an encouraging dream to revive your heart and replenish your soul. This type of prophetic dream gives you an affirmation or perhaps a glimpse into a future blessing or victory. Look at Judges 7:13–15:

> And when Gideon had come, there was a man telling a dream to his companion. He said, "I have had a dream: To my surprise, a loaf of barley bread tumbled into the camp of Midian; it came to a tent and struck it so that it fell and overturned, and the tent collapsed."
>
> Then his companion answered and said, "This is nothing else but the sword of Gideon the son of Joash, a man of Israel! Into his hand God has delivered Midian and the whole camp."
>
> And so it was, when Gideon heard the telling of the dream and its interpretation, that he worshiped. He returned to the camp of Israel, and said, "Arise, for the LORD has delivered the camp of Midian into your hand."

Okay, be honest. If you had a dream about a tumbling barley loaf, would you interpret it to mean victory in battle? This proves that odd symbols can edify when interpreted well. If I saw a loaf of bread tumbling into my house, I would think that my provisions were about to increase or that I was about to receive a financial blessing (as in *dough* or *bread*). If you yourself dreamed about it, it might have a whole separate interpretation, such as a reference to cooking or maybe to Jesus as the Bread of Life. But for Gideon, it meant victory, and it made him bow down and worship God even before the battle began. And he was not even the dreamer or the interpreter. Just the overhearer.

The story has three players, and all of them were encouraged. In addition, a whole nation was saved through the bravery and courage that came through a prophetic dream that encouraged them to "get up" and fight.

I cannot begin to count the hundreds of encouraging dreams I have had. I remember once during a dark time when I felt there was no fruit or answered prayer in my life, Chris and I pulled all the kids close one night and had a big slumber party. All eight of us in a big dog pile on the floor. The next morning, I had a waking dream in which I was looking down over this room we were in with an aerial view. The entire floor was covered with fruit. From baseboard to baseboard, piles and piles of fruit were everywhere. Instead of my kids and their sleeping bags, there was fruit salad.

> The entire floor was covered with fruit. From baseboard to baseboard, piles and piles of fruit were everywhere. Instead of my kids and their sleeping bags, there was fruit salad.

It was God's way of reminding me that those children were the best fruit I had ever had, and that I was already a fruitful woman even if I never had another prayer answered. And it was not just six pieces of fruit I saw as I hovered. I am telling you, it was hundreds of pieces of fruit of every variety, so I knew and still know this represented my grandchildren and great-grandchildren. It gave new meaning to "be fruitful and multiply."

To this day, it is why I guard my children's lives, callings, attitudes and personal standards of conduct and holiness with such fierceness. There are many other reasons, too, but this hovering image I cannot shake and never will. Even if my adult children are tempted to feel they no longer need my guardianship, and even though other moms are glad when their kids move out and do not need it, I will always guard my children attentively. In God's eyes—from His aerial view—they and their children after them are evidently on the floor of my house forever.

I also remember many encouraging dreams that came during some trying years of my life when I was plagued by constant, unexpected and very violent convulsions. Once, I dreamed that I was in a hospital bed and David came to visit me. He never told me who he was, but somehow, I just knew. Sometimes as the dreamer, you will "know things in your knower," as I have often jokingly explained to others who are growing in dream interpretation and discernment. But aside from that "knowing," David was also just as Scripture described him: "Now he was ruddy and had beautiful eyes and was handsome" (1 Samuel 16:12 ESV). Ruddy as in red hair, and yes, he was so very handsome. I had never thought of him as anything but King David, yet in the dream he was not a king. He was just David paying me a hospital visit. He came to my bed and leaned over with a wide, winsome smile. Squinting his eyes, he said, "I am so proud of you."

Coming from such a famous warrior and worshiper, that meant a lot. It encouraged me to get up and keep warring and worshiping and trusting. My journey toward freedom from those convulsions was a long road. Before they ended, I often recounted that "hospital visit from David" dream for encouragement. I will know those brown eyes in heaven one day, for sure.

Another time when I had been badly bruised after a seizure, I awoke after a dream about Dwight Eisenhower. I saw him in his army attire, his jacket loaded with colorful medals. *Why on earth would I dream about Dwight Eisenhower?* I wondered. I would have rather seen Jesus or the archangel Michael, not bald Ike. But as I researched him the next day, I discovered that Eisenhower was the most decorated war general of all time. Other countries even awarded him medals.

After this dream, I knew that God was saying He did not see bruises when He looked at me, but medals. Suddenly, my bruises were colorful badges of honor, and I did not feel so sorry for myself. God said that the enemy had not wanted my health that night, but my life, and that I had won. That perspective shift turned me from the victim to the victor. It made me stop complaining. It made me get up and fight like a highly decorated war general. It encouraged me, meaning I was filled with courage.

I knew that God was saying He did not see bruises when He looked at me, but medals.

I cannot tell you how often prophetic dreams have saved my life. I surely would have lain down and died many times over without seeing God's voice just at the right moment each time. His love for me sometimes makes me weak in the knees.

4. Audible Dreams ("Dark Speeches")

If audible dreams were punctuation, they would be "quotation marks."

The Bible refers to "dark speeches" in Numbers 12:8 (KJV): "With him [Moses] will I speak mouth to mouth, even apparently, and not in dark speeches." Through this we see that God speaks face-to-face in broad daylight, but also concealed in the dark, like in a dream at night. "Dark speeches" is the Hebrew word *chiydah* and means "riddle, parable, dark obscure utterance, enigma to be guessed." That would definitely describe dreams, since they are often obscure parables, but when your heart hears God's voice clearly in a dream, it might as well be an audible experience to your ears.

Just look at the word again: "H-EAR-T." It has been said that the heart has a mind of its own, but never neglect that it has ears of its own as well.

We see several of these mysterious "dark obscure utterances" in Scripture. In 1 Samuel 3, the boy Samuel has been taken to the Temple by his mother, Hannah, and left to serve with the high priest, Eli. Verse 1 is one of the saddest verses in the Bible: "And the word of the LORD was precious in those days; there was no open vision" (KJV). A spiritual blindness was over the nation. Likewise, verse 2 tells us Eli's eyes had begun to grow dim in the natural—a physical manifestation of a larger spiritual vision problem.

God called Samuel three times audibly in the night, until Eli explained to him that it was the Lord. This shows that sometimes you hear a voice in a dream but are not aware that the voice is God's. Pay attention to voices you hear in your dreams. Seek counsel, as Samuel did, from a godly leader you can trust to help you interpret.

> The final blow came. But because God had prepared me in an audible dream, I faced it with joy and without devastation.

I have awakened to the sound of my name before. It was a precious call to immediately come pray. I call that "listening prayer." No agenda. No grocery list of things I need. Just waiting on the Lord. It is good for a soul, no matter who you are. Whenever you hear your name called in a dream, do what Samuel did. Physically get up out of bed. Quiet yourself alone somewhere in a "here I am, Lord" posture, as Samuel did, and pray. Then listen.

In a dream in June 2002, I heard a voice say, "The next fourteen months are going to drastically change your life." What an odd and specific time frame, and boy, did it come to pass. I mention this in the "dreams for now" category because the word that came immediately affected the left-foot-right-foot of my life. I could not refuse the grace for change as it came because God had announced it was coming. I wrote the following poem thirteen months later, in July 2003, just one month shy of the time line the Lord audibly gave me in my dream. By the time I wrote the poem, things indeed were drastically different in my life, relationships, ministry and even my family. Some of it came with an intense tearing away, and that was hard. And in

August 2003, which was exactly the fourteenth month, the final blow came. But because God had prepared me in an audible dream, I faced it with joy and without devastation. Hardly any tears at all. And on the heels of it came unthinkable laughter and rebirth.

"Drastic"

Changes are coming; it's going to be drastic
God, Himself, said it, in a dream quite fantastic
So why are my insides, then, doing gymnastics?
I guess I just know Him by now

He speaks and your heart gets all enthusiastic
You view it one way, purely ecclesiastic
Before long it's doctrine that's interscholastic
As you teach it and preach it and wait

Your prayer life goes deep and becomes quite monastic
You laminate words and protect them in plastic
Your insides explode with a hope that's bombastic!
. . . and I guess all that's really okay

But time stretches on and the word gets elastic
Your hope gets deferred and your spirit, sarcastic
You bury the word in a deep, doubtful casket
And question yourself, it, and Him

Then just as your spirit is blowing a gasket
As friends looking in start to say you've gone spastic
God realigns all with His sage chiropractics
And the word you laid down stands back up

As if that alone isn't totally drastic
Your world starts to change by proportions galactic
And then, in an end that's augustly climactic
That word you first heard all comes true.

And then some.

© Laura Harris Smith, July 3–4, 2003

5. Pizza Dreams

If pizza dreams were punctuation, they would simply be a space
. . . because they seem as if they are from *outer space*!

I already mentioned in chapter 1 how Ezekiel could have dismissed the illogical, disorderly symbols he saw as pizza dreams. But what is a pizza dream? It is a general phrase people use as a label for a nonsensical dream. But I also observe that some people use it as an excuse to shrug off a perfectly good prophetic dream. With a little prayer and a little probing, their dream would make perfect sense and even provide some instruction.

So why did I list pizza dreams as a type of prophetic dream? One, to challenge people to redefine what they attribute to pizza, and two, because I have another explanation for why the mind dreams crazy things (dreams that are genuinely crazy and not helpful).

You see, Ecclesiastes 5:3 (NLT) says, "Too much activity gives you restless dreams." Other translations replace "too much activity" with "many cares," "too much worry" or "abundance of business." So a restless, crazy dream that we call a pizza dream might actually be God's predesigned way of telling us we are worrying too much, have too many cares or are too busy with business. They are announcements that we are stressed out. Remember, we learned in chapter 1 that *nabi*, one of the basic words in prophetic definitions, means "to announce." In that light, I think even our pizza dreams are announcing something.

Eating too much before bedtime and having erratic sleep schedules can also cause nonsensical dreams. In the end, a crazy pizza dream might be a signpost from God telling you to slow down, rest more, eat healthier and take better care of the temple He is trying to occupy. A pizza dream can save you future strife in life, proving that this type of dream can be highly prophetic and useful after all.

With that in mind, yes, I am one of those people who think all dreams—no matter how bizarre—are somehow from God.

Dreaming itself is from Him, so I never dismiss a dream without praying first.

Seek the Giver, Not the Gift

As I close this chapter by praying for you and your dreams, I want to remind you that we are to seek the Giver of gifts and not the gifts themselves. I say *gifts* metaphorically, too, since we have established that dreams are not a gift of the Spirit, but a form of communication with God. Communication with Him is your birthright as His child.

Also, I do not see it recorded once in Scripture that someone asked God for a dream. However, I do see it recorded that Jesus said, "If you believe, you will receive whatever you ask for in prayer" (Matthew 21:22 NIV). I also see that James said, "Ye have not, because ye ask not" (James 4:2 ASV). We are going to ask with confidence, believing God will see that our pure intent in praying for these things is merely to know Him more. He will not despise that motive. He will answer.

PRAYER

Let's pray out loud together:

God, I want a relationship with You that includes daily communication. I desire more prophetic dreams where You "announce" the future things I need to know today. Holy Spirit, I long for You to speak to me in the nighttime through decision dreams, encouraging dreams, audible dreams with dark speeches and even waking dreams. And show me if what I think is a pizza dream is actually a mysterious invitation to draw near to You for interpretation, as Ezekiel did. Either that, or to teach me to slow down, sleep in and not pig out so much before bedtime, which interferes with my dream life. I pray the prayer of Elisha over my life from 2 Kings 6—open my eyes so that I might see into the spirit realm. Tuck me in each night. I proclaim that the prayer on my lips, based on Song of Solomon 5:2, will be, "I am asleep, but my heart is awake listening for the voice of my Beloved." In Jesus' name, Amen.

IMPARTATION

I release and impart to you the ability to dream "now dreams," to receive the seer anointing and to discern God's intentions. Sweet dreams! (Now open your hands, shut your eyes and receive it.)

3

When Your Dreams
Are for Later

Five Types of Prophetic Dreams for the Future

Just as we determined that prophetic dreams can announce things for you to apply to your life now, there are also those prophetic dreams that you must journal and file away for later. They are prayer homework. Five types of dreams are considered prophetic dreams for the future. Let's take a closer look at each of them and how we can best respond to them.

1. Warning Dreams

If warning dreams were a punctuation mark, they would be an exclamation point!

Warning dreams are exactly what they sound like: dreams that warn of coming danger caused by a person, the evil one or a wrong decision we are about to make. As we read at the start, Job 33:16–18 says about dreams: "Then He opens the ears of men, and seals their instruction. In order to turn man from his deed, and conceal pride from man, He keeps back his soul from the Pit, and his life from perishing by the sword." We see here that God can save us from bad deeds, pride or the pit of hell itself. Sometimes we need saving from an enemy, and sometimes we need saving from ourselves.

> If warning dreams were a punctuation mark, they would be an exclamation point!

But warning dreams are not necessarily "fate," meaning they are not definitely going to come to pass. The world would have us believe that life is one big happenstance full of unavoidable fortunes, and that a stirring dream heralds either coming good or bad luck. Nothing could be further from the truth. God will often show you things in dreams so you will partner with Him and change them. They are given so you can pray and change the plot of the story, or at least avoid the trap set for your feet. Sort of like those movies with alternate endings where you can use your DVD remote to decide the outcome, heeding a solid warning dream can prevent bedlam from breaking out. Plenty of times, I have released to someone a warning dream that did not come true in the end. Did that make it false, or did that mean my commitment to pray helped prevent the imminent danger the enemy had planned for them?

Likewise, when someone delivers a warning dream to me, I have a choice. Either I can accept it as "fate" and adopt an "Oh, it'll be okay, just wait and see" attitude—a prevalent line of thinking even among Christians, and a misuse of the sovereignty of God. A *Que será, será* or "whatever will be, will be" attitude strips us of the responsibility of partnering with God in prayer, especially when He is wooing us through a dream to partner with Him. Or I can get busy praying and realize that God is trying to seal my instruction and save my life from perishing by the sword. I could not survive without God's warning dreams. I would not be alive today without them.

Matthew 2 records two of the most important warning dreams of all time. Without them, the salvation of the world would not have occurred when it did. The first warning dream was to the wise men. Commissioned by Herod to find the Christ child, they did not realize that Herod wanted them to report back to him so he could find Jesus and kill Him. Verse 12 says, "And having been warned in a dream not to go back to Herod, they returned to their country by another route." Then immediately in verse 13, God's protection continued: "When they had gone, an angel of the Lord appeared to Joseph in a dream. 'Get up,' he said, 'take the child and his mother and escape to Egypt. Stay there until I tell you, for Herod is going to search for the child to kill him.'"

Can you imagine it? Your spouse awakens you in the middle of the night and tells you to pack your bags because you are leaving the country immediately. Would you do it, all based on a dream? Or would you tell him or her to roll over and go back to sleep? Later, in verses 19–20, God tells Joseph in another dream that it is safe to return home again, and they do. All of these dreams involved international travel and faith. Not grandiose faith, just simple, childlike faith. And the childlike faith of those involved still profoundly affects your life today.

I have lost count of all the warning dreams God has sent me throughout the years. I am grateful to Him for so many things in my life, like salvation, healing, His love and my family, but in the Top 10 is my gratitude for how He warns me of impending danger and keeps me from *so much harm and heartache* through warning dreams. I am also thankful for how He gives me warning dreams for my friends and family, even though nobody likes to get that warning phone call that is a call to war in the middle of peacetime. But the "war" is merely prayer, so in the end, a warning dream is an invitation to seek God, just as is any other dream.

And this is one of the most important things to remember: You will not always feel a connection to a warning dream ("Oh, that dream could never come to pass in my life!") because it has *not* come to pass and often announces a coming attack in a blind spot. Otherwise, God could trust your usual wisdom or common sense to instruct you.

But regardless of how you feel at the time of a warning dream and regardless of when it is given to you, do not dismiss it, even if it means filing it away in a journal somewhere. Warning dreams are valuable in navigating through life. People often discount them, get pummeled and then shake their fists at God for not protecting them. God tried! Through warning dreams, it is as if God rolls out hell's blueprints in front of you to divulge what the enemy is plotting. After you pray, such a dream winds up altering your steps.

> You will not always feel a connection to a warning dream because it has not come to pass and often announces a coming attack in a blind spot.

My great friend Sue prays for me and our church regularly. As a result, God often gives her warning dreams for us so we will not be caught off guard by challenges. Often, she prays and sees the threat thwarted entirely. She often has tornado dreams to alert us to coming trouble. When she sees me, my family or my church in a dream with a tornado, I take a serious prayer posture and cancel planned activities to spend extra time in prayer. We also take dreams of snow and hail as warnings, since Job 38:22–23 says, "Have you entered the storehouses of the snow or seen the storehouses of the hail, which I reserve for times of trouble, for days of war and battle?" I notice that when it snows or hails, or when I have dreams of snow or hail, if I will spend some extra time in prayer, I will see a major breakthrough in an area of prayer that formerly seemed to have a "lull" in getting answered. It is as if prayers count double on snow days—I do not know how else to explain it.

Warning dreams are an invitation to pray, not to fear or relax. They are announcing a day to win, if we will partner with God. They are like receiving inside information on how to buy stock just before it doubles (legally, of course).

On one occasion, I had a waking dream with another warning symbol in it. It was a Sunday morning, and I saw myself standing in front of my church. Suddenly, I looked up and saw a huge wrecking ball sailing through the air, headed straight for the building (and for me). This was both a waking dream and a warning dream, so I took it very seriously. In the dream I had seen myself standing between the wrecking ball and the church, so I knew this represented how I must stand in the gap in prayer, stand between my people and peril, just as Moses did in Numbers 16:48 when he stood between the living and the dead and stopped the plague. I got up, got dressed and got to church early to meet with the pre-service prayer team.

I must have barged in there like a bull in a china closet. I even called in the elders I could find and the worship pastor. I told them what I saw, and we began to war in prayer for the safety of our church and our people. In that moment, I was thankful for the relationship I had built with my leaders and for how they trusted my prophetic eye. Sure enough, that week a dispute broke out between two key members that easily could have split the church. If either of them had left, it could have devastated interpersonal relationships in our congregation. Chris and I spent extra time in prayer that week and cleared our schedule for plenty of mediation meetings.

When it all hit, we were calm, unemotional and full of peace and authority, all because of one ten-second dream that we heeded. Thanks be to God, the two families reconciled with our guidance and did not leave. Love won. Forgiveness won. Discernment had fondued them all in prayer—saturated them in it—before we even knew who "they" were. The lesson learned is that warning dreams can keep you ahead of the ball, even when it is a wrecking ball. Pay attention to warning dreams and stay alert.

2. Directional Dreams

If directional dreams were a punctuation mark, they would be a period. They show you what to do, period.

They "seal your instruction," as Job 33:16 promises dreams and visions can do. The Bible is full of directional dreams. In Genesis 46:2–3, God tells Jacob in a dream to go to Egypt. In Genesis 31:24, God instructs Laban in a dream to speak kindly to Jacob. In Matthew 1:20, God tells Joseph in a dream to take Mary as his wife. Directional dreams leave you thunderstruck when you awake at the detailed counsel you realize you have just received.

Directional dreams do not always involve warnings; some of them can be quite exciting. Once, Chris and I were leaving to go on a mission trip to Helsinki, Finland, and had not yet raised all of our funds. Then one night, I had a dream in which I saw a blank check made out to me, and I was able to see the name of the signer. I had never met the woman, and you cannot very well go up to a stranger and ask for money. Yet I had this directional dream showing us where to go. Since my daughter Jessica was friends with the wealthy widow's daughter, I shared the dream with Jes, and she passed it along to her friend. We trusted that the dream would find its way to the woman if it was the Lord's will.

> Directional dreams leave you thunderstruck when you awake at the detailed counsel you realize you have just received.

Lo and behold, news of our mission trip made its way back to the woman in a casual, indirect way. She contacted us for a meeting, at the end of which she took out a pen and wrote us a check for the overseas trip for two—in full—just as I had seen in my dream.

In the same dream, I had also seen a huge map with two glowing countries: Finland and Holland. When I called the travel agent to book our flights, I was informed that the route chosen would require an overnight stay in Holland. As I recounted this entire praise report to my Granny Rooks, she divulged that all of my grandfather's people came from Holland, a fact I had never known. Through this directional dream, my instruction was sealed. We were able to travel to the conference in Helsinki, and then I was able to spend a day in Amsterdam, Holland, where my great-greats had hailed from. I spent the day praying and releasing generational blessings over the entire Rooks family and descendants. I felt the Lord had ordained for my feet to go there and bring those blessings back to America with me.

Then there is the directional dream that saved my life. I was hesitant about getting on a certain medication that would curb some horrible seizures, and I had a dream about sitting with a new neurologist and watching him hand me white pills, pink pills and blue pills. Shortly after the dream, I was sitting with a new neurologist and he described a new medication. He offered me samples, and you guessed it—they were white pills, pink pills and blue pills. I knew then I was in the right place at the right time and within God's perfect will. Likewise, God gave me similar dream guidance when, a decade later, His promises for healing began springing forth in my body and it was time to wean down to lesser doses of that same medicine.

God is so good! He wants to be intricately involved in the minutia of your life story, if you will let Him.

3. Recurring Dreams

If recurring dreams were a punctuation mark, they would be the number sign #.

I have talked to people who say they have had the same dream so many times they have lost count. Perhaps it is a dream that started way back in childhood, or a dream with the same plot but slightly different symbols each time. Typically, the people who say this describe their dream with troubled faces. It comes accompanied either with fear, dread or embarrassment. Being in a public place naked. Falling off a tall building. Dying. Definitely with a recurring dream, there is the chance that something is weighing heavily on the mind. But be comforted by the fact that recurring dreams also happened in Scripture.

We already discussed how Joseph was called to interpret Pharaoh's two dreams. They were similar numerically, with their seven cows and seven ears of corn representing the next fourteen years of Egypt's agricultural and economic future, and although they were not the same exact dream, they had the same exact interpretation. Joseph said, "The dreams of Pharaoh are one; God has shown Pharaoh what He is about to do."

Yes, it is possible for a recurring dream with slightly different symbols to have one interpretation. Joseph's next statement introduces the idea that through multiple dreams, God is stressing the point that something is ordained to transpire: "And the dream was repeated to Pharaoh twice because the thing is established by God, and God will shortly bring it to pass" (Genesis 41:32). I do not want to say that the events in a repetitive dream are 100 percent set in stone to occur, but from looking at Joseph's statement, such dreams must be taken seriously and committed to prayer. Not with fear (because God has not given you a spirit of fear) and not with confusion (because God is not a God of confusion), but with priority.

> It is possible for a recurring dream with slightly different symbols to have one interpretation.

I remember once when I was watching a friend of mine die of cancer. At the time I would not say those words, and I constantly told her she was on her "life bed." I refused to entertain the thought of her death. Sheila had stage 4 cancer in seven organs, yet our entire community refused to give up hope. I was the prayer coordinator for her cause and was responsible for rallying thousands to pray. They took their cues from me, so if I demonstrated faith, they did, too. If I exhibited hopelessness or gave in to the gloominess of a certain day's report, they would take an "it's time for her to go home" posture, and we could not afford that. In fact, once someone did express that, and I reprimanded the person sharply.

I kept positive and kept the healing Word in front of everyone; then I would seek God at night to tell me what was going to happen. I have never taken a begging posture with God, because I am His daughter and I have His Word, but many a sleepless night during that season I begged. And then I would lie in bed and whisper, "Lord, what are You going to do? Will You show me? Give me a dream. Is she going to live? Are You going to heal her?" And then I would dream. Just like Pharaoh, I would have the same recurring dream, but with slightly different symbols or settings.

Once, I saw an extravagant house being built for her. But in a closet, tucked away, was a little suitcase. It was Sheila's. She was packed and ready to go somewhere. After waking, I knew the house was the house of prayer we were building for her, and I also knew the tiny suitcase represented her being packed and ready to go to heaven. And while you technically cannot take anything with you when you die, the suitcase was from the mid-sixties (when Sheila was born), and I knew it represented her life.

Another night, I dreamed about the packed suitcase again. This time it was in the driveway. Another night, I saw an open grave with fresh dirt piled up on the side and the shovel stuck in the ground, as if it would soon be shoveling the dirt back in. Then I dreamed what I did not want to dream. My persistent begging with God to see into Sheila's future finally led Him one night to give me a dream that needed no interpretation: I was sitting at her funeral. That one did me in. But I still asked God, "What are You going to do? Are You going to heal her? Are these dreams from the enemy?" Here I had had twice the number of dreams that Joseph had deemed as announcing that something was established by God, but I could not accept it. Why?

Because faith does not quit. I would do things the same way again. But then came the final dream that helped me let Sheila go. I saw her in a room with a bright light. She was totally well and was holding a little baby adoringly. She looked up at me and smiled. Peace was all over her face. And then I remembered she had lost a baby once, before the birth of her first child. Somehow, it was easier for me to release her to Jesus if I knew she had somebody up there waiting for her. She was leaving her children here, but finally going to meet another one she had never been able to hold. This dream also helped me fully grasp the concept that she was going to live forever—something you know deep down, by faith, but God knew I needed to *see* it. Again, another argument for the incalculable value of prophetic dreams.

4. Incubation Dreams

If incubation dreams were punctuation marks, they would be ellipses . . . *dot, dot, dot.*

An incubation dream is one that you have to file away with a "to be continued . . ." status. Not because a part 2 sequel will be coming in another dream, as with recurring dreams, but because what you have seen simply has no immediate application for your life. Perhaps you recognize the people in the dream and the setting and symbols, but you cannot make heads or tails of what it all means. Joseph's story of being a dream interpreter fascinates me. We see him go from being a boy who cannot interpret his own two dreams and save his own neck, to a man who interprets two highly symbolic dreams for a king and saves a whole nation. Suffering did that to him. Prison honed his prophetic eye. It "meeked" him.

Joseph's first mistake was telling a bunch of jealous relatives his dream about them bowing down to him. I can wholeheartedly understand Joseph's enthusiasm in wanting to solve the mystery of his dream, but he was young and should have let this dream incubate a little more instead of committing reputational suicide. Still, look what God did through the process. Joseph was thrown in a pit by his brothers. Sold into slavery in Potiphar's house. Falsely accused by Potiphar's wife. Thrown into prison. Met Pharaoh's baker and cupbearer there and interpreted their dreams. Stood before the king to interpret his dreams. As a result, Jacob, his sons and all of Israel were saved during the horrible famine, and through that family line came the Messiah.

But from the time Joseph left that pit as a slave until he stood before Pharaoh, thirteen years passed. Psalm 105:17–19 says, "He sent a man before them—Joseph—who was sold as a slave. They hurt his feet with fetters, he was laid in irons. Until the time that his word came to pass, the word of the LORD tested him." I love that. The word of the Lord tested him as he was waiting and as his dreams were incubating.

> An incubation dream is one that you have to file away with a "to be continued . . ." status.

I have a lot of dreams I can apply to my life immediately, but I have just as many incubation dreams. Of those that stand out, one was about when my daughter Jessica and new son-in-law, Kyle, moved to Virginia after Kyle was transferred to Fort Lee, where he served as a marine sergeant. They literally got married, packed and left for three years, and it taxed my heart to let them go. The day they drove off in the moving van, we joked that they were going to return with three kids in the back of it, but inside I thought, "No, Lord! I couldn't bear to become a grandmother so far away from the grandbaby!"

Our family is very close, and I could not bear the thought of not being there for my daughter and not doddling a new grandbaby on my knee. But then I had a dream. In it, I was at their home taking care of Jessi after she had had a son, and I saw myself packing up and leaving them to come back home. The emotions upon waking were gut-wrenching—especially the angst I felt in the dream at having to leave Jessica and the baby—but that dream incubated in me and marinated my mother's heart so that when she called nine months later to tell me she was pregnant, I felt as if I had already lived it. I was fine.

And guess what? They *did* move back three years later with three kids in the back of that moving van. How good of God not to show me that all at once. And how good of God not to show me that the first baby boy turned out to be *two* baby boys—twins. I would have been twice as heartsick at not being close by.

I also remember long before we were pastors that I had a few dreams I did not understand. In one, we were at lunch when about thirty of our church friends suddenly came and soberly placed a makeshift crown on my husband's head. It was made of a Thanksgiving cornucopia and had harvest corn coming out of it. I told my pastor at the time about it, with no response. Years later, as that ministry was dissolving and shutting down, that is exactly what happened. About thirty people came to us and said they wanted to stay together and form a church. Plus, it all happened at Thanksgiving time.

But what continued to incubate in me was this one particular couple that was in the dream. They were not with us at the new church, and I could not figure out why the Lord had included them in the dream. Their presence would have been such an affirming mark on our hearts for the new ministry because we respected them so much, and they were actually the ones in the dream who had placed the crown on Chris' head. Lo and behold, six years later, Barry and Fay Wallage showed up and have never left. And interestingly enough, they came home to us on a Thanksgiving weekend.

That incubation dream had both prepared us for being approached to pastor the church and sustained us until everyone in the dream was standing by our side to do it. Fay also became the prayer captain for this book you hold in your hands.

5. Apocalyptic Dreams

If apocalyptic dreams were a punctuation mark, they would be an asterisk * because they are only explained at the end of the story.

Moses, Isaiah, Jeremiah, Daniel, Ezekiel, Zechariah, Zephaniah and Habakkuk all have proven track records of prophetic accuracy when it comes to world events, but they also all have predictions yet to be fulfilled because they deal with the final days of judgment or the end of the world. I can just imagine these men all sitting around the dinner table in heaven and keeping score right now. When yet another dream or vision comes to pass, they high-five and then slide another bead across the prophetic abacus.

> If apocalyptic dreams were a punctuation mark, they would be an asterisk * because they are only explained at the end of the story.

Moses' 3,500-year-old "regathering of Israel" prophecy from Deuteronomy 30:3–5 is materializing before our very eyes, defining what it means to be alive in a prophetic time. Isaiah's prophecy about Jesus setting up a millennial Kingdom in Jerusalem is about 2,800 years old, and I am sure Isaiah is on the edge of his seat, just counting down the days for its fulfillment (see Isaiah 2:4). I wonder if Jeremiah is lamenting and crying over his currently developing prophecies. Hang on, Jeremiah!

I have never personally had any apocalyptic dreams, which is sort of a joke in our family. With all the teaching Mom does on prophecy, and with the number of prophetic dreams I have on a regular basis for myself and others, I have never once dreamed of the rapture, tribulation or anything else eschatological. I feel my prophetic dreams are more practical than mystical, which works well for me since I do a tremendous amount of pastoral counseling every week. But sometimes my mouth waters as I sit and listen to my family tell their dreams of being caught up into the clouds with Christ, or of seeing the events described in Scripture about the heavenly signs that herald the end of the world, such as the moon or stars doing crazy, impossible things.

The Other Side

Remember my waterfall dream at the start of chapter 1? Can you guess which of the ten prophetic dream categories it falls into? And what about Chris' sensible interpretation that calmed my hysteria? Was it correct? Most important, how was my relationship with God after the dream different from before?

The truth is, it is possible for a prophetic dream to be several categories rolled into one, as that dream was. It was an audible, encouraging, warning, waking dream. I was encouraged that God was affirming the leap of faith we had just taken and that He was telling me a great autumn was coming, but I also soberly knew this was most likely a warning of a difficult summer. And that time was indeed difficult—financially and reputationally—due to the repercussions of our decision. We had made the big leap of faith in January and were still on the high from that when the dream came a month later. While a dream at that time about a coming great fall season was *good* news, when the hard summer actually hit, it was *great* news.

Now I see the pattern of how the Lord does this for me. He does not give me scary dreams about impending doom. He gives me positive dreams on the front end to see me through a coming trial. Not that I do not have alarming dreams, but they are pure warning dreams and calls to pray. If I do my job well, the calamity will rarely hit. If for some reason it still comes, I have hope because God has already shown me the other side.

And we did get to the other side. That artist management company we tried starting with musicians, actors, painters, dancers, photographers and other artisans never amounted to anything because it was not supposed to. The name of the company was "The Oikos," and *oikos* is the Greek word in Scripture for "household." We foresaw a household of various genre artists, but it was not supposed to be a business; it was supposed to be a church. So 2,872 days after Chris took the leap and left Reunion Records, we started Eastgate Creative Christian Fellowship in Nashville, Tennessee. It has been one of the greatest joys of our lives. Starting out with a solely creative arts vision, it now houses artists of every kind, as well as those left-brainers gifted at what we call the "administrative arts."

Those seven years that we waited were the worst and the best of our lives as we hung on to each other during the free fall. But we—all eight of us—had our eyes and ears opened in the spirit realm in those years. Mornings at the "Campsmith" breakfast table were usually full of dream sharing and inter-pretations, and to this day, some of the sweetest words I can hear from my adult children are, "Hey, Mom, can I tell you my dream?"

Seeing the voice of God in dreams has changed my life forever, and there is not a single night that I do not crawl into bed excited at the thought that God might speak. He does speak just about every night, and He would like to do the same for you. I do not know if you have a problem with the idea of God speaking directly. I hope not, since hearing from God is what this book is about. And since John 10:27 says that we will know His voice, then we need to expect to. With that said, when I began writing this book, I kept hearing these words resonate in my spirit and sensed strongly that He wanted them stated plainly to you: "Visions and dreams are not a gift of the Spirit. They are mere communi-cation with Me, and communication with Me is the birthright of every believer."

> "Visions and dreams are not a gift of the Spirit. They are mere communication with Me, and communication with Me is the birthright of every believer."

From the time a future prophetic dream comes until the time it comes to pass can sometimes involve years, and as the dreamer, you may experience many stages and emotions along the way—particularly when the dream includes a promise concerning your future. When dreaming "The Impossible Dream" becomes more than a song to you and more like a way of life, be encouraged that millions of dreamers before you have waited upon the Lord and seen their dreams come true as they did.

"Dreaming"

dreaming.
planning.
listening.
praying.
hoping.
testing.
fearing.
swaying.
wondering.
doubting.
running.
crying.
crying.
crying.
crying.
dying.
nothing . . .
awakening.
praising!
believing.
knowing.
trusting.
trying.
pressing.
growing.
claiming.
standing.
rejoicing.
being.
shouting.
laughing.
having.
seeing.

© Laura Harris Smith,
October 1995

PRAYER

Let's pray out loud together:

Father, prepare me for my future, beginning tonight as I sleep. I want to know about upcoming snares set for me, Your secrets and what I can do to minister to others with Your insights. Holy Spirit, I receive any dreams You have for me, including warning dreams, directional dreams, recurring dreams, incubation dreams and apocalyptic dreams. As of today, I vow to You that I will begin a new life of stewarding these types of dreams with more gravity. In Jesus' name, Amen.

IMPARTATION

I release and impart to you the ability to dream "future dreams," the grace to be patient in prayer as you ponder them in your heart, and the intercessor's anointing. (Now open your hands, shut your eyes and receive it.)

4

Sleep: The Mattress of Dreams

For years I was an on-air guest personality at the Shop At Home TV Network, eventually getting hired there as a full-time TV host in 2006. Some of my most fun shows were the bedding shows. Production assistants would re-create an entire bedroom on the set, complete with a platform bed, matching furniture and all the expensive trimmings. It was my job to sell the mattress under me or the pillows beside me, so yes, that meant hopping up on the bed and doing the majority of the show from there. But unlike the shows where I sold matching bedskirts and curtains and could go on for an hour describing the various fabrics and options, selling a plain, white pillow and mattress can only be done by selling the concept of sleep itself.

Some of my buzz phrases were, "You spend a third of your life in bed. Don't you think you owe it to yourself to invest in a good night's sleep?" Or "Create a sanctuary and refuge you can retreat to at the end of every day." Buzz phrases or buzz words were statements hosts could say that would make the phones ring. While you were speaking on-air, you were also listening to the producer in your earpiece, who would tell you what phrases were working for you with today's viewers. Unlike you, the producer knew when the phone lines were lighting up and could draw conclusions as to why.

Another buzz phrase of mine was, "How long do you toss and turn before finding your sweet spot at night, and what if you could find it sooner?" Clever, huh? I guess you could say I was preying on people's fatigue, but if it was a 3:00 a.m. show, then it did not take a rocket scientist to figure out that my viewers were either insomniacs or afraid of the dark. What was the major selling point of the products in those bedding shows? Was it the fabric thread count? Was it the "NASA technology" in the spring foam that absorbed G-forces so well that they started making mattresses out of it? No, it was rest. The idea of a good night's rest was what made the bedding shows work. The phones rang when I talked about sleep. Why?

> You spend a third of your life in bed. Don't you think you owe it to yourself to invest in a good night's sleep?

Because people are not getting enough of it.

Scientists do not understand why we sleep, much less why we dream, but I have decided to devote two entire chapters in this dreams and visions book to the very practical and physical topic of sleep so that you can get more of it. I can just hear my husband and children now, cackling because they know I have always thought that sleep is such a whopping waste of time. Nonetheless, although I hate to sleep, I love to dream, and I know the two go together like a horse and carriage. If I cannot help you sleep, I cannot help you dream—and I do think I can help you dream if you say you are not having dreams.

I also believe I can help you remember your dreams if you normally cannot. I cannot sell you dreams the way I can sell you a mattress, but I am sure going to try, and sleep is the mattress of dreams. In this chapter, we will discuss the stages of sleep, dream sleep, the ramifications of sleep debt and my ABCs for ZZZs guide for a good night's sleep. Then for fun, we will review some free downloadable sleep and dream apps for your iPhone or Android that track your sleeping habits.

Simply put, I have jam-packed the next two chapters with every helpful hint that doctors and studies have confirmed will help you sleep and help you remember your dreams better. (You are welcome.)

Doctor's Orders

Upon making the decision to write this book, I had to look no further than my own biblical research from the last twenty years of eating, sleeping (literally) and breathing this topic. I had taught "Hearing the Voice of God" classes more than a decade before and had even created an eight-part audio series for that. But it was when I began teaching "Seeing the Voice of God" classes in 2005 that people really started responding at a greater level. People who felt unworthy or too intimidated to say "I had a word from the Lord" or "I heard God speak" felt more comfortable saying "I had a dream last night," and then edifying their listeners with what they saw about them in their dream.

But, although I had seen the self-proclaimed spiritually deaf begin to "see" God's voice for themselves and others, and although I had created endless computer files and workbooks on the subject that I could have adapted easily for this book, I knew that to make a book like this complete, there was one thing missing from my research—a medical perspective. As I said before, sleep is the mattress of dreams. After years of studying dreams themselves, I knew it was time for me to pull the covers back and do some fact-finding on the science that embraces the supernatural.

> Sleep is the mattress of dreams.

I already know everything that the dreamer Joseph, the prophet Jeremiah and the apostle Peter had to say about dreams in Scripture, but marrying that with a modern-day medical doctor's knowledge on dream physiology would be, well, a dream come true (pun intended).

To get started, in the summer of 2012 I met with Dr. Jonathan G. W. Evans, M.D., a board-certified pulmonologist at the Middle Tennessee Pulmonary Associates at Skyline Medical Center in Nashville, Tennessee. He specializes in sleep medicine, pulmonary diseases (of the lungs, including sleep apnea), critical care and internal medicine. He knows sleep the way I know dreams, and the verbal collision of our two worlds was, to say the least, fascinating. As I asked him to help me travel into the night hours and discover what we are all doing as we unconsciously lie there apparently doing nothing, I realized that we are not unconsciously lying there doing nothing. With that said, let me set the stage by diverging into a bit of science from what up until this point has been all biblical teaching.

Brain activity during dreams can be studied noninvasively by affixing anywhere from 4 to 256 tiny electrodes to someone's head and then attaching these electrodes to an electroencephalograph, or EEG. "Brain waves" are then marked and measured with wavy lines on a paper graph. Heaven knows, I have had my share of EEG glue in my hair over the last three decades. Back when I was suffering from violent convulsions, reading one of my EEG printouts would have surely been like looking at the erratic scribblings of a hyper toddler with an imposing black marker. But neurologists and scientists have a skillful eye when it comes to determining EEG results. They know what a seizure spike wave looks like versus an eye blink wave versus a sleep wave. And yes, there are even special waves for dreams.

There are also special, specific times each night for dreams (or if you work the nightshift, then you sleep and dream during the day, or even when napping). These times occur during what is called REM (rapid eye movement) sleep, a portion of the sleep cycle where you not only experience darting eye movements, higher blood pressure, accelerated breathing and an inability to maintain a normal body temperature, but also, through a sudden, automatic release to the brain of an amino acid called glycine, you are paralyzed.

And for good reason! If you were not, you would be acting out all those crazy dreams and be a great danger to yourself and to those around you. However, maybe a dream sometimes lingers at the cusp of exiting REM sleep, because one night my husband had a long soccer dream, at the end of which he finally was given the ball and allowed to kick a goal. He must have been given the ball right as he was exiting REM sleep, because the next morning I had the sore shins to prove it.

A complete sleep study involves a PSG, or polysomnogram, which not only studies brain waves but utilizes an EOG (electro-oculogram) to detect the REM eye movements, an EMG (electromyogram) to detect when you move and when you are paralyzed and an ECG (electrocardiogram) to track heart rhythms. As for the EEG monitoring the brain, our brain waves ride a roller coaster all night long as we sleep, into and out of and back into five different stages of sleep.

> Our brain waves ride a roller coaster all night long as we sleep, into and out of and back into five different stages of sleep.

Throughout the day, though, your brain waves are characterized as either alpha or beta waves. Beta waves appear during the normal daily stimuli you encounter (talking, listening, processing information), but alpha waves are slower, wider and typically present during times of relaxation and peacefulness, such as when in quiet introspection or prayer. But during the five nighttime sleep stages, these waves change remarkably. Think of the first four sleep stages (termed N-REM or non-REM sleep) as four gears that drive you to dreamland. As we look at the stages, you will see that sleep is less like one long, consistent journey and more like a trip with many rest stops.

Setting the Stage

The nightly ride you take, using your varied gears to get to these metaphorical rest stops, is what we will now explore.

Stage 1 (N1): You climb into bed. You find your "sweet spot" and close your heavy eyelids, and deep drowsiness sets in. You fade in and out of a relaxed state of early sleep, but if awakened by a shutting door or conversation, you will deny ever being asleep. However, your brain waves paint a different picture. They are already slowing down, your eyes are moving very slowly and your muscle activity reduces. Many people experience muscle jerkings and twitches called hypnic myoclonia at this time because their muscles are reacting to a sensation of falling as they relax and unclench. Brain waves during this stage are characterized by theta waves, which are even slower and wider on a graph than our daily alpha and beta waves. Stage 1 lasts between five and ten minutes. Think of it like first gear.

Stage 2 (N2): Your eyes stop moving, as does your body. Your heart rate slows, and your body temperature decreases. Your brain waves become even slower, continuing with theta waves, but with the periodic occurrence of a phenomenon termed *sleep spindles*, which are 1-second to 2-second bursts of electrical activity. *K complexes* also occur, which EEG readings show are sizable peak and valley brain waves. Some scientists believe both of these types of brain waves help us turn off the outside world and its sounds. Since the elderly seem to have fewer sleep spindles, this could explain why they are such light sleepers. If you are prone to sleeptalking (somniloquy), it usually occurs during this stage. Your body is preparing to enter deep sleep, and after about 15–20 minutes in this second gear, you do.

Stage 3 (N3): You are totally separated now from the cognizant world around you, your problems, worries and all stress. Your brain activity is more synchronized and seems eagerly unified to reach its destination of deep sleep. The theta waves become delta waves, which are the slowest and strongest waves our brains produce.

Many sleep study specialists now combine stage 3 and stage 4 into one stage called N3, but the slight difference in the stages is that stage 3 contains only 20 percent to 50 percent of these deep sleep delta waves, whereas stage 4 is marked by a majority of delta activity. This non-dreaming sleep in stage 3 is the time at which you are most likely to sleepwalk (somnambulism). Dr. Evans says this occurs in up to 40 percent of children, peaking around the ages of 11–12. (Having had six children, I can attest to this statistic with many comical accounts.) Although it is difficult to predict how long a person will spend in stage 3 before drifting off into its near twin, stage 4, it is known that we enter this "third gear" about 35–40 minutes after falling asleep.

Stage 4 (still considered N3): Now you are in slow delta wave deep sleep and are utterly oblivious to any external stimuli. Your body, bringing all that ails it, is happy to be here since this is the slice of night when restorative sleep occurs. During delta deep sleep, a phenomenon occurs that is nothing short of miraculous: The pineal gland automatically releases growth hormone, which in children results in bone and muscle growth, but in adults provides tissue repair and total body rejuvenation. And since the body also decreases its breakdown of proteins during deep sleep—proteins you need to have stick around and repair damage from the day's stress and ultraviolet rays—it is also thought that deep sleep is your "beauty sleep." Prolactin and gonadotropin are also secreted, which makes the precious time spent in this stage a phase of healing and rehabilitation. If awakened during stage 4 (deep N3) sleep, you will be very disoriented and may even appear drunk. It is also during this stage that most bedwetting occurs.

Then, before you shift into our proverbial "fifth gear," which is REM dream sleep, the other stages actually reverse and you downshift gears, going from stage 4 back to stage 3 and then landing at stage 2—as if you are moving back up the charts toward awakening, but you never do. It is as if you are pushing up a hill in second gear, reach the top and then begin to coast downward—fast. Before you know it, you have skipped all the other gears and have shifted immediately into a proverbial fifth gear, REM. Ah . . . dreamland!

Your first complete sleep cycle is stage 1 to 2 to 3 to 4, then back to 3, then 2 . . . then finally into the final phase, REM dream sleep. That is one sleep cycle down and only four or five more to go before sunrise. Each of these full sleep cycles lasts between 90–120 minutes, and after the first cycle, each of the remaining cycles shifts gears in a little different order. As the night goes on, you spend less time in N3 deep restoration sleep and more time in N2 and REM sleep. In the first sleep cycle, you only spend about 10 minutes at the end in REM dream sleep, but like some dangling carrot intended to lure you to get more sleep, the latter sleep cycles have you in almost solid REM dream sleep.

> With a full eight hours of sleep, you are experiencing between an hour and a half and two hours of dreaming. That is like watching a full-length movie each night as you sleep!

Each night, with a full eight hours of sleep, you are experiencing between an hour and a half and two hours of dreaming. That is like watching a full-length movie each night as you sleep!

Sleep Debt

It is not normal for a healthy adult to board an airplane before lunch and fall asleep within five minutes in an uncomfortable chair, surrounded by strangers, but we do. Why? Because we are starved for sleep. The world seems to be spinning faster every day, full of opportunities and activities vying for our attention. The way we respond to those opportunities is to sleep deprive ourselves and seize them.

"Sleep debt" is exactly what it sounds like: accumulated sleep deprivation for which the body will pay a great price. When you hear that you owe it to yourself to rest, it is true. Count sheep or get overdrawn at the sleep bank. Sooner or later, your body will insist the debt be paid.

Lack of sleep will alter your sleep stages, resulting in what is called REM rebound, the lengthening and intensifying of REM sleep after stretches of sleep deprivation. If you crawl into bed exhausted, having accrued recent sleep debt, you will bypass the first few sleep stages and jump right into REM dream sleep. But recalling these REM rebound dreams becomes difficult because your body's need for deep sleep wins out and you sleep like a rock, spending the majority of the night in N3. Thus, sleep deprivation is a dream stealer in terms of recall.

While you can acclimate your mind to a sleep-deprived schedule, your body cannot adjust and function at peak performance. The sleep debt will show up in your delayed reaction times, poor judgment and other impaired functions. And not only do you harm yourself when you scrimp and catch only twenty winks; you also endanger others. The National Sleep Foundation's website says that according to the National Highway Traffic Safety Administration, about 100,000 police-reported crashes annually are due to driver fatigue, resulting in around 71,000 injuries, more than 1,500 deaths and $12.5 billion in economic losses.[1]

In addition, in 2007 the Division of Sleep Medicine at Harvard University published an article entitled "Sleep Performance and Public Safety" that disclosed how lack of sleep quality or quantity can lead to costly workplace miscalculations and blunders that endanger lives and the environment around us. Listen to this:

> Investigators have ruled that sleep deprivation was a significant factor in the 1979 nuclear accident at Three Mile Island, as well as the 1986 nuclear meltdown at Chernobyl.
>
> Investigations of the grounding of the Exxon Valdez oil tanker, as well as the explosion of the space shuttle *Challenger*, have concluded that sleep deprivation also played a critical role in these accidents. In both cases, those in charge of the operations and required to make critical decisions were operating under extreme sleep deprivation. While the *Challenger* disaster put the

multi-billion dollar shuttle program in peril, the Exxon Valdez oil spill resulted in incalculable ecological, environmental, and economic damage.[2]

The Chernobyl meltdown or the *Challenger* explosion may not have affected you, but sleep-deprivation disasters affect your doctors and local hospitals. Between 50,000 and 100,000 deaths and over 1 million needless injuries take place annually as a direct consequence of medical mishaps, according to the Institutes of Medicine, and they report that many of those are the product of insufficient sleep.[3]

And after med school, it is the newest doctor graduates completing their internships who are often called on to work back-to-back shifts of 24 to 36 hours with little or no sleep. Interestingly enough, when I sat with Dr. Evans in Nashville last summer for our interview, the first piece of information he volunteered was a testimony about his own sleep debt during medical school and afterward, during his residency. For three years he worked 36-hour shifts, which were, as he put it, "interrupted by 0–3 hours of fragmented sleep." At the conclusion of the 36 hours, he would sleep like a rock for 11–12 hours and then do it all over again. Granted, he was only a resident, but by the end of each week he had totaled 120 hours on duty, more often than not. Although he smiled and said he did fine grabbing those fragmented hours of sleep when he could, I find it ironic that after such sleep deprivation, he completed that residency and went on to specialize in sleep medicine during his fellowship at George Washington University, where he studied to become a pulmonologist. (And I will take a sleep doctor over a sleepy doctor any day of the week.)

Likewise, Harvard Medical School's Division of Sleep Medicine issued a study led by Dr. Charles Czeisler divulging that hospitals could reduce their medical mistakes and oversights by an outstanding 36 percent by limiting doctors' shifts to no more than 16 hours at a time, with a weekly work load not to exceed 80 hours.[4] This was a fact Dr. Evans also alluded to during our conversation, when he said that just a few years after he graduated, studies were done that prompted government intervention to regulate hospital shifts, promptly putting an end to such long rotations for the students following in Dr. Evans's footsteps.

And let's not forget the Colgan Air crash on February 12, 2009, that killed all 49 people on board and someone in the house the plane hit. That crash, later linked to pilot fatigue, prompted a string of investigations of all the major regional airlines in America. The victims' families took their voices to Capitol Hill and asked the government to pick up the airlines' slack if they were not going to regulate pilot schedules and commuter demands, and also pay pilots enough so that they did not have to sleep on crew lounge sofas the night before a flight. Or worse, in "pilot crash pads," tiny near-airport apartments lined with dozens of bunk beds crowded together in often unsanitary conditions. These accommodations are often all a starter pilot making $16K per year can afford to rent. In February 2011, the ABC News program *Nightline* broadcast a story on the two-year anniversary of the Colgan crash to see if these airline amendments had been enforced. The story reported that "little has changed."[5]

> Just as fewer than fifty years ago we did not understand the deadly effects of tobacco, we also have not fully understood the deadly effects of too little sleep until now.

But fear not, the tide will turn. Just as fewer than fifty years ago we did not understand the deadly effects of tobacco, we also have not fully understood the deadly effects of too little sleep until now. But the world is waking up to it. Are you in your own life?

If you typically fall asleep within five minutes of lying down—whether at night or for a nap—you may have a sleep debt and be suffering from extreme sleep deprivation. According to Dr. Evans, sleep debt is not cleared up with one night's good sleep. Sometimes it takes two or more. He says the first night you will spend in N3 deep sleep, and on the second night you will regain your REM cycles. That is another argument to either support getting ample sleep or quit complaining that you never dream.

Just for Fun

If you are curious about your own sleeping habits and cycles but do not need a doctor-supervised sleep study, why not try out one of the many downloadable sleep cycle apps on your iPhone or Android? I typed "sleep cycles" in the search field of my iPhone's App Store and came up with over a hundred apps. Then I typed in "sleep" and came up with two thousand more. The same was true for Androids, and I am about to suggest a dozen popular choices for both types of smartphones (all of which were available at the time of this book's publication). Some are free, but none of them cost more than a few dollars.

How do these apps work? Using your Android or iPhone's extremely sensitive accelerometer, they monitor your movements during sleep when you place the phone near (but not under) your pillow. After spending a summer studying EMFs (electromagnetic fields), I am not a fan of sleeping near electronics, and I worked on ridding my home of "dirty electricity" and rearranging it to have less concentrated "hot spots." But when I weighed the risks against investing just a few nights in finding ways to improve my sleep (and therefore my overall health), I went for it. Here are a dozen app suggestions for you if you're curious about that third of your life you have been missing.

For the iPhone, I downloaded Sleep Checker, Sleep Time, Smart Alarm Clock, Sleep Cycle, Sleep Lab Snore Monitor and my personal favorite, Sleep Bot, which not only allows you to keep up with your sleep trends in a history log but also emails them to you for further study. But most impressively, it educates you about sleep debt and helps you calculate and control yours, while also offering dietary suggestions of foods that will help you go to sleep (or stay awake when need be).

For Android, there is Sleep Diary, Sleep Right, 90 Minutes, Sleep Cycles, Electric Sleep and Sleep As Android, which is getting rave reviews and already boasts between 1 million and 5 million downloads. Sleep As Android includes sleeptalk recording, go-to-bed notifications, antisnoring features, sleep graph history, deep sleep stats, nature alarm sounds and even lullabies for sleep.

Most of these apps aim to track your sleep stages in order to avoid awakening you during deep sleep, because waking up during this stage can be the reason you are groggy and hard to rouse each morning (even when you sleep a full forty winks). You set a thirty-minute wake-up time window, and the app smartly adjusts the wake-up time once it senses the smaller movements of a lighter sleep stage. Some of the apps even claim that after a few nights, they can learn your REM cycles and wake you up during the final one so that you can remember those vivid dreams.

Some of the apps only wake you, some only lull you to sleep, but some will do everything but drag you out of bed and make you breakfast. The interfaces on many of these apps are slick. The most humorous sleep app award from me goes to Help I Can't Sleep's "Dream Recorder," a hilarious animated app that pokes fun at the dream app theory and posts amusing (and often embarrassing) made-up dreams from you on Facebook and Twitter. Not on your life!

Some of the apps are based on the theory that if a normal night's sleep consists of four to six full 90-minute sleep cycles, then an app can predict when you need to awaken and have the alarm sound during your lightest sleep phase of the final cycle. Trouble is, not every full sleep cycle is 90 minutes. Some of these apps are therefore ineffectual, but nonetheless amusing. Hey, if something has a chance of turning me into a morning person, I am all for it.

If you are in the mood to lay down $150 for a watch/wristband that claims to track your sleep cycles within 95 percent of the accuracy of sleep monitors used in professional sleep studies, then the SleepTracker is for you. It was even voted Invention of the Year by *Time* magazine.

None of these apps can replace a more sophisticated sleep study, and none will reveal sleep apneas or other sleep disorders. They will, however, give you an inside glance into a third of your life that you have never cognitively experienced. Using one to monitor your sleep is like reading a postcard from yourself to yourself the next morning.

Please avoid apps that promote lucid dreaming or hypnotherapy, however, as well as those that play preprogrammed phrases and tones while you sleep. You could be throwing wide open a door in your spirit and asking for trouble. (Check out the personal interview on lucid dreaming in chapter 10.)

"Sleep Sound" Advice

Circadian rhythms are our miraculous inner wirings toward a schedule, sort of like a biological clock. *Circadian* is Latin for "around a day" and means "recurring naturally on a twenty-four-hour cycle, even in the absence of light fluctuations: a circadian rhythm."[6] But because light has so much influence on us, people's internal clocks changed drastically with the invention of electricity. Now we do not have to go to bed when the sun goes down because we can flip a switch and stay up for hours longer.

Trouble is, the sun still rises the next morning, and our bodies begin responding before we ever awaken. Why? Because light shuts off the production of melatonin, a hormone that increases at dark and produces drowsiness. Light, with all of its signals, hits your retinas, crosses your optic nerves, travels to the hypothalamus and into your suprachiasmatic nucleus (or SCN), where about twenty thousand neurons are waiting to take those signals and dead-end at your pineal gland. *Wham!* The pineal gland tells the melatonin its job is done and shuts down production. All of a sudden, you are not drowsy anymore. This is why it is so important that if you get up for that middle-of-the-night bathroom break, you leave the lights off so that you can remain drowsy.

So many factors alter our body rhythms, such as alarm clocks, the neighbor dog's annoying barking, the baby needing that 2:00 a.m. feeding or even the timing of our meals. Circadian rhythms are even responsible for that sluggish feeling you suffer when you cross into another time zone. You call it jet lag.

Laura's ABCs for ZZZs Sleep Tips

Earlier we compared the sleep stages to gears, so think of your nightly descent toward bedtime as starting the engine of a car. Here are some keys to use for a great ride into dreamland:

A. *Abstain from all caffeine, nicotine and alcohol since they can lead to insomnia.* Caffeine is lurking in many things including chocolate, soft drinks, nonherbal teas, diet pills, energy drinks and of course, coffee. And remember, alcohol in any form may sometimes help you fall asleep, but you will not stay asleep. For deep sleep, skip the nightcap. Finally, consider that smoking is not just bad for your lungs, but bad for sleep cycles due to waking up with nicotine withdrawals. Let this be the year that you rid your body of all such habit-forming, life-altering substances.

B. *Bedtime Math.* Consider your required wake-up time the next morning and subtract at least 8½ hours from it to determine your bedtime. That allows 15 minutes to wind down (doing my Sleep ABCs for ZZZs), 15 minutes to actually fall asleep and 8 hours to actually sleep. If you need to rise at 6:00 a.m., then be done with your Sleep ABCs and in bed no later than 9:45 p.m. You can adjust the times to fit your schedule. Midnight to 8:00 a.m. has always served my schedule well, but my challenge as a writer is that once I am finally enjoying a quiet house late

> Be good to yourself and create your own bedtime traditions. Sleep time is a sacred time.

at night, it is easy to get a second wind and breeze right past midnight. Make promises to yourself to be at step C (which follows) 15 minutes before bedtime each night.

C. *Create room atmosphere and temperature.* As you are beginning your descent toward bedtime and heading to the bedroom or bathroom to prepare, use soft lighting to begin adjusting your circadian rhythms, which signals your brain to pump out the drowsy juice, melatonin. Adjust the temperature to a bit cooler than during the day, but remember that too hot or too cold causes constant tossing and turning. Perhaps turn on a fan for some white noise.

D. *De-stress for 5 minutes before climbing into bed.* You can use a warm face wash, an Epsom salt bath (which is pure magnesium sulfate and aids sleep), essential oils on your pillow or any favorite relaxation routine to train your body that sleep is near. Be good to yourself and create your own bedtime traditions. Sleep time is a sacred time.

E. *Enter.* Time to transition into your bed clothes, bedroom and bed itself. Lie down, close your eyes and enter into peace. Ask God to enter your heart if you never have; then ask Him to enter your dreams and speak to you tonight.

F. *Forgive.* You have cleansed the atmosphere in your room, and now it is time to cleanse the atmosphere of your heart. "Don't let the sun go down while you are still angry, for anger gives a foothold to the devil" (Ephesians 4:26–27 NLT). It is time to forgive whoever ruined your day or night, especially if it is the person lying next to you. What you go to bed with, you wake up with, so choose love. Then ask God's forgiveness for yourself for whatever He brings to mind, and receive it. Finally, forgive yourself and determine to start fresh again tomorrow.

G. *Go to sleep.* Find your "sweet spot" sleeping position. If you cannot fall asleep, try slowing down your breathing. This mirrors what happens anyway during N1 and N2; you are basically tricking your brain into thinking you are there and causing your brain waves to slow down and widen (I have done this for years). If you still cannot fall asleep, try keeping a gratitude journal that you write in at this time each night, listing just three things you are thankful for that day. Or try reading, but use an actual book and not your Kindle, iPad or other tablet because the direct lights will cue your pineal gland to quit making melatonin and will wake you up. You would not want to have to start the whole winding-down process again. Also, pray Psalm 127:2 over yourself: "For so He gives His beloved sleep."

Experts will tell you that the best way to get a good night's sleep is not to set an alarm clock, but most working people must set an alarm. Considering what we learned earlier about circadian rhythms and light's power to shut down melatonin production (thus waking you up), the key to living with an alarm clock is to turn on bright lights as quickly as possible each morning. Even Mr. Rooster knows that light is an alarm clock's best friend. And if you sense some sleep debt coming on, get an extra hour of sleep as soon as possible. But go to bed an hour earlier at night since somehow a morning "sleeping in" does not cut it. In fact, sometimes it leaves you feeling even more sluggish. Have you ever experienced "sleep-in hangover"?

Remember, too, that daily exercise—even just twenty minutes a few times a week—is a great cure for insomnia. Just do not exercise before bedtime.

After all of my ABCs for ZZZs, if you still have trouble falling asleep night after night, or if you are constantly tired during the day, consider seeing a sleep doctor. There is nothing wrong with asking for the help of a good physician, just as long as you filter his or her wisdom through the higher wisdom of the Great Physician.

The Battle of the Bed

I want to end this chapter with a night owl's confession by giving you my own near-deadly sleep deprivation testimony, not just because it will save someone's life, but because it will reiterate my previous teaching about the power of warning dreams.

I was consistently drained each morning not because of a sleep disorder, but because of a "sleep defiance." I had a lifelong habit of getting four or five hours of sleep each night. Because I had endless energy and the metabolism of a grasshopper, I could get a second wind at midnight, put in two or three more hours of writing, and then be back up at 7:30–8:00 a.m. for another homeschool day with my six children. Night after night I did this for years, wearing my ability to operate so efficiently like a badge. Ignorance and sheer will kept me from seeing all the sleep debt warning signs in my body. I was robbing Peter to pay Paul and slowly killing myself. Creative types must be very careful not to let their genius be the death of them.

> Ignorance and sheer will kept me from seeing all the sleep debt warning signs in my body. I was robbing Peter to pay Paul and slowly killing myself.

My sleep defiance finally caught up with me and I wore my adrenal system out, meaning I had no adrenaline left for the bursts of energy necessary for motherhood and grandmotherhood (not to mention ministry, business and teaching). I also had no cortisol left to get me through each day's stresses and calm me down. Because of my strong constitution, I never really felt exhausted, but my insides felt it. At five foot two and 107 pounds in my early forties, my sugar levels and cholesterol suddenly shot up, and my metabolism and adrenals started shutting down—as did my thyroid, all my hormones and my entire reproductive system. My lack of sleep began to affect just about every organ system in my body, but we caught it on the brink of being too late. A sleep debt that had taken thirty years to accumulate had only taken three years to make my once-healthy body fall into a deep sleep, one organ at a time. If I would not sleep externally, the organs in my body decided they would sleep anyway, internally. Adrenal exhaustion has four stages, the fourth of which is adrenal failure—when your organs shut down. I was in stage 3.

I learned that with serious focus I could turn my condition around, so we got to work, but not before the warning dreams started coming. Some of them even came *before* the grave diagnosis or the slightest hint of it. They came to me, to friends and to family, and they all had the same message: death. Caskets, funerals, my family in mourning—you name it. We did not even tell our younger children about the frightening dreams. They are hearing about them for the first time right here, along with you. So when the diagnosis did come, I was all ears. I was told that if I did not turn this around, I would die.

A precious friend, mentor and classy Nashville businesswoman, Trish, had gotten me on the waiting list with her five-star Christian nutritionist for a general visit months before all this. This master nutritionist always had a multimonth waiting list, but by God's grace, I got my diagnosis ten days before my visit, changing the nature of the appointment entirely. During those ten days before the visit, Trish baby-stepped me through the vitamin regimen that had helped her years earlier, when she had been diagnosed with stage 3 adrenal burnout. By this point, I could not even stand up without almost passing out, so Trish was my lifeline during that week of angst between the diagnosis and the nutritionist appointment.

I had to rebuild my system with the extensive and expensive supervision of many different medical professionals, including doctors, but in the end, it was the nutritionist who saved my life and changed it forever. I already ate all my vegetables, went to the YMCA daily and watched bad fats. But without sleep, my body was not in the mood to give me any brownie points for it. I held up my nutritionist's wisdom to my lifestyle as a measuring stick and realized I had not been wholeheartedly taking care of God's temple, my body. "I was given a reed like a measuring rod and was told, 'Go and measure the temple of God'" (Revelation 11:1 NIV). I repented. I started again.

I had missed all the warning signs and hints from heaven. God had been trying as far back as my early thirties to get me to sleep more. Some good friends had even given us a $1,200 mattress, and I still did not take God's hint. I had not heard myself, either, as I stood there each night on Shop At Home TV *telling millions and millions of people they needed to invest in their rest.* Sad to say, but it took years of health struggles and then some scary warning dreams about death to get my attention. The seriousness of my condition stopped me in my tracks and made me change my lifestyle. It also made me get busy praying to live. The enemy wanted me dead; God did not. The warning dreams were not showing me my future, but my assignment. They were wake-up calls. Wake-up calls to get more sleep!

About a week after my life-changing visit to the nutritionist's office, I suddenly remembered something Dr. Jonathan Evans had said to me as I was feverishly typing during my interview with him the summer before: "The biggest metabolic changes that occur from sleep deprivation are hormonal. You get sick when you don't sleep." I had sat there listening to one of the best and most passionate sleep doctors anywhere (his medical sleep books were as highlighted and ragged as my Bible), yet I had missed this attempt at divine intervention. I had every major hormonal system in my body going awry and I knew it sitting there, but even with his words, I did not make the connection. Surely sleep doctors were just for people with apnea. I was exempt. I was covered by God's grace. I was a minister, so God had my back. That warped thinking was part of my undoing. What a slap in God's face.

The diagnosis, the warning dreams, my friend Trish, the nutritionist and Dr. Evans were the five fingers on God's hand that finally shook some sense into me. And how clever of God to make me have to study sleep for my work since He knew work was what was keeping me from sleep.

In a way, this book helped save my life. I hope it does the same for you, so please do not wait until things go so far before you change your sleeping habits. At the risk of offending you, I hope God will make you miserable until you treat your body better. Do not ask God for healing to come through the front door when your bad health choices are ushering it right out the back. Let this be the year you get healthy. In the past you have heard "diet and exercise," but now it is "diet, exercise and sleep."

Now that you understand the science of sleep and will be sleeping smarter, let's look in the next chapter at the predominant reasons why you may have poor dream recall. Of course, God can speak to you in a dream anyway in the supernatural realm, but also remember that you can hinder that process by not taking care of your body in the natural realm. God created you to dream, but He also created you to sleep. He wants your sleep to be sweet. He even made it one of the Ten Commandments for you to take one whole day a week to rest, and He set the example by resting on the seventh day after the creation of the world. Be a Sabbath keeper and live.

As it turns out, sleep is not the titanic time waster I mistook it for. In fact, I think sleep doctors could put all the other doctors out of business with the ailments they cure when they help a person find sleep. Think about it—from the moment your head hits the pillow each night, your body begins setting the stage for the next day of your life, and it is trying to deliver you there healthy. The regimen sleep follows is nothing short of miraculous, and to interrupt it—or cheat it—will result in poor health, and more relevant to our topic, an altered dream journey.

> In the past you have heard "diet and exercise," but now it is "diet, exercise and sleep."

Now I lay me down to sleep
I pray the Lord I don't count sheep
And if I dream before I wake
I pray it sticks for heaven's sake.
Amen.

© Laura Harris Smith,
February 4, 2013

PRAYER

Let's pray out loud together:

> God, *where do I start? I am sorry for abusing my body, for not taking care of it and for every vow and resolution I've ever broken to better care for it, Your temple. I pray that You will forgive me and give me a strategy and schedule for optimum health. God, make my sleep sweet. Pay my sleep debt and rejuvenate my body. Not just nightly, but once a week as I participate in Your Sabbath rest. I receive Your healing. I receive Your peace. In Jesus' name, Amen.*

IMPARTATION

Right now, I release and impart to you the ability to go to sleep, stay asleep, sleep deeply and dream. (Now open your hands, shut your eyes and receive it.)

5

Dream Recall

Austrian psychoanalyst Sigmund Freud said that we only remember the dreams we want to remember. Many African tribes believe that real life is lived in dreams and that our waking hours are the illusion. Bolivian philosopher Oscar Ichazo depicted dream reality as like the night stars and said they are always there, but that the brightness of the sun and the consciousness of the day blot them out. Many American scientists believe that the only purpose for dreams is to process the events of one's day and consolidate memories. What do you believe? Have you ever really given much thought to this phenomenon of dreams?

Freud, Jewish by birth and atheist by choice, had some deep insight on dreams, but his dreams were monochrome at best because he chose to exclude the Giver of them. That is like believing in milk but denying the cow. You could analyze the milk, its nutrients and its benefits with utmost scientific accuracy, but without knowing the source and your connection to it, and without nourishing that source, the quality of the milk would not only suffer, but your cup would eventually run dry.

Freud's *The Interpretation of Dreams*, published in 1900, took eight years to sell out of its first six hundred copies, and evidently he was only paid $209. But as the public intrigue with dreams increased, seven more successful editions followed.[1] Since he was an atheist until the day of his death, you may wonder why I am interested in Freud's thoughts on dreams, but the truth is that he and I both had a preoccupation with the topic of dreams and wrote books about it. He was so close! All the answers were right in front of him, but he still missed it— not the dreams, but the dream Giver. He thought of belief in God as a collective neurosis (mental disorder). He called it "longing for a father." So close again, since God *is* our Father, but still so far because Freud did not know Him and made no bones about not seeing the need.

> By day, you may think in your mind you are an atheist, a Buddhist, an agnostic or whatever, but by night, as your spirit stays awake with your body and mind asleep, you are God's child and He is still drawing you.

We know that Freud dreamed because much of his work involved self-analysis of his own dreams. I fully believe God tried to reach him in the night hours. At night, you are God's. Your body and mind are resting, but as I said at the start, your spirit is awake all night. Your spirit is the part of you that hears God. Therefore, by day, you may think in your mind you are an atheist, a Buddhist, an agnostic or whatever, but by night, as your spirit stays awake with your body and mind asleep, you are God's child and He is still drawing you. Take heart in that fact if you have loved ones who are adamantly anti-God or who have become entangled with false doctrine that compromises their once-pure faith.

On how quickly dreams slip from your grasp and get left behind, Freud and I agree. He said this:

That a dream fades away in the morning is proverbial. It is, indeed, possible to recall it. For we know the dream, of course, only by recalling it after waking; but we very often believe that we remember it incompletely, that during the night there was more of it than we remember. On the other hand, it often happens that dreams manifest an extraordinary power of maintaining themselves in the memory. I have had occasion to analyse, with my patients, dreams which occurred to them twenty-five years or more previously, and I can remember a dream of my own which is divided from the present day by at least thirty-seven years, and yet has lost nothing of its freshness in my memory.[2]

Forget Me Not

If you wake up immediately after a dream, you have an 80 percent chance of remembering it, according to a 1953 study done by University of Chicago researcher Dr. Nathaniel Kleitman, Ph.D., and two of his students, William C. Dement and Eugene Aserinsky. Suspicious that darting eye movements were associated with dreaming, they did a test and awoke subjects during various sleep stages, to discover that 80 percent of them reported having dreams and only 7 percent did not. I am not sure what the other 13 percent reported—perhaps they were unsure—but for certain on that night, REM sleep was discovered and linked to dreaming. Dr. William Dement, now known in the medical community as the father of modern sleep medicine, said of that night in his book *Some Must Watch While Some Must Sleep,*

> The vivid recall that could be elicited in the middle of the night when a subject was awakened while his eyes were moving rapidly was nothing short of miraculous. It [seemed to open] . . . an exciting new world to the subjects whose only previous dream memories had been the vague morning-after recall. Now, instead of perhaps some fleeting glimpse into the dream world each night, the subjects could be tuned into the middle of as many as ten or twelve dreams every night.[3]

Dr. Dement is also quoted as saying, "The simplest definition of REM sleep is a highly active brain in a paralyzed body." That is why in my gears analogy in chapter 4, although it would have seemed more logical to label the sleep stages as moving from fourth gear downward to first since the subject is winding down toward sleep, that would have meant interpreting the fifth stage as "park," and the brain is in anything but "park" during REM sleep! In fact, REM dream brain waves look more similar to waking brain waves than any of the other brain waves of sleep—beta, alpha or delta.

Interestingly enough, the same Dr. Evans whom I interviewed for chapter 4 says that if he phones someone in the middle of the night and awakens them, he can tell which stage of sleep they are in. If they are in REM dream sleep and get awakened, they can immediately engage in conversation, but if they are in deep sleep, they will hardly be able to talk and may not even remember the call the next day. He adds, "It's because the mind is ON during REM sleep and OFF during deep sleep."

The National Institute of Neurological Disorders and Stroke (NINDS) in Bethesda, Maryland, states it like this:

> This sleep-related form of amnesia is the reason people often forget telephone calls or conversations they've had in the middle of the night. It also explains why we often do not remember our alarms ringing in the morning if we go right back to sleep after turning them off.[4]

In the sixty years since that 1953 University of Chicago study, it has been tested, proven and printed hundreds of times over that there are four to six of these 90-minute to 120-minute cycles each night, with each cycle containing four to six dreams. Thus, you could be having up to 36 dreams each night. You have the potential of dreaming over 13,000 dreams per year. That means that by age 75, with proper sleep, you could have dreamed almost one million dreams.

Then why aren't you remembering your dreams, or even most of them? Would you like to? I ask because I am amazed at how many people have resigned themselves to a dreamless life. You do not have to.

The number-one line I hear when I begin discussing dreams with people is, "Oh, I never dream." The experience seems gated to them, and they have accepted it as part of who they are. But it is not who they are, nor who you are. You do dream every night. If babies dream and the blind dream and animals dream (check out our FAQ page at the end of the book), then why would God snub you? Not only is it scientifically impossible for you to opt out of the REM dream sleep cycle, but it is not within God's nature to exclude you from what is potentially His greatest opportunity to get you still and speak to you.

> By age 75, with proper sleep, you could have dreamed almost one million dreams.

No one can say he or she does not dream. Every one of us dreams. Every night. Multiple times a night. In fact, you may be dreaming as many as three dozen dreams each night. So all of you who say "I never dream" can stop saying it. The real issue to address now is not the dreaming, but the trouble remembering those dreams.

Get serious about taking back your dreams.

Sick and Tired

We spend about 8 hours daily, 56 hours weekly, 240 hours monthly and 2,920 hours annually doing it. That is right . . . *sleeping.* Live 45 years and you will have slept 15 of them. Live 75 years and you will have slept for a quarter of a century!

In 1960, a survey by the American Cancer Society asked 1 million Americans how much sleep they got per night. The median answer was 8 hours. Today that number has fallen to 6.7 hours. That is a decrease of more than 15 percent in less than a lifetime.[5]

According to *Web*MD and its various physician sources, the amount of sleep we need varies from person to person and depends on various lifestyle factors. Babies usually need 16–18 hours of sleep per day (and it is mainly all REM sleep), while teens need about 9. Most adults should get between 7–8 hours of sleep each night.[6]

As we age, we still need the same amount of sleep, but our sleep tends to get lighter and shorter. N-REM stages 3 and 4 (N3, deep sleep) sometimes shorten or stop completely in the aged. So we have to ask ourselves, is diminishing health just a part of old age, or does it develop as a result of diminishing deep sleep? One thing is for sure: Even a young adult's health will diminish more quickly if a sleep disorder is present that prohibits restorative sleep.

Sleepless in America

According to the NINDS, at least 40 million Americans suffer from sleep disorders and another 20 million encounter them periodically. The sleep medicine business is a $16 billion a year industry involving more than 70 identified sleep disorders. Most of those can be treated, returning the sleepless to a good night's sleep.[7] Let's look at two of the most common sleep disorders.

Insomnia

Simply put, insomnia is the inability to sleep, or consistent sleeplessness. We are not talking *Sleepless in Seattle* or the occasional inability to fall asleep, but chronic sleeplessness. There is also sleep-maintenance insomnia, which is the inability to stay asleep after falling asleep. Insomniacs rarely awake feeling refreshed, and the nightly tossing and turning leaves its imprint on their entire day.

Dr. Evans says that in his experience, women suffer from insomnia more than men. He offers promising opinions about treatment and says that whereas a primary care doctor would prescribe a sleeping aid and perhaps refer you to a psychologist, in his line of work he tries to determine the tangible, physical reasons you are not sleeping and correct them so that you are not dependent on medications. One of the results of taking sleep aids can be iatrogenic (physician induced) insomnia, which is when a patient develops a tolerance to a sleep aid and requires larger and larger doses, or is advised to stop taking sleep aids and then develops severe insomnia as a withdrawal symptom. This causes the patient to return to sleep aids in a vicious cycle that is hard to beat.[8]

Dr. Evans says that REM sleep should account for approximately 25 percent of your total sleep time each night. A downside to sleeping pills is that they depress brain functions and interfere with sleep cycles. In fact, they make REM sleep less likely, period.[9]

In my line of work, ministry, I have another approach to helping those who have tried everything medical but still toss and turn each night. Oftentimes, there is nothing physically wrong with them, because their insomnia is actually an invitation. An invitation to deal with their anxieties, fears and guilt. An invitation to pray and draw close to their Creator while He has their full attention, to be still and know that He is God. An invitation to pray for someone else, after which sleep often comes.

One time, I met a little girl named Maci whose story moved me to tears. At an Epilepsy Forum at Vanderbilt University Medical Center in Nashville, her mother, Katie, stood and told hospital doctors how Maci—who struggled with seizures and was on a variety of medicines—could not sleep. Maci's life had been one of frequent doctor visits with infrequent solid answers, and it was taking its toll on her. Her insomnia was affecting the entire household, not to mention intensifying Maci's seizure activity since sleep deprivation is a major seizure trigger. The smartest minds in the room had no concrete answers for her. I knew I needed to tell Katie what had helped me, but I could not interrupt the speakers. I took out my pen:

> I can tell you what helped me. . . . I pray the last part of
> Psalm 127:2 over myself and somehow, supernaturally, I honestly

sleep. . . . May God bless your daughter and the mommy who gets up with her. Don't give up if it doesn't work at first. Keep believing. . . .

Psalm 127:2 says, "So He gives His beloved sleep."

I had never had insomnia. As I mentioned previously, I did not have a sleep disorder, but rather a sleep defiance. Still, getting to sleep that way had worked for me in years past, and I felt the need to share it. I put my email address down just in case Katie needed prayer, but I did not think I would ever hear from her again.

> Psalm 127:2 says, "So He gives His beloved sleep."

Then one day, an email came. Katie had prayed Psalm 127:2 with Maci each night before bed, and Maci had begun to sleep. More and more, the tide turned. Maci's health stabilized as a result, as did the household. It so impacted their lives that Katie—an artist—painted a large mural in Maci's room with this Scripture on it, and she attached a picture for me to see. I sat at my desk, stared at it and just cried. What no doctor of medicine or psychologist could do for little Maci, God's Word did when applied with faith. The faith of a child.

Apnea

Approximately 18 million Americans have sleep apnea, a sleep disorder in many forms that results in the cessation of breathing, especially at night and all throughout the night. Some of apnea's defining characteristics are loud snoring, obesity, morning headaches, waking up with a sore or dry throat, waking during the night with a choking or gasping sensation, restless sleep and more.

The week I began writing this chapter, a good friend, Lisa, had made the decision to get tested for sleep apnea. Having heard that sleep apnea can be a real dream stealer (because sufferers often do not reach REM dream sleep), I wondered if Lisa would allow me to study the results of her sleep study test. An accurate dreamer, Lisa had brought some dreams to me over the years that contained information she could not have known except through divine means. I knew the information was counsel from God, and we applied it, with positive outcomes each time. Knowing that frequent waking episodes of apnea could be preventing Lisa from finding much REM dream sleep, I was curious to see if Lisa's dreams would increase if the apnea was resolved.

Sure enough, Lisa was diagnosed with severe obstructive sleep apnea/hypopnea and sleep-related hypoxia. She had 46 "events" per hour, meaning that she stopped breathing 46 times an hour, one time for 46.2 seconds. Halfway through the night, they awakened Lisa and fitted her with a sleep mask that provided streams of oxygen to keep her air passages open while sleeping. Not only did she have 0 events afterward, but her dreams doubled. Without her sleep mask, she spent only 23 minutes dreaming during the first half of the night. Afterward, she dreamed for 58 minutes.

This breakthrough medical remedy for sleepless (and therefore, dreamless) nights could not have been better invested in anyone—Lisa is such an eager dreamer, interpreter and friend. Could God have bypassed modern medicine, overridden her REM cycles and given Lisa dreams anyway? Yes, and He obviously did on occasion. But now, because she dealt with her physical sleep disorder, her dreams will increase. She may even need to observe my dream recall tips to remember them all. I think the main reason God did not make a habit of overriding Lisa's disorder to give her dreams is that He wanted her to sleep. Remember, He gives His beloved sleep. (Sweet dreams, Lisa.)

Other sleep disturbances include restless leg syndrome, bedwetting, COPD and difficulty breathing, snoring, sleeptalking, sleepwalking, sleep-eating, teeth grinding and night terrors (nightmares).

Sleep deprivation—self-induced or involuntary—is not only a dream killer, but a life killer. CBS News broadcast a study a few years ago in which several young, healthy, fit patients were allowed only four hours of sleep for six nights. It was discovered that after only six nights, the subjects had already reached a prediabetic state. A chemical called leptin, which tells your brain when you are full, is suppressed without ample sleep. The researchers noticed that the subjects ate more when they slept less and were unable to metabolize sugar as effectively. It was reported that this could be a major factor contributing to the American obesity epidemic. It also explains the "freshman ten," which are those extra ten pounds that college freshman notoriously gain once Mom is no longer in their ear, enforcing bedtime. Sleep deprivation leads to weight gain, plain and simple.

Sleep deprivation—self-induced or involuntary—is not only a dream killer, but a life killer.

CBS's Lesley Stahl reported afterward, "Several large-scale studies from all over the world have reported a link between short sleep times and obesity, as well as heart disease, high blood pressure, and stroke." The experiment was spearheaded by an endocrinologist at the University of Chicago School of Medicine, Dr. Eve Van Cauter. Her conclusion was, "I think it tells us that sleep deprivation is not a challenge for which biology has wired us. There's no other mammal that sleep deprives itself [other] than the human."[10]

Food for Thought

Whether you are awake or asleep, both states are affected by the neurotransmission signals of your brain. Therefore, the foods you eat and the nutrients you ingest (or the lack thereof) alter them. A prime example would be caffeine. Caffeinated coffees, teas, soft drinks and energy drinks stimulate certain portions of the brain and result in eventual insomnia and needless tossing and turning at night.

Other stimulants are diet pills, decongestants and even sugar. It has also been proven that antidepressants suppress REM dream sleep, as does smoking. Smokers tend to sleep for only a few hours before their sleep is interrupted with nicotine withdrawal. Quit smoking and dream more.

Many people try to solve the insomnia battle with a nightcap by drinking a glass of wine or other alcohol, and studies have shown that alcohol does help people go to sleep—but not stay asleep. Alcohol can help people reach a very early stage light sleep, but it prohibits them from reaching REM dream sleep or the restorative stage of deep sleep so crucial for good health. Therefore, nightcap users will definitely fall asleep, but will not stay asleep for the entire night.[11]

Vitamins, Minerals and Dream Recall

What should you consume for a good night's sleep? Is there any nutrient that can help you remember your dreams? Yes! Let's look at some vitamins and minerals that help improve dream recall.

Vitamin B6

The National Center for Biotechnology Information reported on a placebo, double-blind study done to investigate numerous reports of the effects vitamin B6 (pyridoxine) has on dreaming.[12] For a period of five consecutive days, twelve students were given 100 milligrams (mg) of B6 before bedtime and then interviewed each morning about their dreams. After a two-day washout to allow elimination of the vitamin from their systems, they were given 250 mg of B6 and once again interviewed the next morning. After another two-day washout, they were given a placebo for five nights and then interviewed the next morning.

On a scale that measured vividness, bizarreness, emotionality and color, morning self-reports revealed a marked difference between the time the students were given a placebo and the time they were given 250 mg of B6. The data proposed that vitamin B6 may act by increasing cortical arousal during periods of rapid eye movement (REM) dream sleep, and that it plays a role in converting tryptophan (which, according to the Cambridge University journals, appears to show some promise in treating depression)[13] into serotonin (which, according to Mayo Clinic, acts as a neurotransmitter to the brain).[14]

> The hypothesis is that vitamin B6 "wakes up" the brain during REM dream sleep, assisting the mind in intensifying and evaluating what it is seeing as it sees it.

What does this mean? The hypothesis is that vitamin B6 "wakes up" the brain during REM dream sleep, assisting the mind in intensifying and evaluating what it is seeing as it sees it.

Because I generally take a phosphorylated version of the B vitamins for optimum absorption and conversion to energy, and because I typically take it during the day, I was curious about whether it would interfere with my sleep if I took it at night. I found it did not, although other people's results will vary due to lifestyle, sleep times and even illnesses. Livestrong.com, a journalistic byproduct of Demand Media and the Livestrong Foundation, lists comments by both the *New York Times* and the Hypoglycemic Health Association of Australia that address this:

> The energy effects of B vitamins may last through the night if you take supplements during the evening. According to the "New York Times," vitamins B6 and B12 directly affect the hormones melatonin and serotonin, which can affect your sleep. Taking vitamin B6 at night can cause vivid dreams that lead to a restless sleep. The "Times" argues that there is some evidence that taking vitamins can increase hormone production, resulting in sleep difficulties. At the same time, your brain relies on these hormones to go to sleep. The Hypoglycemic Health Association of Australia explains that sufficient melatonin is necessary for the brain to go into sleep mode for a restful night. Vitamin B6 helps create serotonin, which then creates melatonin.[15]

Although the study was done at a university and not in a sleep laboratory, it was still featured on PubMed.gov, a database maintained by the U.S. National Library of Medicine at the National Institutes of Health. PubMed contains 22 million citations for biomedical literature from Medline.

Vitamin B6 is also listed on Mayo Clinic's website under "Uses Based on Tradition or Theory: The following uses are based on tradition or scientific theories," where the site states that "dream recall and sleep enhancement" is one of the uses for vitamin B.[16]

Always discuss with your doctor, pharmacist or nutritionist what vitamin levels are right for you. The 250 mg amount of B6 used in the aforementioned study is an excessive dose, and you would not want toxicity to occur. Daily recommended dietary allowances (RDAs) of vitamin B6 taken orally are as follows: males and females 19–50 years old, 1.3 mg; males 51 and older, 1.7 mg; females 51 and older, 1.5 mg. (Many researchers think these RDAs should be increased for all ages.) Like vitamin C, B vitamins are water-soluble, meaning that the body uses them right away and excretes excessive amounts through the urine. Vitamin B12 is the exception; it can stay in the liver for years.[17]

The recommended maximum daily intake of vitamin B6 by mouth for adults, and for pregnant and lactating women (over 18 years old), is 100 mg. I use a little more than that daily, because I take a medicine that depletes it, plus I eat a lot of protein. Both of those factors consume B6 in my system, and I like to build it back up before I start another day. Ask your doctor or pharmacist about doses right for you. You will know you are getting too much vitamin B6 if you begin to feel numbness due to nerve damage, or if you experience lack of coordination or changes in sensory perception. But do not worry, because according to the National Institutes of Health Office of Dietary Supplements, the side effects of a B6 overdose are usually alleviated once supplementation stops.[18]

The busy Bs have many names: thiamine (B1), riboflavin (B2), niacin (B3), pantothenic acid (B5), pyridoxine (B6), biotin (B7), folic acid (B9) and cobalamin (B12). If for some reason you are not comfortable taking an over-the-counter vitamin B supplement despite countless reports of this family of vitamin's healing properties, just remember to include more of the following foods in your diet: bananas, cereal grains, legumes, vegetables (especially carrots, spinach and peas), potatoes, milk, cheese, eggs, fish and sunflower seeds. Enriched cereals supposedly put vitamins back in after refining them all out, and those always include Vitamin B6, but to get the 100 mg nightly dosage, we are talking 32 bowls of Cheerios before bed.[19] Uh, I will take the supplement, thank you.

Magnesium

I am not a doctor (nor did I play one on TV), but I know that magnesium has changed my life and my brain health. Part of my healing journey for relief from the seizures and for lowering the high doses of acidic medicine I was on involved high daily doses of magnesium. After years of anticonvulsants that were unable to offer me relief, my neurologist was pleased when we found how much magnesium helped me when I took a thera-peutic dose. I was able to cut my seizure medicine by two-thirds, in fact. Why?

Simply put, magnesium is nature's tranquilizer for the brain, and for the whole body. What do you think Epsom salts are? Magnesium sulfate. And they relax everything from the pro athlete's injury to Grandma's sore feet. What do hospitals give pregnant mothers by IV when they are in premature labor? Magnesium. Because of its calming effects on contractions, it stops them. And you will know when you have had too much magnesium because it will loosen your stools considerably. After all, what is the laxative Milk of Magnesia? Magnesium.

Likewise for the nighttime brain, magnesium calms your nerve activity and helps you go to sleep and stay asleep, thus ensuring that you go smoothly from your N-REM sleep stages into dreamland. Magnesium is necessary for more than 300 biochemical reactions in your body and gives you energy for metabolism. It also helps your heart, muscles, immune system, bones, blood sugar levels and blood pressure. There is a concern among doctors because, according to data from the 1999–2000 National Health and Nutrition Examination Survey, substantial numbers of adults in the United States do not have enough body stores of magnesium because dietary intake may not be high enough.[20] The RDA of magnesium is 400 mg for men 19–30; 310 mg for women 19–30; 420 mg for men 31 and older; 320 mg for women 31 and older. To find out what is right for you, do your research, and then ask your pharmacist, nutritionist or doctor.

Magnesium comes in many forms and doses, including a 1000 mg tablet. I have a good friend who swears by this dose as the occasional cure for insomnia and for getting a great night's sleep. But since magnesium exits the body through the kidneys, you want to avoid high doses if you have kidney issues. For brain help during the day, I take 250 mg each morning and 500 mg each night of magnesium taurate, which combines the power of magnesium with taurine (another brain booster). I go for the chelated versions—those that end in *ate* such as glycin*ate*, mal*ate* and taur*ate*, versus oxide and chloride versions. It has been shown that the chelation process results in better absorption by the body.[21] Simply put, magnesium is my ritual nightcap.

> Since magnesium comes from the ocean floor, my young daughter says it is as if God made the ocean to be one big, relaxing Epsom salt bath.

While foods like almonds, sesame seeds, spinach and all green leafy vegetables (which are green because their center is the chlorophyll molecule that contains magnesium) are great sources, changing your diet alone is not going to solve your insomnia or give you better dream retention. Levels of at least 100 mg of B6, 600 mg of calcium (we will cover calcium in a moment) and 300 mg of magnesium are usually needed to produce a result. Since magnesium comes from the ocean floor, my young daughter says it is as if God made the ocean to be one big, relaxing Epsom salt bath. Why didn't I think of that? (So thanks to my daughter Jenesis, you now know why the ocean is salty.) Maybe this is one of the more scientific explanations for why trips to the beach are so relaxing.

Zinc

The Institute for Optimum Nutrition (ION), one of Europe's leading providers of nutritional therapy and education (based in Richmond, South West London), published an article on sleep and dreams that cited research from Dr. Carl Pfeiffer, a Princeton researcher with ties to the CIA. The article said,

> When researching the signs and symptoms of vitamin B6 and zinc deficiency Dr. Carl Pfeiffer, from the Brain Bio Center in New Jersey, found that an alarming proportion of deficient people couldn't recall their dreams. After supplementing with B6 and zinc, often in doses as high as 1,000 mg of B6 and 100 mg of zinc, dream recall would return. If they took too much B6 and zinc dreams became too vivid and the person would wake up in the night. B6 and zinc also affected the quality of dreams. . . .
>
> So if you don't think you dream it's worth supplementing B6 and zinc gradually increasing the dose up to 500 mg B6 and 50 mg of zinc. (It is best not to take more without the advice of a nutritionist.)[22]

Many bodily functions are affected by zinc's influence on numerous enzymes, and zinc may increase REM sleep, as well. As with the B vitamins, many people do not consume sufficient zinc in their diets, so supplementation is smart. Foods high in zinc include pumpkin seeds, salmon, dark chocolate, garlic, organic beef, lima beans, egg yolks, mushrooms, turkey, spinach, peanuts and brown rice. For nighttime, you might try sucking on a zinc lozenge about ten minutes before bed.

These findings line up with those of Dr. Charlene Gamaldo of Johns Hopkins Medicine, who says that magnesium and zinc deficiencies have been linked to sleeping problems.[23] The Institute for Optimum Nutrition put out a list titled the *Best Bedtime Vitamin/Mineral Combo for Dream Recall*. According to ION's list, here is how to fall asleep and stay asleep:

- Avoid all stimulants after 4:00 p.m. and take 2 x L-tryptophan 500 mg (if still necessary).
- Daily eat calcium rich and magnesium rich foods.
- Supplement B6 100 mg and zinc 10 mg (and more if no dream recall).
- Supplement three dolomite tablets in the evening.[24]

Calcium

Dolomite tablets are calcium magnesium carbonate. Calcium is perfect for a good night's sleep. After all, babies love it! A warm cup of milk does wonders. Turns out it is not just the warmth, but the calcium. Calcium has a calming effect on the nervous system and is a natural relaxant. Typically, 500 mg daily is helpful. Keep in mind that soft drinks for dinner can deplete calcium, not to mention keep you awake if caffeinated. Check with your pharmacist or doctor about the calcium dosage that is right for you in your stage of life.

Vitamin D3

I had heard the rumor that taking large doses of vitamin D before bedtime would give you bizarre dreams, so I tried it. It did. I dreamed the most nonsensical things, and trust me, I can get a good interpretation out of almost any dream scene. But remember, you do not want to take supplements that give you more dreams. You just want to remember the ones you are already having. Let's not confuse matters or waste time sorting through outlandish dreams.

So why did I include vitamin D here? Mainly to address the dreams rumor, and also because you do need vitamin D in your diet in the D3 form since it is more potent and long lasting. The Harvard School of Public Health reported in an article entitled

Go ahead and get plenty of vitamin D in your diet, but just remember not to take the sunshine vitamin at night.

"Vitamin D and Health" that being "D-ficient" has been linked to multiple ailments. Once the deficiency is corrected, there is a reduction in bone fractures, heart disease, cancer, type-1 diabetes and multiple sclerosis—not to mention that vitamin D possibly prevents the common cold.[25] Go ahead and get plenty of vitamin D in your diet, but just remember not to take the sunshine vitamin at night.

Melatonin

We talked in chapter 4 about circadian rhythms and how melatonin, "the drowsy hormone," is released in the body. But you can also buy it over the counter in a supplement, although I have never tried it. It is a neurotransmitter/hormone that is only active when you are sleeping and is being metabolized from serotonin, a neurotransmitter whose predecessor is tryptophan.

Melatonin increases N-REM sleep. You do fall asleep faster if you are taking it, but then something risky happens. After reaching the N-REM sleep cycles sooner, a sort of rebound effect occurs that throws you into unusually vivid dreams. Personally, I do not want to play with my dreams like this. I just want to supplement my body with the right nutrients so that I can better remember the dreams I am naturally having. Lucid dreamers often take melatonin to manipulate their dreams. Be careful not to train your body to need melatonin supplements nightly, lest you begin to mistake vivid dream rebound for true prophetic dreams.[26]

Many scientists support the idea that nutritional deficiency is why people do not remember their dreams. In a survey I cited earlier from ION, they discovered that more than 40 percent of people had no dream recall or poor dream recall. While the federal government's 2010 *Dietary Guidelines for Americans* notes that "nutrients should come primarily from foods," there is nothing wrong with supplementing your diet with over-the-counter bottled vitamins and nutrients to ensure you get them—and to assist with sleep and promote healthy REM dream sleep. Always consult your pharmacist, doctor or nutritionist for dosage amounts.

Herbs and Teas

Livestrong.com lists the following as great herbal combinations for better dream recall and aid in sleeping:[27]

Valerian and Passionflower

Valerian is a relaxant that helps you fall asleep faster. This shorter sleep latency time results in more nightly time to complete N-REM cycles and move efficiently into REM dream sleep. Valerian is often taken in combination with passionflower for what are said to be magnified results. Passionflower is often used for insomnia. The herb leaves no narcotic-type hangover symptoms the morning after.

Lemon Balm and California Poppy

Lemon balm helps normalize your breathing and circulation. When taken together with California poppy, lemon balm helps normalize both your N-REM and REM sleep patterns and facilitates sleep depth. California poppy helps by restoring sleep patterns in those who wake up frequently during the night or wake up earlier than necessary in the morning.

Red Spider Lily and Daffodil

Spider lily is an herb native to China and Japan that can be used to assist your REM dream cycle and even to help with dream recall. Galanthamine is a chemical derived from the extracts of red spider lily and common daffodil bulbs. According to a 2004 trial published in "The Journal of the American Medical Association, galanthamine (or "galantamine") shortens the amount of time between N-REM cycles and dream sleep, and also increases REM-state density.[28]

Other Helpful Herbs

You can also try the following herbs in capsule form or as a tea: chamomile, spearmint, hibiscus, cinnamon, peppermint, mugwort, Saint John's wort, licorice root, jasmine, honeysuckle, orange blossom, bee pollen, skullcap, rose blossoms, mimosa, lavender, passionflower, cardamom, marigold, nutmeg and turmeric.

Combination teas at your local grocer:

Bigelow Sweet Dreams Herb Tea: chamomile, hibiscus, peppermint leaves, rose blossoms, spearmint leaves, spice, orange blossom.

Celestial Seasonings Sleepytime Herbal Tea: chamomile, spearmint, West Indian lemongrass, tilia flowers, blackberry leaves, orange blossoms, hawthorn, rosebuds.

Turns out Peter Rabbit's mother was right after all a hundred years ago, when she gave the overexcited bunny some chamomile tea to calm him before bed.

According to the University of Maryland Medical Center, the following herbs and supplements are beneficial for improving memory, period: Asian ginseng, carnitine (L-carnitine), ginkgo biloba, green tea (decaf if at bedtime), rosemary and siberian ginseng.[29]

Please avoid the following potent dream-inducing herbs that are often used by shamans for hallucinatory, witchcraft purposes: alepidea amatymbica, calae zacatechichi, whole leaf African dream root and silene capensis synaptolepis. Also abstain from dream oil magic pills or any other substance that claims to help you control your own dreams, such as is done in lucid dreaming.

> Turns out Peter Rabbit's mother was right after all a hundred years ago, when she gave the overexcited bunny some chamomile tea to calm him before bed.

Essential Oils

Essential oils have many benefits. They can relieve stress and anxiety, soothe a busy mind and help you fall asleep and stay asleep. Essential oils never have serious side effects; they work with the body to support its God-given healing capabilities. Proverbs 7:17 mentions a few oils when it says, "I have perfumed my bed with myrrh, aloes, and cinnamon."

To name a few other helpful nighttime oils, there are lavender, frankincense, chamomile, marjoram, orange, patchouli, valerian, chamomile roman, clary sage, sandalwood, lemon and nutmeg. You can also promote peaceful rest with clove oil. Add a few drops of any of these oils to a spray bottle and spritz your room, or use a few drops in a room diffuser. I also put some drops on a tissue inside my pillowcase. I personally enjoy a few drops of pink grapefruit oil under my pillowcase after a stressful day, as does my husband. I keep it by the bed and reach for it at the first sign of a burdened brow, enjoying the smile that comes to his sleepy face when he settles in and takes that first deep breath.

Here are some helpful oil recipes for relieving insomnia. For babies, boil water and place some in a bowl with one drop each of chamomile Roman and geranium oil. Put the bowl under the child's crib (but not under baby's head), and keep the door almost closed to retain the aroma molecules in the room. Slowly, over time, the baby's sleeping patterns will change.

For children 12 months old to 5 years, help insomnia by placing the child in a warm bath that contains 1 drop per year (up to 3 drops maximum) of these oils: mandarin, chamomile Roman, lavender and palma rosa.

For children 5–12 years old, do the same as for younger children, except add these oils to the bath as well: geranium, nutmeg and clary sage, in the amounts of 3 drops for up to 7 years old, 4 drops for 7–10 year olds and 5 drops for 11–12 year olds.[30]

Increasing Prayer and Worship

Have you ever thought about why you seem to dream more on Sunday nights or Monday mornings? Years ago, I began to recognize this pattern with myself and soon realized why. I had spent time in worship on Sunday morning at church, and sadly, had not done so any other day of the week. I was praying, but not truly spending time in thanksgiving and adoration of the Lord. Some people have never been taught to sit still long enough to practice God's presence, but if you will wait on God, you will notice a change in your spirit. It may not be in that moment of worship and you may be tempted to think it is time wasted, but it is not.

In fact, what happens as you sit there in prayer is that you make a deposit into yourself and into your inner man (or woman). Tomorrow or the next day or the next, when you are presented with a situation in which an immediate decision must be made, you instantly will be able to make a withdrawal and choose rightly. There will be a sudden wisdom that you cannot explain, or a "knowing" about how you should proceed. It came from God, and it came while you sat with Him and—by faith—allowed Him to pour His divine nature into you.

It is a supernatural exchange that many miss these days because they are too busy and too distracted. These very people fall into bed exhausted, needing counsel, often begging God to speak to them at night with a dream, but no dream comes. Not because God is unkind, but because these people never prepared their spirit to hear from God that day. And because, on the practical side, they were so exhausted and had such a sleep debt that they spent much of the night in a deep N-REM dreamless sleep.

Healing Is Here

As I look back at this list of vitamins, minerals, herbs and oils, I marvel at how just about everything we need to take care of our bodies was created on day 3 of Creation. On that day, God made the land (from where we get minerals from rocks and dirt), the sea (from where we get many things, including fish oil and magnesium) and then vegetation (where we get all our herbs, vitamins and vegetables). How miraculous. "The earth is the LORD's, and the fullness thereof; the world, and they that dwell therein" (Psalm 24:1 KJV).

But before you run to your local drugstore and clear their shelves so that you can better hear from God through dreams, remember that this is a total-package lifestyle change. You can take all the proven vitamins, guzzle all the proper teas and lather on all the ordained essential oils, but if you are sleep deprived, your sleep stages will not flow as God intends. Many of us are unreachable, except for the occasional crisis-intervention dream. Wouldn't you much rather hear from God on a regular basis in times of nonconflict and perhaps even avoid the conflict?

> As I look back at this list of vitamins, minerals, herbs and oils, I marvel at how just about everything we need to take care of our bodies was created on day 3 of Creation.

You often hear God called the "Great Physician," and Jesus the "Balm of Gilead." Jeremiah 8:22 (NIV) asks, "Is there no balm in Gilead? Is there no physician there? Why then is there no healing for the wound of my people?" I hope that after the evidence about sleep debt (and sleep defiance) I have presented in the last two chapters, you will see just how many of your wounds are self-inflicted. Find healing through God.

I will close with a testimony of such healing. During the writing of these last two chapters (which at first was one chapter that grew and doubled), I encountered incredible opposition from what seemed like hell itself to get this information to you. In fact, I encountered opposition to the whole book when I was diagnosed with adrenal burnout just weeks after signing the publishing contract and turning in a sample chapter.

Things noticeably intensified, however, when I began to pen these actual medical pages. At home, while chatting with my beautiful daughter-in-love Brittany that week, I fell backward onto a glass-and-wrought-iron coffee table, breaking a rib, puncturing a lung, spraining a ligament and bruising more ribs. I have had six children and yet have never known such pain. On a deadline to finish the book, I refused to quit writing, but I also refused painkillers because I did not want to be groggy during the process. I was told to go home and rest for 6–8 weeks and breathe deeply if I wanted to avoid surgery to reinflate my lung (which had already started to collapse). They called it a pneumothorax. To make matters worse, a few days later I caught a nasty stomach flu and my sainted husband had to hold in my ribs for me each time I got sick during the night.

Since the ER doctors and the fall's adrenal experts all seemed to be saying the same exact phrase to me, *"Go home and rest,"* and since I was contracted to sit and write a book, I decided to look at these physical hurdles less like an illness or injury and more like an invitation. We turned my bed into my new desk, our church cooked us meals and my daughters served them to me in bed. Even my "co-mothers" helped (both of my sons' mothers-in-law). Debb, the Virginian mother of my beautiful daughter-in-love Sarah, bought me some bright jammies that lured me to rest, and WenDee, Brittany's mom, sent me cards and "thinking of you" texts from Texas that seemed to come at the exact moment when bed rest was getting painfully lonely. I had been cornered by God—who uses for good what the enemy intends for evil—and had been given no choice at all but to sit and focus on this book. How ironic, though, that I was pecking out these medical chapters while hunched over a pillow, on my stomach, with iced back ribs.

But 3 days into the 6–8 weeks, I cried out to Jesus. Easing myself down to the ground in my closet to avoid more pain, I had a very frank conversation with God *and* with my enemy. I have done it thousands of times in this same closet over the last 23 years—but this time, something was different. This time, I had an audience in that closet with me . . . you. I asked God to back me up so that I could testify to you about His healing power, and I forbade the devil from interfering.

After a few minutes of just waiting on the Lord, I felt peace and decided to get up, carefully pulling myself to a standing position and leaving the closet. As I bent over to get something, I noticed, *Hey, did I just bend over to pick something up?* Without any fireworks or apparent signs of the Holy Spirit's activity, my body was merely doing things it could not have done just moments before.

I walked up to a full mirror, bent down and touched my toes, then stood back up, twisted my rib cage from side to side and jumped up and down three times. No pain. An hour before, it had taken me fifteen minutes to get in and out of bed, during which there were many shrieks and yelps. Now I could still feel a pulled muscle or something at the point of impact, but suddenly my ribs were not screaming at me for looking at them the wrong way, and breathing deeply did not hurt anymore. *Wait, did I just breathe deeply?*

On day five, I went for another X-ray. It showed that my lung was entirely reinflated, and you could not even see where the rib break had been. In the words of the doctor, "Your pneumothorax is healed." The before-and-after X-rays flooded Facebook.

My nutritionist told me soon after that my adrenal issues must be improving ahead of schedule, too, because of how well my body handled the trauma and bounced back. A body on the brink of adrenal failure cannot handle even a little trauma, but mine did, emerging from it like Superman out of his phone booth. Honestly, as I write this I can say that I have not felt this good in years. Even those pesky extra ten pounds are gone now that I have paid my sleep debt.

These chapters have cost me something, but an amazing calm has come after their completion. I even had a powerful dream near the end of the writing in which I saw my son Jhason racing toward me in utter joy. His name means "healing," and that is exactly what happened to me through this fast healing. The enemy lost. What he intended for evil, God used for good. I became more focused, more determined and even more productive, researching and writing so much for you that the one medical chapter I started with had to be turned into two chapters that I hope will change your life, body and spirit.

> The night belongs to God
> The sleep belongs to me
> The dream that's gained is preordained
> To heal and set me free.
>
> © Laura Harris Smith, February 8, 2013

PRAYER

Let's pray out loud together:

Father, You are the Great Physician. I ask You to heal my body so it can sleep, then heal my mind so it can dream. Finally, I ask You to heal my spirit so it might receive from You, starting tonight. In Jesus' name, Amen.

IMPARTATION

Right now, I release and impart to you the seer anointing, the ability to dream, the ability to remember, the ability to interpret and the ability to see God's voice as you rest and value this sacred thing called sleep. (Now open your hands, shut your eyes and receive it.)

6

Visions

will never forget where I was standing the day I admitted to someone that I was seeing visions. I had told no one but Chris. Whom would I tell in my conservative church? Having had no teaching about visions, I thought surely it was all in my head, and although I had read about visions in many Bible stories, they were . . . well, just Bible stories. Did that kind of thing even still happen today?

As I was playing putt-putt golf that day with my good friend Beth, she began describing a new book she was reading called *This Present Darkness*. The author, Frank Peretti, wove a tale about the heavenly realms and its key players, angels and demons. As my friend described this one hideous demon from the book, I stopped in midswing. "Beth, I've seen that. It. Him. I saw one of those."

Out it all spilled as I explained about this demon I had seen in my mirror as I stood doing my makeup one day. It had stepped out from behind me and stared me down in the mirror. I felt no fear or shock, nor the need to spin around and see if it was really there. It just was.

But it did not bring with it instincts of fleeing, as I might have experienced if a burglar had snuck up behind me. It was as though someone had lifted a veil and opened my eyes into the spirit realm. Standing there, I, too, was in the spirit and was therefore totally unafraid. No emotions at all, in fact. Next thing I knew, I was "back," and it was just me in the mirror.

Beth did not even bat an eyelash. She wanted to know more. Thank God for Beth. Thank God for Frank Peretti. That game of miniature golf majorly impacted the rest of my life and ministry.

I have since heard people say, "That thing in the mirror would totally freak me out!" I would have said that, too, before I experienced it. But it was not as if he had invaded my world. It was as if I had invaded his. My main question was, *Why is that thing in my house at all?* It drew me to my knees in prayer to ask God if any open door in my life had let him in. If you had seen him, you would have asked the same question and dug deeply for the answer. But I could not think of anything that would have opened a door.

Once the body dies, our spirit lives on. We will all live forever; it is just a matter of where.

What I did not understand at the time is that we are not the main show down here, but that we—in an earthly shell—are merely passing through to a spiritual world that is very real and very eternal. A world to which our eyes are closed unless God decides to lift that veil and open them for some purpose. A world to which we will all transition one day. As the saying goes, "You don't have a soul. You are a soul. You have a body." Once the body dies, our spirit lives on. We will all live forever; it is just a matter of where.

But before we travel too far down the freeway of seeing angels and demons, I want to discuss first what visions are and how they occur. If you have never had a vision, I do not want to scare you by implying that your first vision will involve seeing a demon. I am just "lucky," I guess.

Cut!

One of my favorite pastimes is video editing. You will not find it anywhere on my résumé, but for the last fifteen years I have edited everything from television shows to commercials to short themed musical videos for special events. None of it was done for a living, but merely because one project after another fell into my lap, so I reinvented myself to accomplish each one for some worthy cause or ministry. Along the way, I mastered various editing softwares, and probably as an extension of my writing abilities, I also learned that I had a natural feel for emotive timing and viewer satisfaction. Video editing is the perfect occupation if you want to maneuver people's emotions without getting in trouble for it.

But I am glad that I ventured into that visual world, and not just because I have a couple of sons who were onlookers to Mom's small beginnings with her meager tools. They went on to establish the capability for having a career in film themselves, and in the eldest's case, he is realizing that goal while combining it with the inheritance of his father's musical sensibilities.

I am also glad because it has forced me to begin to think of God as a master editor and of my seer experiences as a timeline to which He is constantly contributing and cutting. In fact, it is the best analogy I can think of to begin describing to you what happens when I see a vision.

Next time you watch your favorite movie or television show, make note of the transitions between shots and scenes. Dissolve, cross-fade, overlap, iris, page-peel, cube, slide, dip-to-color and wipe are just a few of the transitions that can move you from one scene or frame to another. Their job is to subtly reinforce the emotion of that moment in your story without drawing attention to themselves. I always find that long, slow transitions elicit more heartfelt emotions and that not using a transition keeps the momentum at a steady pace. And of course, nothing says "the end" like a fade to black. But the rule is to keep it simple. Never use a transition when a cut will do.

A vision—for me—is like having a new frame dropped into my timeline with no transition between the real-life action that preceded or followed it. The clouds do not part, the angels do not sing and the trumpets do not blow. There is no zooming in or fading out, and no blips in the audio, for that matter.

Disney used to have a comedy television show about a teenage psychic who was always coming in and out of what she called visions. Whenever one commenced, she would jerk her head sharply toward the camera and get a wide-eyed look as shafts of light shot out of a close-up of one of her pupils. Reverse that upon exiting the vision, topped off with an "I've just been struck by lightning" look left on her face. All I can say is I am so glad God does not do that to me, because if He did, I might just have to resign. The Holy Spirit is a gentleman. A vision definitely interrupts what I am doing, but it is never intrusive, nor does it cause me to act dementedly or become emotionally unhinged. That would only be bad publicity for God. If you were sitting with me, you would not even know what had happened.

From my perspective, if I were in conversation with you, there would be your face . . . then another very brief scene during which I would not be aware that you were there . . . and then your face again. No transitions, no fireworks. And if you are wondering what happens when the vision goes on so long that I am not cognizant enough to keep the conversation going (thus freaking the other person out as I stare into space), my answer is that God has never—not once—done that to me. As I said, He is a gentleman.

Like dropping a new, unexpected photo into my slideshow video timeline, visions for me are clean, transitionless cuts. And even when I have seen horrendous things in them, visions are peaceful. Calm warnings come, and I am either to use them in prayer for the intended party or to release what I have seen to him or her. Of course, once my mind begins processing what I have seen, I may sometimes have to wrestle my way back to peace, especially if a vision involves a loved one who is in urgent peril.

Visions definitely happen independently, with no help from me. Visions do not involve the imagination, and you do not get a running start and daydream your way into one. I definitely have no control over when they come or how long they are. And even though my eyes are open in the example I just gave, I do not consider that an open vision. (I will explain more about open visions shortly.)

> Visions do not involve the imagination, and you do not get a running start and daydream your way into one.

I have heard of other people who have very long visions, some of which I would consider translations. (We will discuss biblical translations later, too, where a person was transported to another place for a specific reason.) But whereas my dreams are often quite long, my visions are not. Usually, even though they include motion and speech, I call them snapshots or frames, and they are no more than four to five seconds long. Everyone's visions are different, including yours now and to come, but now you know what mine feel like.

Hopefully, what I have said here cuts through the obscurity of how a vision might feel to a seer. Now let's explore where a vision comes from and what the Bible says about visions—important, because otherwise, your visions can become more about the visions themselves than about the Giver of them, quickly stagnating them and stopping their pure flow of accuracy.

Visions in Scripture

Take a look at this partial list of visions in Scripture. There is no substitute for savoring them one by one, so get up and go get your Bible. I will wait for you. . . .

Genesis 15:1—God consoles Abram with a promise
Genesis 46:2—Jacob is told in a "vision in the night" to move to Egypt

Numbers 24:1–25—Balaam sees a vision for Israel

1 Samuel 3—Samuel hears God's audible voice, but it is called a "vision" (verse 15)

2 Samuel 7—Nathan establishes David's royal throne and commissions the Temple

Isaiah 1—Isaiah describes a vision of Jerusalem and Judah

Isaiah 21:2—Isaiah receives a dreadful vision of judgment

Isaiah 29:11—Isaiah delivers a vision to a sinful people

Ezekiel 1:1—Ezekiel sees a vision of the four living creatures

Ezekiel 7—Ezekiel tells Israel of his vision for them

Ezekiel 8—Ezekiel is taken to Jerusalem in a "vision"

Ezekiel 13:7—Ezekiel warns of vain visions and divination

Ezekiel 40—Ezekiel's visions of Israel

Ezekiel 43—Ezekiel has another vision of the glory of the Lord

Daniel 2:19–45—Daniel gets the king's dream revealed to him in a night vision

Daniel 8—Daniel sees the archangel Gabriel and a vision about the end times

Daniel 9:21—Daniel gets a vision and a message from the archangel Gabriel

Daniel 10—Daniel is visited by the archangel Michael after a 21-day fast

Obadiah 1—Obadiah receives a vision for his people

Nahum 1—Nahum's vision and message to his people

Zechariah 1:8—Zechariah's vision of the red horse

Matthew 17:9—the Mount of Transfiguration is called a vision (in many translations)

Luke 1:22—Zechariah realizes his vision in the temple

Acts 9:10–11—Ananias has a vision to go pray for Paul's healing

Acts 9:12—through a vision Paul has already seen that Ananias is coming

Acts 10—Cornelius has a vision telling him to send for Peter, and Peter has a vision in a *trance* that prepares him for his visit (the lowered sheet vision)

Acts 16:9–10—Paul has a vision about a man from Macedonia beckoning him

Acts 18:9—Paul's vision and direction from the Lord

Revelation 9—John's vision of the horses and riders

> "And it shall come to pass in the last days, says God, that I will pour out of My Spirit on all flesh; your sons and your daughters shall prophesy, your young men shall see visions, your old men shall dream dreams."

Throughout history, the Holy Spirit has guided God's people through dreams, visions and prophecy. But according to Acts 2—where Peter quoted the prophet Joel—we are on the verge of a major intensification of this type of activity. In fact, it has already begun. That is why we must be educated and refuse counterfeits.

But this is what was spoken by the prophet Joel:

> "And it shall come to pass in the last days, says God,
> That I will pour out of My Spirit on all flesh;
> Your sons and your daughters shall prophesy,
> Your young men shall see visions,
> Your old men shall dream dreams.
> And on My menservants and on My maidservants
> I will pour out My Spirit in those days;
> And they shall prophesy."
>
> Acts 2:16–18

As I said in chapter 2, no one in the Bible ever asked God to give them a dream. They were just busy seeking Him, and the dreams came. But if God says He is going to increase this form of communication with us as Jesus' Second Coming nears, then there is nothing wrong with positioning yourself to be a recipient.

As you read through each of these visions, first be mindful of the humanity of each seer. Imagine what it took to deliver these visual sermons, including the risking of one's own reputation. It is no different today, whether the seer is being called on by the president of the United States, submitting a message to his or her pastor or lovingly confronting a friend about a hidden area of his or her life that God has revealed to the seer. First lesson for every seer: Learn tact.

The words *vision* and *visions* are mentioned more than 120 times in the Bible, and rarely are they used in a figurative sense. And not all of these visions fall into one category. In fact, for our one little English word *vision*, there are nine possible Hebrew words and six possible Greek or Aramaic words that compare to it. While I would love to tell you that you could merely look up which Hebrew word is used with a certain prophet's vision and it would tell you whether it was an open vision, night vision or waking vision, that is not the case. I am about to show you more than a dozen definitions and derivatives that ambiguously mirror one another.[1]

In fact, it is so hard to find a variation in one over the other that I daresay they are more like synonyms. Sort of like in an English thesaurus, the word *vision* in the Bible might include *mirage, illusion, ecstasy* or *apparition*. These words are in many ways equal, and we must rely solely upon the seer's description to distinguish categories. Trouble is, the seers were so riveted by what they were seeing that the last thing on their minds was giving us a written side lesson in visionary protocol. You will notice in the following breakdown that some stories are mentioned twice (such as Daniel 8 and 10). This is because Daniel uses the different synonyms for *vision* interchangeably while telling his story.

Visions

In some instances, the word *vision* was actually just being used to describe a mode of revelation, such as in 1 Samuel 3 when little Samuel hears God's audible voice, yet refers to it as a vision. If you will note the following definition of *mar'ah*, you will discover that "seeing" and "hearing" are sometimes interchangeable and are often irrelevant details when communicating with God. I suppose this thought also lends believability—and perhaps legitimacy—to the very title of this book, *Seeing the Voice of God*.

> Chazah: to see, perceive, look, behold, prophesy, provide, to see as a seer in the ecstatic state, perceive with the intelligence, to see (by experience).

Hebrew Word #1:

chazown: vision, vision in ecstatic state, vision in the night, oracle, prophecy (in divine communication), vision as title of book of prophecy—see from visions list Isaiah 1; Ezekiel 7; Daniel 8; Daniel 9:21; Obadiah 1; Nahum 1.

chizzayown: vision, vision in ecstatic state, valley of vision, vision in the night, oracle, prophecy (in divine communication)—see from visions list 2 Samuel 7.

chazuwth: vision, conspicuousness, oracle of a prophet, agreement, conspicuousness in appearance—see from visions list Isaiah 21:2; Isaiah 29:11.

machazeh: vision in ecstatic state—see from visions list Genesis 15:1; Numbers 24:1–25; Ezekiel 13:7.

Root—*Chazah*: to see, perceive, look, behold, prophesy, provide, to see as a seer in the ecstatic state, perceive with the intelligence, to see (by experience).

Hebrew Word #2:

ro'eh: seer, prophet, prophetic vision—see 1 Chronicles 26:28; 2 Chronicles 16:7; Isaiah 28:7 (not on visions list).

mar'eh: sight, appearance, vision, phenomenon, spectacle, appearance, what is seen, a vision that is supernatural, sight, vision as in the power of seeing—see from visions list Ezekiel 8; Daniel 10.

mar'ah: vision, mode of revelation, mirror—see from visions list Genesis 46:2; 1 Samuel 3; Ezekiel 1; Ezekiel 8; Ezekiel 40; Ezekiel 43; Daniel 8; Daniel 10.

Root—*Ra'ah*: to see, look at, inspect, perceive, consider, have vision, regard, look after, see after, learn about, observe, watch, look upon, look out, find out, give attention to, discern, distinguish, gaze at, to appear, present oneself, to be seen, to be visible, to cause to see, show, to cause to look intently at, behold, cause to gaze at, to be caused to see, be shown, to be exhibited to, to look at each other, face—see from visions list Zechariah 1:8.

127

Greek Word #1:

horama: that which is seen, spectacle, a sight divinely granted in an ecstasy or in a sleep, a vision—see from visions list Matthew 17; Acts 9:12; Acts 10; Acts 16:9–10; Acts 18:9.

horasis: the act of seeing, the sense of sight, the eyes, appearance, visible form, a vision, an appearance divinely granted in an ecstasy or dream—see from visions list Revelation 9.

Root—*Horao*: to see with the eyes, to see with the mind, to perceive, know, to see as in become acquainted with by experience, to experience, to see, to look to, to take heed, beware, to care for, pay heed to, or as in "I was seen," "showed myself," "appeared."

Greek Word #2:

optasia: the act of exhibiting oneself to view, a sight, a vision, an appearance presented to one whether asleep or awake—see from visions list Luke 1:22.

Root—*Optanomai*: to look at, behold, to allow oneself to be seen, to appear.

Aramaic Word:

chezev: vision, appearance—see from visions list Daniel 2:19–45.

As you read the aforementioned visions in Scripture, note each seer's description of which type of visionary experience it was—vision of the night, open vision and the like. Of course, it is the message itself that the seer would want us to focus on, but I do want us to explore their modes of revelation so that we can know what to expect for ourselves today.

Waking Visions

Like waking dreams, waking visions are hard to shake. Knowing what we now know about sleep stages, I would say that these visions happen just as you have left stage 1 (N1) sleep, in the seconds just before waking up. You most likely have not yet opened your eyes for the morning or have not even had a cognizant thought about where you are or what the day holds, yet you are not asleep, either. I used to describe this fleeting stage with the word *twilighting* until the vampires got hold of it (in the popular *Twilight Saga* movies), but now I just say waking visions.

But here is the thing—because it is your first real thought for the day, you may have a hard time distinguishing between the two realms, asleep and awake. The two waking visions I am about to describe fall into that category. One involves seeing writing on the bedroom wall in front of me. Because the wall I saw with my spiritual eyes was the actual wall in my line of vision as I opened my human eyes, it *felt* as though I had seen this literally, as if my eyes had already been opened for the morning. The veil is so thin during these seconds of the morning that to this day, I do not quite know how to tell the story. So for this type of vision, I say, "One morning, I awoke and saw . . ." because whether your human eyes are open or closed, you are awake regardless, so it is a waking vision.

"*Hebrews 12:10*" said the writing on my wall. I had never seen such a thing, and I excitedly jumped out of bed and grabbed a Bible to see what encouraging message God had for me. But my excitement was short-lived. It was a word about discipline:

> For they [our earthly fathers] indeed for a few days chastened us as seemed best to them, but He for our profit, that we may be partakers of His holiness. Now no chastening seems to be joyful for the present, but painful; nevertheless, afterward it yields the peaceable fruit of righteousness to those who have been trained by it.
>
> Hebrews 12:10–11

It was 1994, and I had dived headlong into the world of a Spirit-filled walk with God. Although I had been sealed with the Holy Spirit on the day of my salvation almost twenty years earlier and had become a Bible teacher, church leader and even a Christian author, I awoke one morning to the realization that the Holy Spirit had been the most neglected member of the Trinity in my life. So I immersed myself in studying His spiritual gifts to me and all the trimmings. I said yes to all of them: prophecy, faith, speaking in tongues, interpreting tongues, praying for healings and miracles. . . . But on this morning, the Lord was reminding me that the Holy Spirit's main job was to make me holy. More like God. Less like the world. He was saying I was about to enter a season of discipline so that I might partake in His holiness. Sounds all fluffy, but boy was it rough.

Disciples have to be disciplined, though, so I tried hard to obey every little prompting after seeing this on my wall. Pray. Read. Forgive. Apologize. Speak out. Shut up. Be grateful sooner. Surrender a desire. I felt as if God had me on a very short leash. He had given me fair and very visible warning, so I had no wiggle room. Sometimes I still look up at that wall and envision the words there as a reminder that my holiness is a big deal to the Holy Spirit. He cannot dwell with sin or compromise. I must decrease so He can increase. (See John 3:30.)

> Holiness is a big deal to the Holy Spirit. He cannot dwell with sin or compromise. I must decrease so He can increase.

Another waking vision took place in 1993, on a day when I was very discouraged. I do not "do discouraged" anymore because it is a ginormous waste of time, but even that was part of disciplining my flesh during this season. As Chris was leaving for work that morning (with me still in bed), he heard the Lord say in the driveway, "A spirit of discouragement is coming after Laura. Pray for her." To this day I find it puzzling why God would not just fight off that spirit for me, but it makes sense that He would want to include my husband in the process. Besides, what happened next changed my life forever, so I would not have had it any other way (and I am crying now even retelling the story).

I awoke and saw a cloud beside my bed, out of which extended a hand reaching out to me. The arm and hand (palm up) were actual size, and the cloud was swirling actively. And then it was gone. No message.

First of all, it got my mind off myself, and then, after lying there and coming up with no interpretation on my own, I jumped up to grab a Bible, which turned my discouraged mind toward God. The teacher in me turned to every verse on "hands" I could think of: "Therefore humble yourselves under the mighty hand of God, that He may exalt you in due time" (1 Peter 5:6) and many others. But nothing clicked. It is important to weigh every vision with Scripture, and of course, no Scripture is ever ill-timed when you read it. But at that moment, none seemed to fit the vision. So I left it to simmer and got up to dress, passing by a daily perpetual prayer calendar I kept by my bed. I flipped over the day's page, and there it was: "Can a woman forget her nursing child, and not have compassion on the son of her womb? Surely they may forget, yet I will not forget you. See, I have inscribed you on the palms of My hands" (Isaiah 49:15–16).

If you had told me that morning that exactly twenty years later, I would be sitting in that same spot on the bed, writing a book on my laptop about the experience (and that the unanswered prayer I was discouraged about at the time would still have a bit to go in being fully answered), I might have crawled back under the covers. But Laura Harris Smith became Laura Harris Smith during these last twenty years. And God has not forgotten me! Plus, He has made sure a lot of other people have not, either. There has been steady headway as proof, and I know the best is yet to come.

You do not forget being awakened with the hand of God in your face. This vision has twenty years of mileage under its belt, yet still summons the same tears, emotions, weight and courage as it did the day it came. *That* is the power and importance of visions. Tell the Holy Spirit you welcome them into your life.

Next, I am going to explain what seem to be the more abstract visionary events. But whatever you do, do not label them as the Ph.D. of all optic experiences, or you will think they will never happen to you. God does not play favorites. You can have just as much of Him as the next guy, even if the guy is a prophet.

Open Visions

I described in my previous video editing analogy how a vision feels for me. But even though I said my eyes were open during these types of visions, I do not consider them open visions. If I saw visions of actual people coming into the exact room that my human eyes were already viewing, I would consider that an open vision, where the two worlds interact. But in my typical short snapshot, moving visions, I am totally unaware of the real images that my human eyes are supposed to be seeing at that moment. I am "gone" for a second. So with that definition in mind, I will now describe some open visions I *have* experienced.

When I was quite young in things of this nature, in an instance where Chris and I were in prayer with a couple, I saw a scarlet letter "A" hovering over the husband's head. It was a private prayer time, so I blurted out what I saw. The man looked mortified. I had totally forgotten about reading *The Scarlet Letter* in high school, Nathaniel Hawthorne's book about a Puritan woman found guilty of adultery who suffered the shame of the conviction by wearing a scarlet-colored "A" on her dress. The man broke and admitted his affair to his wife, and she forgave him. To this day they are still together, but it was important that it come out that night and God made sure it did (using me, His clueless vessel).

Also, I often have open visions of angels standing next to people. Or I will see them over people's heads, hovering. In those instances, the two realms are definitely overlapping, and I am totally aware of the room I am in as the angel is added to it. Each seer sees them differently depending on how God chooses to have them manifest.

Night Visions

What is the difference between a night vision and a dream? It depends on whom you ask. Some would say that a night vision is merely a regular vision that happens after the sun goes down. I have had plenty of night visions, and I know that they are different for me than dreams. I have had night visions while in bed, while praying in my closet or while at an event or a friend's house for supper, times when I was not expecting a vision at all. If you are trying to turn to Scripture to secure a solid definition for a night vision, you might need night vision goggles to do it. In fact, you could even ask two different Old Testament prophets and get two different answers. Let's try it.

In 2 Samuel 7, the prophet Nathan recounts this extremely long word God gave him for King David. At the end he tacks on the phrase, "In accordance with all these words and all this *vision*, so Nathan spoke to David" (verse 17 NASB, emphasis added). But it begins with "In the same night the *word* of the LORD came to Nathan" (verse 4 NASB, emphasis added). This leads you to couple those together and classify it as a night vision since the Hebrew word used is *chizzayown*, which can mean "vision in the night." It was not a dream because nowhere does it mention anything about him being asleep. But only the King James Version, New American Standard Version and New Living Translation of the Bible use the word *vision*, whereas the others chose an alternate English definition such as "oracle, prophecy (in divine communication)." Nathan's choice of words is fuzzy. It is doubtful that Samuel actually wrote 2 Samuel because he dies in 1 Samuel 25, so many think either Nathan wrote it or a scribe with access to his notes did. But the bottom line is, the prophecy still proves true 'til this day.

> "For God may speak in one way, or in another, yet man does not perceive it. In a dream, in a vision of the night, when deep sleep falls upon men, while slumbering on their beds, then He opens the ears of men, and seals their instruction."
>
> Job 33:14–16

We see the phrase "night vision" used again in Daniel 2:19–45 (depending on your translation; some say "vision of the night"), and yet the word used is an Aramaic one that has no connection whatsoever with night visions. It is *chezev*, which means "vision, appearance." So we may never know concretely what a night vision is or is not, or if it is merely a dream.

Let's not forget our Job passage from chapter 1:

> "For God may speak in one way, or in another,
> Yet man does not perceive it.
> In a dream, in a *vision of the night*,
> When deep sleep falls upon men,
> While slumbering on their beds,
> Then He opens the ears of men,
> And seals their instruction."
>
> Job 33:14–16, emphasis added

This makes it sound as though a vision of the night is a dream and that both occur while slumbering on the bed. The world may never know. Just take comfort in the fact that if even the prophets of old did not know proper definitions, it is okay that you do not either.

Translations

Depending on which Bible version you are reading, the word for "translation" might be *trance*. That is right, trances are in the Bible. But they were not and are not hypnotic trances such as we will discuss in chapter 10. These are bona fide "pick you up in one spot and take you to another location" expeditions. Some biblical examples of translations are:

Ezekiel—Ezekiel lifted up to Tel Abib (3:14–15), Jerusalem (8:3), Babylon (11:24) and Israel (chapter 40)

Acts 10—Peter falls into a trance and then has a vision (also 11:5)

Acts 22:17—Paul's vision of the Lord in the Temple through a trance

2 Corinthians 12—Paul describes being taken up into the third heaven

A couple of those are also listed under the preceding visions section, but that is because the author/prophet also used the word *vision*, thus showing us that sometimes visions happen during trances (while being taken to another location). It is hard to nail down a Hebrew word for this phenomenon. One example of how it was handled is in Ezekiel 40:2: "In the visions of God He *took me* into the land of Israel" (emphasis added). Once again, the seer was taken somewhere (translated supernaturally) during a vision. But the New Testament Greek gives us a bit more clarity, as in the definition that follows, and we already put it to good use in Acts 10, 11 and 22:17.

> *ekstasis*—1) any casting down of a thing from its proper place or state, displacement 2) a throwing of the mind out of its normal state, alienation of mind, whether such as makes a lunatic or that of a man who by some sudden emotion is transported as it were out of himself, so that in this rapt condition, although he is awake, his mind is drawn off from all surrounding objects and wholly fixed on things divine that he sees nothing but the forms and images lying within, and thinks that he perceives with his bodily eyes and ears realities shown him by God. 3) amazement, the state of one who, either owing to the importance or the novelty of an event, is thrown into a state of blended fear and wonderment.[2]

Now, *that* is a definition! I have experienced this *ekstatis* before (especially #2 and #3), which is where we get the word *ecstasy*. My husband, however, has a translation story that still leaves my mouth watering, in which the Lord "took him" to Italy to baptize him in His Holy Spirit. My Spirit baptism happened in my den on grubby carpet! His translation—which occurred while he was on a business trip to Canada in 1994—had much to do with what we now see was a commissioning to minister to the people of Italy. We are now connected to Italian missionaries there, such as Gaetano Sottile in Rome, but it all began with that translation from a ritzy Canadian hotel room to a craggy cave in Italia, where Chris Smith became a different man.

There in that cave, Chris saw people, angels and the Lord Himself. And they all knew him. He "came to" on his bed praying in tongues—something he had never done and was afraid to do—and then he slid off the bed and crawled to the bathroom to look in the mirror and see if his physical appearance had changed. He said he was afraid he was going to look like Charlton Heston as Moses, with platinum hair, but instead he looked just like himself. Same old Chris on the outside, but a different Chris on the inside. Little did he know that ten years later, he would be pastoring a Spirit-filled church and funding missionaries in countries all over the world, including Italy. All because in 1992–1993 he started raising his hands and saying, "More, Lord." In hindsight, those were very dangerous prayers.

Hebrews 11:5 (KJV) says, "By faith Enoch was *translated* that he should not see death; and was not found, because God had *translated* him: for before his *translation* he had this testimony, that he pleased God" (emphasis added). In this example, the Greek word for *translated* is this:

> *metatithemi*—1) to transpose (two things, one of which is put in place of the other), to transfer, to change, to transfer one's self or suffer one's self to be transferred, to go or pass over, 2) to fall away or desert from one person or thing to another.[3]

Visitations

Whereas a translation involves you supernaturally visiting another place, a visitation is when a heavenly entity or being *visits you*.

About fifteen years ago, I was in prayer one night in my bedroom, praying about my health. Many times in my life's health journey I have felt I narrowly escaped death or was trying to, and this was one of those nights when I was reminding

God (and my own heart) that He said He would not forget me
and that I was dependent on His protection. Suddenly, on my
knees in prayer, I lifted my head and saw I
was entirely encircled by a massive pair of
angel's wings that reached all the way down
to the floor. It was like I was inside an igloo,
an igloo made of cupped angel's wings.

I had always read about "pinions" in
Scripture, but now I could see them up
close in each feather of each wing. God
also disclosed three things He was giving
me as I knelt there, things that began to
manifest very quickly after the experience
and are still blossoming today. Since that
open vision, I have never once doubted
my bodily protection. Another argument
for the power of visions in your Christian
journey. I suppose this angelic encounter
could be classified an open vision, too. Or maybe even included
in our chapter 10 section "Seeing Angels and Demons." Now
you see why the seers in the Bible had a hard time categorizing
their visions. In the end, does it really matter?

Some more visitations in Scripture are:

Daniel 8—the archangel Gabriel visits Daniel (also 9:21–23)

Daniel 10—the archangel Michael visits a fasting Daniel and
promises relief

Matthew 17:1–9—Peter, James and John see Elijah and Moses
on the Mount of Transfiguration with Jesus

Mark 16:9–12—Jesus visits Mary Magdalene and others after
His resurrection

John 20:26—Jesus appears to the disciples after His resurrection

Acts 12:8–9—an angel rescues Peter from prison

Acts 22:6–11—Paul encounters Jesus on the road to Damascus

> On my knees in prayer, I lifted my head and saw I was entirely encircled by a massive pair of angel's wings that reached all the way down to the floor. It was like I was inside an igloo, an igloo made of cupped angel's wings.

Revelation—the entire book of John's visitations, visions and revelations

I have included here the Mount of Transfiguration story, where Jesus takes Peter, James and John and they rendezvous with Moses and Elijah. This encounter is a perfect example of categorization difficulty. Was it a vision? A translation? A visitation? Probably all three. Can you imagine seeing Jesus standing there talking to two dead people, not to mention that they were two of the greatest prophets the world has ever known? But what I find interesting is that Jesus did not just walk into this party. He had to be transfigured first. Transformed. The message here is that we, too, must be transformed (spiritually) before we can experience this heavenly realm.

I will never tire of telling you that you do not need a visitation, a vision or a dream to believe the Bible. Even if you experienced every supernatural encounter and translation possible, afterward you would still be right back living in your same old shoes and having to choose to walk by faith or not. But God, in His mercy and at His choosing, will occasionally decide to open your eyes. You will never be the same afterward, even if it only happens to you once.

In closing, here is a poem that I wrote in 2005, while spending the night in an ICU waiting room with a dear friend, Stacey, while her husband, Bobby, was hospitalized. I was writing a poem a day that year, so that day's got documented. I had a waking vision, and in it, I saw a phone number. I felt the Lord saying I needed to call it and encourage the person to keep moving forward and not give up, and to remind the person to come to Jesus for his or her every need. Trouble was, I could not remember the last digit. I narrowed it down to three numbers and decided to call them all. Boy, am I glad I did. "You don't know me, but I awoke to a vision of your phone number this morning. . . ." I delivered the message to all, and all three were grateful. One even confessed that she was about to take her life. Thank God for waking visions!

Stepping out to make a call
Will I touch one? Will I touch all?
A number "seen." No, two. No, three.
I'll phone them all. We soon shall see . . .

© Laura Harris Smith, May 4, 2005

PRAYER

Let's pray out loud together:

God, open the eyes of my heart right now. At the times of Your choosing, I ask You to speak to me in visions of all kinds, whether they be open, waking or night visions. I submit to what You want and have made up my mind not to be afraid of any good and scriptural gift You want to give me, including visitations, translations or even sighting heavenly beings. I trust You. In Jesus' name, Amen.

IMPARTATION

Right now, I pray the words of the prophet Elisha over you from 2 Kings 6:17: "And Elisha prayed, and said, 'Lord, I pray, open his eyes that he may see.'" (Or if you are one of my sisters in the Lord, I pray, "Open her eyes that she may see.") I also declare over you the promise of spiritual gifts made to you in 1 Corinthians 14, including "discernment of spirits." Not just to discern the presence of angels and other spirits, but to be able to know for certain when the Holy Spirit is near, who is the most important Spirit deserving of your focus. I break fear off you in Jesus' name. Scripture says if you ask God for bread He will not give you a stone, and that if you ask Him for a fish He will not give you a serpent. As you ask Him for these things here, you will not receive a counterfeit. Knowing God led me to write this book, and knowing He led you to read it, I impart to you every good gift He has given to me and ask that He multiply those gifts to you this very day. (Now open your hands, shut your eyes and receive it.)

7

Interpretations
and Dream Dictionary

I have had a dream that troubles me and I want to know what
it means.

Daniel 2:3 NIV

I t is with great sobriety that I compile this chapter, knowing that for years to come, people will turn to it and use it
to make life decisions. Groggy-eyed risers will wake from a
dream, turn to this chapter and try to make sense of enigmatic
symbols that they hope will unravel their distresses. Long after
you have finished reading *Seeing the Voice of God*, chapter 7 is
what will keep it on your nightstand or a nearby shelf for years
down the road, and that is a lot of weight for this little author
and Kingdom nobody who still cannot believe God uses her to
teach about these things she once doubted existed.

Seers—those who often dream and/or see visions—must stay
connected to the Body of Christ (and I want the image burned

into your mind of a beautiful pair of eyes plucked out and sitting on a desk, far from both the muscles that empower them and the blind body that needs their sight). We will talk more about that connection in chapter 10, but as you seek interpretation for your dreams and visions here, just know this chapter is not intended to replace the godly counsel of the local shepherd in whose field God has called you to feed. Remember: Seers are sheep, too. And every sheep needs a shepherd.

These pages also cannot replace prayer following a dream or vision, because dream interpretations without God's help get flaky fast. To use this chapter like a slot machine would be to reduce it to new-age witchery, old-school psychology or the countless psychic manuals available today for dream interpretations. I once visited what seemed like a harmless secular dream interpretation website, and the first two symbols proposed that dreaming of biscuits indicated pent-up emotions and that a woman dreaming of pickles meant she was unambitious in her career. Seriously?

> Remember: Seers are sheep, too. And every sheep needs a shepherd.

Remember that the best interpreter is the Holy Spirit within you. The same symbol could speak different things to different people, and only you live in your life's story and know for sure. For example, once at one of my classes on dreams and visions, I poured salt in each person's palm and asked them to share what it meant to them. One woman said, "We are the salt of the earth." Another said, "Elisha healed the waters with salt." The man next to her mentioned his high blood pressure. Yet another said, "Let your speech be gracious, seasoned with salt." Finally, one woman with a terrified look on her face exclaimed, "Lot's wife!"

Another time, I had a dream with three symbols: a friend with the last name of Brothers, Johnny Carson and my iPhone. I told Chris, "Mark my words, something will happen with one of my brothers that will involve my iPhone, and it will happen tonight." (The only thing Johnny Carson brought to mind was

The Tonight Show.) I prayed and forgot about it. Turns out, that very night I got involved in a detailed, very personal text conversation with someone who I thought was my brother-in-law because I had an old cell number for him in my phone. The man, who now had that number, wound up being a stranger who called to say he was interested in meeting and getting to know me. I was really alarmed. But I knew that God's warning dream had prompted me to pray, and therefore I would be safe.

The next day I told my family about it. My sister-in-law, Susan, exclaimed, "So Johnny Carson means 'tonight'?"

I said, "Only to me, not to everyone."

I was glad she asked, because it made me mindful about explaining here that God will use symbols unique to the experiences of the dreamer. You will dream plenty of dreams that no dictionary can assist you with because the symbols mean nothing to anyone but you. For instance, my brother is a successful banker. When God drops him down in the middle of a dream unrelated to him, He knows I will understand that it is a financial dream. Likewise, when my earthly father appears in a dream where he normally does not seem to "fit" (like with a group of my friends he does not know), it usually symbolizes my heavenly Father.

If one of the definitions that follow does not seem to fit your dream or vision, then seek God and phone a Christian friend who interprets. I often find that God will give one person the dream and another person the interpretation because it keeps us connected and interdependent, fostering family.

Also, these interpretations that follow will treat your symbols figuratively and not literally. In other words, if you dream that someone has died, you will find herein what that means symbolically (death to a dream or spiritual death, for example), but it is always a good idea to go ahead and also pray literal prayers of protection over that person's life. It is an airtight, winning combination.

I have also included a reference list for numeric symbolisms in Scripture. It follows the dream symbols section of the dictionary. Many people do not believe that God is concerned with numbers, but my answer to that is, "There's a whole book in the Bible called Numbers!" I am strict with my interpretations of numbers and take them only from Scripture. In other words, if the number 5 symbolizes grace, I do not believe that 10 indicates double grace. The number 10 has enough literal beauty of its own without us needing to manipulate something better out of it.

Keep in mind that sometimes a symbol can be used positively or negatively. For instance, let's say you see a snake in your dream. Snakes represent evil and demonic influence, but a snake was also raised up on a stick in the desert by Moses and used as an instrument of healing—which John 3:14 says foreshadowed Jesus being raised up on the cross for our healing. Which is the right interpretation for your dream? Satan or Jesus? Either would be spiritually grounded. At that moment, you must consider your soul (your emotions). If you are fearful, then the dream was from the enemy. If you are at peace afterward, then it was from the Lord, even if it was exposing a demonic influence at work. And even when I awake under the fear of the Lord, I am not afraid of God but am consumed with reverence and total peace.

Dream interpretations vary from dictionary to dictionary, and that can be confusing. But my friend Stephanie once said something insightful concerning this. I questioned if a particular interpretation of a symbol she had read in a book was the one she should go with, and her answer was, "When God gave me the dream, He knew I had this book and would be turning to it, so I believe He used symbols and interpretations I could find in it." I have never forgotten that, and I hope this book of mine will be your "go-to" book that God uses for you as you interpret.

Dream Dictionary

What you will find: I felt the need to include a Bible verse for each symbol I give, but sometimes Scripture does not include a modern symbol. In that case, I relied on decades of interpretations that have come through fasting prayer. If the symbol is literally in Scripture, then I list in normal type at least one verse where it is found. If it is not, then I give a tried-and-true, universal interpretation and then list a verse *in italics* to help you with the issue the symbol introduces, or at least to show you that someone else in Scripture was in the same boat. The same italics rule applies if the symbol is in Scripture but the interpretation has a modern relevance and is not in Scripture.

All 1000+ symbols are supported by God's Word, though. Some come directly from His *logos* (written Word), and some come from His *rhema* (spoken Word), supported by His *logos*. A good example of this would be the symbol of a rearview mirror. Although not in Scripture, a rearview mirror is a clear indicator from the Lord in a dream that someone is focusing on the past and is in danger of not moving forward. Alongside that definition, I would place *Philippians 3:13* in italics since it advises us to forget that which lies behind and look forward to that which lies ahead.

What you will not find: You will not find the word *feeling* in this dictionary. Secular symbol dictionaries will say this-or-that symbol reveals how you are *feeling* about this-or-that situation. That is not my goal. You already know how you are feeling about your situation. What you need to know is what God says about it. My symbols are intended for you to pray with and find faith. For instance, "buried alive" symbolizes sudden helplessness. Whereas a secular dream symbols dictionary would say this reveals that you are feeling overwhelmed by a current situation, I would say it is God revealing the enemy's intent to overwhelm you, but that you can *and will* experience the resurrection power of Jesus to rise up and overcome, if you will pray. Who wants to reaffirm misery? This dictionary reaffirms your faith.

Symbols and Interpretations

Note: For Scripture references, unless I recommend a specific Bible translation[1] for a particular symbol, you can use the translation of your choice.

abandoned car: a stalled or neglected move of God (*Acts 17:28a; Isa. 66:20*)

actor: someone playing a role (1 Kings 14:6 NASB; 2 Sam. 14:2; Prov. 13:7)

adoption: the gift of family, coming into God's family (Rom. 8:15; Eph. 1:5)

adultery: spiritual affair/idolatry (James 4:4a); pornography (Matt. 5:28; Exod. 20:14)

aging: spiritually exhausted if aging too soon (Ruth 4:15a); wisdom (Deut. 32:7)

air force: high-ranking spiritual warfare in the heavenlies (*Eph. 1:20–21; 6:12*)

airplane: huge move of God—holds many and occupies the heavens; favor (*Isa. 60:8–10*)

airport: waiting for takeoff, departure, deadline, runway for ministry (*Isa. 40:31*)

alarm: a wake-up call to action (Num. 10:5)

alcohol: controlled by something other than God; foolish (Prov. 23:19–35; Rom. 14:21)

alligator/crocodile: lurking danger; jaws of death (Ps. 9:13 NLT; Lev. 11:29 DARBY)

altar: a place of sacrifice or the laying down of one's will (Exod. 20:24)

ambulance: emergency spiritual or physical intervention (*Ps. 71:12*)

amusement park/fair: carefree fun, but also amusement (*Exod. 32:25*)

anaconda: see python

anchor: hope; fixed, steady (Heb. 6:19a)

angel: messenger (Job 33:23); protectors, guardians, ministering spirits (Heb. 1:14)

ant: a hardworking attitude, diligence (Prov. 6:6–8)

antenna: a call to pay closer attention to God and to tune in (*Prov. 1:8–9*)

antiques: something old or outdated (*Isa. 42:9*)

apple: favor (Ps. 17:8); temptation (Gen. 3:6)

apron: serving others (John 13:4–5); miracle prayer cloths (Acts 19:12)

aquarium w/fish: a church or ministry, we are to be fishers of men (*Matt. 4:19*)

ark: refuge; salvation during life's storms (Gen. 7:1 23)

arm: God's might and power (Ps. 89:13; Isa. 62:8)

armor: promised protection by God for all Christians (Eph. 6:11)

army: an organized group with a cause, godly or evil (Joel 2:11; Eph. 6:12)

army tank: opposite of a move of God; a corporate move of the enemy in war (2 Cor. 10:4)

arrow: children (Ps. 127:3–4); poisoned arrows are grief (Job 6:2–4); lies (Jer. 9:8)

ashes: repentance (Luke 10:13); mourning (Esther 4:1)

aspirin: see medicine

assassins: demonic forces with a special mission to kill and steal (*John 10:10; Ps. 38:12*)

astrological signs: pagan influences/witchcraft (Jer. 10:2–3; Isa. 42:8 NLT); see zodiac

athlete: a competitive spirit, good or bad (1 Cor. 9:24–26)

ATM: mass production; unlimited financial access (*Phil. 4:19*)

attic: a high place of sacrificial prayer and worship (*2 Chron. 33:17*)

attorney: intercessor, one who mediates through prayer (1 John 2:1; Rom. 8:34)

ax: the end of a thing; pruning (Matt. 3:10)

babies: spiritual infants (1 Cor. 3:1; 1 Pet. 2:2); birthing new things (*Isa. 42:9*)

baby food: if eaten in a dream, symbolizes a need for the meat of the Word (*1 Cor. 3:2; Heb. 5:14*)

back door: if entering through, conveys secrecy or a sneak attack (*Gen. 4:7*)

backpack: life situations/weight on a person's back slowing them down (*Heb. 12:1*)

backsliding: losing progress spiritually, emotionally and/or physically (Prov. 14:14)

backstage: behind the scenes, hidden, waiting to be revealed (*1 Cor. 4:5*)

bait: something intended to lure one into a trap (*Amos 3:5*)

baking/bakery: producing something; sustenance (Lev. 7:9; James 1:3 NASB)

balancing: needing order in one's life (*Dan. 5:27*)

balding hair: being uncovered—not having adequate prayer or protection (*1 Cor. 11:15*)

Band-Aid: remedying a big problem with small resources (*Hos. 6:1*)

bandage: needing to cover a wound to promote healing (Isa. 1:6)

banker: an accountant, a money manager or angel (*Luke 19:23*)

bankrupt: spiritual or emotional depletion; collapse (*Ps. 94:11* NET; *Gal. 4:9* NET)

banner: victory and rejoicing in Christ (Ps. 20:5); love (Song 2:4)

banquet: Jesus' love (Song 2:4); affirmation in the presence of our enemies (Ps. 23:5)

bar: an atmosphere of sinfulness (*Rom. 13:13; Luke 21:34; 1 Cor. 6:9–10*)

barn: a storehouse (Luke 12:18); blessing (Mal. 3:10)

barrel: being "over a barrel" means helpless in someone's power (*Ps. 10:12; 2 Chron. 14:11*)

baseball: pay attention to running bases and "sliding home" (*1 Cor. 9:25*)

basement: to be abased (*Phil. 4:12* KJV); humility (*Matt. 23:12; Ezra 9:5* NIV)

basket: delivery of provision (Matt. 16:9); escape (Acts 9:25)

bat: unclean, demonic distraction (Lev. 11:13–19)

bathing: cleansing for holiness (Exod. 30:19–21); cleansing from sin (Ps. 51:2–3)

bathrooms: cleansing; the "rest room" (*Gen. 18:4; Heb. 4:9*)

battery: power, energy (*Ps. 21:1*)

battle: every battle is God's to win (1 Sam. 17:47); spiritual warfare (Eph. 6:12–13)

battleship: may symbolize a future attack to thwart in prayer (*Dan. 11:40; Isa. 54:17*)

bears: the fear of the Lord, reverence, respect (2 Kings 2:24)

beaten: demonic attack (2 Cor. 4:9); punishment of the foolish (Prov. 10:13)

beaver: a diligent worker (*Prov. 10:4*)

bed: rest and healing (Ps. 41:3); the marriage bed (Heb. 13:4); a refuge (Prov. 7:17)

bedroom: a private area (2 Kings 6:12; 11:2); a place of relaxation (Ps. 63:6)

bees: swarming foes (Ps. 118:12); stinging words, gossip, busybodies (*1 Tim. 5:13*)

behead/head injury: rebellion against authority or the head (Luke 9:9; Mark 12:2–4)

bells: announcing a thing; a call to holiness (Exod. 28:33–36)

belly: appetites and lusts (Rom. 16:18); worldly desires (Phil. 3:18–19)

belt: the truth, the whole truth and nothing but the truth (Eph. 6:14)

Bible: a call to study God's Word; ultimate authority (Heb. 4:12)

bike: personal progress or a move of God in one's personal life (*Acts 17:28a*)

bird: see eagle, owl, vulture, mockingbird or dove

birth control pills: controlling one's own life, not letting God (*Ps. 127:3; Prov. 16:9*)

birth/labor: announces bringing forth a new thing (*Isa. 42:9*)

birthday presents: coming gifts from God (*James 1:17*); spiritual gifts (*1 Cor. 12:1–11*)

bite: attack (Acts 28:3); backbiting (Prov. 25:23 NASB); alcohol's consequences (Prov. 23:31–35)

black: modern symbolism death, night, evil or sin; biblical symbolism plague (Exod. 10:15)

black belt: spiritual warfare expertise in prayer (*Ps. 35:1; 1 Tim. 6:12; Eph. 6:14*)

black cat: could symbolize witchcraft in context (*Mic. 5:12; Rev. 21:8*)

black horse: can represent famine (Rev. 6:5); see horse

black sheep: an outcast (Gen. 30:35)

black widow spider: demonic attack or judgment (*Isa. 59:4–5*); see spider

blanket: spiritual covering or protection (Gen. 9:23)

bleeding: suffering (Deut. 21:8 ASV); if nosebleeds, strife, quarrels (Prov. 30:33)

blind: spiritually sightless (Matt. 15:14; John 9:39; Prov. 29:18 KJV)

blind spot: being unable to see one's own faults (*Ps. 19:12*)

blood: life itself (Lev. 17:11a); if on the ground, a curse (Gen. 4:10; Rev. 6:10; Ps. 106:38)

blossoms: coming fruit in one's life (Gen. 40:10); favor (Num. 17:5–8)

blue: holiness (Exod. 39:22), modern—symbolizes a boy

blueprints: strategy or plans for one's life or situation (*Jer. 29:11–13*)

boat: a place of testing if in a storm (Matt. 8:24); faith, if stepping out of boat (Matt. 14:29)

body odor: a call to better care for oneself (*Rom. 12:1*)

boils: judgment (Deut. 28:27; Exod. 9:11); testing and suffering (Job 7:5)

bombs: Holy Ghost power (*Acts 1:8*); anger (*Ps. 76:7 NLT*)

bones (broken): a broken spirit (Prov. 17:22); grief (Ps. 31:10); envy (Prov. 14:30)

book: learning (Deut. 31:12 NLT)

boomerang: returning or coming back (*Jer. 29:10; 1 Cor. 15:34 NIV*)

bows and arrows: bitter words (Ps. 64:2–4); prepared for war (Isa. 5:28)

brake failure: lack of self-control (*Prov. 25:28 NIV*); defeat or death (*Exod. 14:23*)

bread: Jesus (John 6:51); provision, money (Prov. 12:11 KJV); body of Jesus (Luke 22:19)

bricks: building; slavery or bondage (Exod. 5:8, 18–19)

bride: the Bride of Christ, the Church of Jesus (Rev. 21:9)

bridegroom: Jesus Christ (Matt. 9:15)

bridge: crossing over to a new place (*Deut. 3:18 NASB*)

briefcase: business (*Matt. 25:14–18 NIV*)

broom: cleaning of sin (Isa. 14:23); if broomstick, witchcraft, evil curses (Isa. 14:23)

brother: if not literal, a dear friend (Matt. 12:48)

bruise: affliction (Isa. 53:10); result of battling the enemy (Gen. 3:15)

brush/comb: caring for one's covering (*Matt. 6:17*; 1 Cor. 11:15)

bugs/insects: destruction, ruin (Ps. 105:31; Deut. 28:42)

building (1st floor): the natural, physical realm where we live under heaven (*John 3:31*)

building (2nd floor): the 2nd heaven, where angels war, fueled by our prayer (*Eph. 3:10*)

building (3rd floor): the 3rd heaven, where we visit with God in paradise (2 Cor. 12:2–4)

bull: danger (Ps. 22:12); pray for safety from intimidation (Ps. 12:5)

bulldog: stubbornness (*Isa. 46:12*; *Isa. 66:3–4*)

bullets: words or information used during gossip (*Isa. 54:17*)

burglar/robber/thief: a thieving spirit; the enemy, Satan (John 10:10)

buried alive: sudden helplessness (Num. 16:33)

burning bush: announces a supernatural commissioning and sign (Exod. 3)

burns (bodily): burning desires of the flesh; financial oppression (James 5:3)

bus (moving): large move of God in ministry (*Isa. 66:20 NIV*)

bus station: waiting for departure; a center for ministry or deliverance (*Deut. 16:3–6*)

butterfly: change; emergence after metamorphosis (2 Cor. 5:17; Rom. 12:2)

buttons on mouth: keeping quiet (*Prov. 30:32 NKJV*)

buzzard: unclean, impure and ravaged (Lev. 11:13 NASB)

cab/taxi: a temporary mode of travel on your journey (*Judg. 18:6 NIV*)

cage: being trapped (Jer. 5:26–27)

calculator: counting the costs, estimating something (*Luke 14:28*)

calendar: the timing of a promised thing (*Job 14:13*)

camels: something impossible without God's help (Luke 18:25)

camera: memories, capturing a moment (1 *Thess. 3:6*)

camouflage/fatigues: to be hidden in Christ (*Col. 3:3*)

camp or campgrounds: something temporary; passing through (*Heb. 11:8–10*)

cancer: something potentially emotionally deadly that can spread (2 *Tim. 2:17 NLT*)

candle: one's life (Matt. 5:15 KJV)

candy: may represent immaturity if the mainstay of one's diet in a dream (1 Cor. 13:11)

cannon: substantial, far-reaching verbal assault; see guns

captain: the one in charge (Num. 31:48)

car (moving): move of God, varying sizes depending on vehicle; ministry (*Acts 17:28a*)

car crash: a hindrance in ministry or to one's personal destination; see cars

cardinal: seeing cardinals is a sign of very high importance (1 Cor. 15:3 NIV)

carpenter: the Builder of your life (Isa. 44:13; Matt. 13:55)

carried (in a dream): in need of rescuing or carrying (Ps. 28:9)

casino: gambling at life (*Isa. 36:8 ISV*)

casket/coffin: death (Gen. 50:26 NIV; 2 Chron. 16:14 NASB)

caterpillar: a season of hiddenness before transformation; see butterfly

cathedral: old religion (*Luke 21:5–6*)

Catholicism: religious traditions (*Mark 7:8*)

cave: a place of escape and refuge (1 Sam. 22:1)

cemetery: death of a dream or a desire, etc. (Job 21:33 NLT)

censer: prayer (Rev. 8:3)

chains: can represent addictions; imprisoned, in bondage (Acts 12:6)

chair: a seat of authority (Ps. 107:32 DARBY; 2 Sam. 23:8 DARBY)

chapel: a place of intimate personal worship (Amos 7:13 KJV)

chariot: a vehicle of war (1 Kings 20:25 NIV)

chased: being pursued by enemies (Deut. 1:44)

check: money or currency (*Num. 3:47*)

cheerleader: an encourager or rallier (*John 16:33 KJV*)

chewing gum: represents chewing but never digesting spiritual truths (*Rev. 10:9*)

chicken: fear or timidity (*2 Tim. 1:7*)

children: innocence; God's blessing, heritage, legacy (Ps. 127:3)

choking: worries over money and other life cares (Matt. 13:22)

Christmas tree: holiday symbols are only time lines for when a thing may occur

cigarette: addictive behavior (*Gal. 5:1*)

civil war: division on a large scale (James 4:1)

clay: molded by God the Potter (Rom. 9:21)

climbing: struggling, contending (Joel 2:7 NASB); moving upward (Isa. 14:14 NLT)

clock: God's timing (2 Pet. 3:9)

closet: a place of private prayer (Matt. 6:6)

clothes: if dirty, dead works or sin (Isa. 64:6); if white, righteousness (Rev. 3:5)

clouds (of rain): favor (Prov. 16:15); if dark, doom and gloom (Job 3:5 NLT)

coals: on lips, anointed speech (Isa. 6:6–7); blowing on, fanning flame (Isa. 54:16)

clown: a demonic mocker (*Prov. 1:26*)

coat: covering, endorsement (2 Kings 9:13 GW); multicolored, favor (Gen. 37:23)

coffee: a need for awakening (*Rom. 13:11*)

coins: if two, poverty (Mark 12:42); stewardship, currency, debt (Matt. 18:28)

college: higher education and learning of life lessons (*Acts 19:9*)

comforter: the Comforter, the Holy Spirit (Jer. 8:18 NIV)

communion: unity within the Body of Christ—"come union" (2 Cor. 13:14 KJV)

compass: one's life direction (*Ps. 119:59 NLT*)

computer: information (*1 Sam. 23:22a; Job 42:4 HCSB*)

construction worker: building or edifying oneself (*Rom. 14:19 KJV*)

conveyer belt: production line of many things, whatever is shown (*Luke 12:16 NASB*)

cooking: preparing spiritual food (Luke 10:40; Ezek. 46:24 NIV)

cornered: put in a compromising position of helplessness (2 Sam. 21:16 NLT)

cornucopia (horn of plenty): Thanksgiving time, or gratitude (*Col. 3:16 NIV*)

costume: pretending you are someone you are not (Ps. 102:26)

couch: relaxing (Ezek. 23:41 NASB)

covering: protection, shield, security (Prov. 10:12 NIV)

cows: a gluttonous woman or wife (Amos 4:1 NIV); improperly holy in some countries

crawling: to sneak; to cower in shame (Isa. 2:21 NLT; Mic. 7:17 NIV)

cross: death; Christ's crucifixion (John 19:17; Matt. 10:38)

crowing: denial of Christ (John 18:27); see rooster

crown: reward (1 Peter 5:4); victory (1 Cor. 9:25 NIV); if thorns, mockery (John 19:2)

crucifix: Christ's death before resurrection (Matt. 16:24)

crutches: vices, coping mechanisms (*Prov. 3:5 NIV; 2 Sam. 3:29*)

crying: needy (Prov. 21:13); sorrow or mourning (Rev. 21:4)

crystal ball: divination or sorcery (*Zech. 10:2 NLT; Acts 16:16*)

cup: partaking or participating (1 Cor. 10:21)

dam: a blockage (Deut. 22:7 KJV); a barrier (Prov. 17:14 NIV)

dancing: celebration or joy (Ps. 30:11; Eccles. 3:4)

death: a need for a spiritual awakening (Eph. 2:5); death to a dream (Heb. 2:14 NIV)

debt: an outstanding obligation owed (Matt. 18:27)

deer: incredible ability, sure-footedness (Hab. 3:19 NIV); longing for God (Ps. 42:1)

demon: an evil spirit (Mark 9:38)

dentist: help with mouth and words (*Prov. 16:24, 27*)

desert: isolation, barrenness (Deut. 32:10); a place of testing (Matt. 4:11)

desk: a place to conduct business (Luke 5:27 ISV)

devil: threatening demonic activity (James 4:7)

diamonds: beauty and strength (Zech. 7:12 ESV); may represent April (birthstone)

diaper: if soiled, sin; immaturity (*Eph. 4:14 NLT*)

digging: hard labor for that which is hidden (Luke 16:3; Deut. 8:9)

dimes: tenfold or ten times over (*Luke 19:16 NLT*)

dinosaur: something outdated or disappearing (*Heb. 8:13 NIV*)

diploma: recognition of completion or mastery (*1 Cor. 9:25 KJV*)

directions (north, south, east, west): a place to watch in prayer or a move (Gen. 28:14)

disease/infirmity: literal ailments (Matt. 4:23); sin and sicknesses (Isa. 53:5 NIV)

dishes: if dirty, sin, hypocrisy (Matt. 23:25)

Disney World: see amusement park/fair

ditch: supply, a place for provision (Isa. 22:11 KJV); deterrent (Luke 6:39 KJV)

diving: falling headlong into danger (Ps. 37:24 NASB)

divorce: a division or disillusionment of any two people or an enterprise (Mal. 2:16)

doctor: the Great Physician, Jesus (Jer. 8:22)

dog (growling): a wicked sentinel/guard dog (Ps. 22:16)

dog bites: attack by an evil spirit; see dog

donkey: a stubborn person (Hos. 4:16 ISV), stupidity (Job 11:12)

door: opportunity (1 Cor. 16:9); if locked or blocked, hindrance (Rev. 3:8)

dove: the Holy Spirit (John 1:32); peace and rest (Ps. 55:6)

dragon: Satan, the devil (Rev. 12:9)

dripping faucet: disagreements/argument (Prov. 19:13)

driving: the one in charge of ministry or leading a move of God; see car

driving backward: losing progress or backsliding (*Jer. 3:22; 2 Pet. 2:21 ESV*)

drowning: sorrow, grief, overwhelming difficulty (Isa. 43:2 NLT)

drugs: if illegal, a sign of addiction; if prescription, a cure (Mark 15:23 NLT)

drums: an instrument with unifying force in battle or worship (Exod. 15:20 NET)

Dumpster: see garbage

dung: unclean and useless (Jer. 16:4 NIV)

dynamite/explosion: danger; a coming emotional explosion (*Ps. 76:7 NLT*)

eagle: leading; of highest authority (2 Sam. 1:23)

ears: being attentive; listening (Rev. 2:17; Ps. 116:2; Mark 4:9)

earmuffs: spiritual deafness (*Zech. 7:11 NIV*)

earring: wisdom/counsel (Prov. 25:12)

earthquake: the shaking of one's life foundation (Ezek. 38:19 NIV)

eating: consuming spiritual food or truths (Mark 14:22)

egg: incubation, gestation, waiting (Isa. 34:15)

Egypt: a place representing slavery and bondage (Exod. 2:23)

elementary school: learning the primary essentials (*Heb. 6:1 NASB*)

elephant: a large, un-dealt-with sin that cannot be concealed (*Prov. 28:13 NASB; Num. 32:23*)

elevator: implies travel between the natural and spiritual realms; see building levels

emeralds: royalty (Rev. 4:3); may be a time line for the month of May (birthstone)

emotions: emotions in your dreams are literal (*Gen. 43:30 NLT*)

engine: great power (*Eph. 1:19–20*)

envy: jealousy with vengeance, revealing covetousness in one's life (James 4:2 DARBY)

escape: fleeing from danger (Jer. 46:6)

ex (spouse, love): may reveal lingering emotions or be a time line of the past (*Phil. 3:13*)

exam/tests: being tested in life (James 1:3)

exercise: increasing strength and exercising godliness (1 Tim. 4:8 KJV)

exorcism: a need for deliverance, the casting out of demons (Luke 4:35)

explosion: see bombs or dynamite

eyes: being watchful in prayer (Col. 4:2); prophetic vision (Prov. 29:18 NASB)

factory: see conveyer belt

fainting: a lack of spiritual or emotional strength (Jer. 8:18 NIV; Gal. 6:9 NKJV)

fairy: a hovering, familiar spirit (*Deut. 18:11–12 KJV*)

fall/autumn: symbolizes a time to reap; a time of reward (Gal. 6:9)

falling: if stumbling, due to sin (Prov. 24:16); if free-falling, see diving

fame: widespread favor for whoever is shown in the dream (1 Chron. 14:17)

family (deceased): revealing generational curses or blessings (*Exod. 20:5–6*)

famous people: ponder what they mean to you; research name meaning (*Ezek. 16:15 NLT*)

fangs: vicious verbal attacks (Ps. 58:6)

farm/farmers: the process of sowing and reaping (Mark 4)

farsighted: cannot see things at hand, cannot see what is right in front of you (Zeph. 1:17)

fear: nightmares or fearful dreams are not of God (2 Tim. 1:7 KJV)

feather/pinions: evidence of angelic protection (Ps. 91:4)

feast: time of plenty (Eccles. 10:19; Hos. 2:11 NASB)

feet/toes: if dirty, sin; if washing, humility (John 13:14); implies your journey (Josh. 1:3)

fence: marks territory (Mark 12:1); barricades to overcome (Eccles. 10:8 ERV)

ferry: an event carrying you to your destination/destiny (2 Sam. 19:18 KJV)

fever: fighting off spiritual or demonic infection (Job 30:30)

fighter jet: high-ranking spiritual warfare from the heavenlies; see air force

fighting: spiritual warfare or struggles in one's faith (1 Tim. 6:12)

fig tree: a sign to rid one's life of something not bearing fruit (Matt. 21:19)

files: a collection of memories or facts (2 Cor. 10:7 NLT)

fingers: creativity (Ps. 8:3 NIV)

fire: destruction (Isa. 47:14); continual worship (Lev. 6:12); tested, pure (Zech. 13:9)

fire extinguisher: extinguishing trouble (2 Sam. 14:7 NKJV)

firefighter: the person who fights trouble and destruction (Isa. 43:17 NKJV)

fish (fishing): evangelism, being fishers of men (Mark 1:17)

fishhook: being hooked or caught (Job 41:1)

flag: emblem of a specific nation or group of people (Isa. 62:10 NLT); see banner

flesh: earthly desires (Matt. 26:41)

flies: rottenness and demonic attack (Eccles. 10:1)

floating: to rise above one's problems (Isa. 60:8)

floods: troubles or grief (Ps. 32:6; 69:1–2)

floor: being on the floor means humility or humiliation (Lam. 2:10)

flowers: a budding or blossoming situation (Song 2:12)

flushing/toilet: ridding oneself of a situation or thing (James 1:21 NIV)

flying: overcoming life's burdens and escaping (Jer. 48:9 NLT)

flying near power lines: flirting with danger; imprudence (Prov. 27:12)

food: spiritual nourishment (Mark 14:22)

fool's gold: a counterfeit in relationship or religion (Col. 2:23 NIV)

fork: ability to feed oneself or another spiritually (Matt. 25:37)

forest: an urgent need to be "out of the woods" (Ps. 104:20)

fort: a place of safety in battle (2 Chron. 27:4 NIV)

fountain: a source of refreshment (Deut. 8:7 NKJV); flowing wisdom (Prov. 18:4)

fox: a deceptive individual, especially little foxes (Song 2:15)

frog: plagued with unclean spirits (Exod. 8:2)

front porch: an altar of fellowship (2 Chron. 15:8 NASB)

fruit: results or blessings (Luke 6:43)

fumble: dropping the ball; a mistake (Matt. 22:29)

funeral: death or despair over the end of a situation or a desire (Eccles. 2:20 NLT)

games: living the game of life (Luke 7:32 NLT; 1 Tim. 6:12 NET)

gangs/gangsters: groupings of demons (Hos. 7:1)

garbage: rejected as worthless (1 Cor. 4:13); to discard (Lam. 3:45 NLT)

gardening: the process of sowing and reaping (Mark 4); see farm

gasoline: fuel for the fire, good or bad (Ezek. 21:32 NIV)

gate: opportunity requiring permission to enter (Gen. 19:1 NIV)

gavel: a determined judgment (Ps. 1:5)

general: high-ranking military chief, good or evil (2 Sam. 24:2 DARBY; Rev. 16:16 NLT)

ghosts: symbolic of demonic spirits (Rev. 16:14)

giant: any spiritual opponent or overwhelming situation (1 Sam. 17:4)

gifts: spiritual gifts or coming reward (1 Cor. 12; 14)

glass: fragility and transparency (Rev. 21:21)

glasses/contacts: a need for corrected spiritual vision; see eyes

globe: Earth and its people (Isa. 40:22 DARBY)

goat: the lost/unsaved (Matt. 25:33)

God: heavenly Father is often symbolized by one's earthly father (Heb. 12:9–10)

going bald: the loss of spiritual covering in one's life; see hair

gold: of highest value and wealth (1 Kings 10:18)

golden calf: idolatry in one's life (Ps. 106:19)

golf: a "hole in one" represents success (Eccles. 10:10 KJV)

gong: works without love (1 Cor. 13:1)

government: a call to pray for man's government or God's (Rom. 13:1)

grave: burying an issue, "laying it to rest" (Job 17:1); if literal, death (Hos. 13:14 NIV)

gray hair: wisdom (Prov. 16:31)

green: new life (Job 8:16 KJV); money (1 Tim. 6:10)

grenade: a sudden explosive situation; see bomb

Grim Reaper: pray against a literal and untimely death when seen (1 Cor. 15:55)

grocery: a place/ministry that provides spiritual nourishment (Mark 14:22)

groom: Jesus, the Bridegroom (John 3:29)

guards: protectors or angels (Ps. 91:11)

gun: gossiping, slander and words used as weapons (Ps. 10:7; Isa. 54:17)

gum: see chewing gum

gymnastics: hard work through much practice (1 Tim 4:8 NIV)

gypsy/vagrant: one who never settles down or commits (Gen. 4:12 NASB)

hail: sudden war declared by God, with promise of victory if we pray (Job 38:22–23)

hair: spiritual covering (1 Cor. 11:14–15)

hallway of doors: many choices/opportunity (1 Cor. 16:9; Ps. 25:12; Col. 4:5 NIV)

halo: holiness (Ezek. 1:28 NLT)

hand: if right, victory, long life (Ps. 20:6); if left, riches, wisdom, honor (Prov. 3:16)

handcuffs: restricting behavior or progress (Matt. 16:19)

hanging on: a long wait for help or change (Heb. 6:15)

harlot: a seductive, tempting situation or person (Prov. 7:10)

hat: a symbol of authority for women (1 Cor. 11:6); a covering (Exod. 39:28)

hawks: something unclean trying to alight (Lev. 11:16)

head: authority (Isa. 9:15)

hearse: nearing the death of a relationship, person or situation (2 Sam. 3:31 ISV)

heart: the condition of your life or intents (Ezek. 36:26; Ps. 57:7; Matt. 15:19)

helmet: protection of authority, salvation (Eph. 6:17)

hemorrhage: slowly losing one's faith, livelihood or strength (Luke 8:43)

herbs: nutrition (Gen. 1:29 KJV); if bitter, grief (Lam. 3:15 NIV)

hiking: see climbing

hills: challenges in life (Luke 3:5); where help comes from (Ps. 121:1 KJV)

hissing: a harassing spirit (Ezek. 27:36 KJV; Job 27:23)

holding hands: being in agreement with someone; to foster with touch (Mark 9:27)

hole: a pit (Ps. 7:15 NIV); hiding place (Matt. 25:18); if in a garment, repair (Mark 2:21)

home run: sliding into home = "safe!"; run home; winning the game of life (*Phil. 2:16*)

homeless person: an evil spirit searching for a home (Luke 8:27 NLT)

homosexual: in a dream, symbolizes a perverse spirit or person (Lev. 18:22 NLT)

honey: sweetness in life, a situation or with God (Ps. 19:7–10)

honking horn: impatience or an impatient person (*Job 21:4 NLT*)

horn: power, especially governmentally (2 Sam. 22:3 NIV; Dan. 7:24 NIV)

hornets: spiritually confused, blindsided or stung (Exod. 23:27–28)

horse: a means of fast travel in battle (Prov. 21:31); if white, Christ's return (Rev. 6:2)

hospital: a place to stay and heal, ministry (*Ps. 147:3*)

hotel/motel: a temporary situation or location (Luke 10:35 NKJV)

hourglass: fleeting time and deadlines (*Ps. 39:4 NLT*)

house: house of prayer (Matt. 21:13); a symbol of one's choices (Matt. 7:26; Prov. 14:1)

hovering: see floating

howling/wolves: an evil person's or spirit's voice (Mark 5:2–5 NLT)

hunger: spiritual desire (Matt. 5:6); spiritually malnourished (Ps. 107:5 NKJV)

hurricane: sudden disaster and trouble in life (*Ps. 107:28–29*)

hyena: ridiculed or laughed at, "laughing hyena" (*Job 12:4 KJV; Isa. 13:22 NASB*)

hyssop: the need for cleansing (Exod. 12:22; Ps. 51:7 KJV)

ice: dangerous while driving; danger of losing one's footing (Ps. 73:18; Jer. 23:12)

ice cream: enjoying the milk of God's Word (*1 Pet. 2:2*)

ice water: to receive refreshment where spiritually parched (Prov. 25:25)

iceberg: an unforeseen, emerging danger (*Acts 19:40; 27:9*)

ICU: a need to be in a spiritual or emotional intensive care unit; see hospital

idols: distractions from serving God (Jer. 10:8)

immunization: a need for strength to resist spiritual infirmities (*1 Pet. 5:9*)

incense: the sweet aroma of prayer (Ps. 141:2)

incest: influence by a family member's perversions (*Exod. 20:5–6; Gen. 19:31–36*)

income: finances related to work (Luke 10:7)

Indians: a literal call to prayer for sins against Native Americans (*Isa. 10:2; Job 5:16*)

inheritance: spiritual blessings from one generation to another (Prov. 13:22)

injury: a spiritual or emotional wounding (Jer. 30:15)

insects: see bugs

insurance: the need for protection from loss (*Eccles. 7:12*)

interior designer: getting your house in order spiritually/relationally (*1 Tim. 3:12; 5:14*)

invitation: a request from God to you (Isa. 55:1)

iron: the strength of men; accountability promoting Christian growth (Prov. 27:17)

iron bars: a symbol of arguments (Prov. 18:19)

island: seclusion or seasonal isolation (*1 Sam. 19:2; Ps. 68:6*)

Israel: a call to pray for Israel, or pray for the Jews to receive their Messiah (Ps. 122:6)

ivory: luxury and lavishness (Amos 3:15)

jail: circumstantially imprisoned or a loss of freedoms (Gen. 39:20)

jail keeper: a spiritual oppressor (Matt. 18:34)

janitor: a servant who cleans up others' emotional messes (*Prov. 14:35; 1 Chron. 9:22–26*)

jawbone: superhuman strength (Judg. 15:15)

jaws: whether on animal or machine, symbolizes entrapment (Ps. 141:9)

Jesus: an invitation, i.e., toward salvation, healing, restoration (Rom. 10:9–10)

jewels: rewards and favor, especially in a crown (Zech. 9:16)

journey/trip: the path of life toward a destination (Luke 9:3)

joy (or someone named Joy in a dream): happiness in the Spirit (Gal. 5:22)

judge: one who can decide your fate (James 4:12)

juggling: overactivity, doing too many things at once

jugular vein (being cut): a threat to your life (Lev. 17:11)

junk food: an improper spiritual diet; a call to read God's Word more (*Rom. 14:17*)

junkyard: a place to discard worthless emotions; see garbage

jury: those who pass judgment (James 5:9)

karate: skilled and honed spiritual warfare (*2 Cor. 10:4*)

keg: drunkenness and sin (*1 Pet. 4:3*)

kernel: seemingly small or insignificant beginnings (Amos 9:9 NLT)

keyhole: needing the right key for a way in or out; see keys

keys: the unlocking of doors of opportunity or progress (Rev. 1:18)

kicking: to be on the defensive in a struggle (Acts 26:14 NIV)

kidnapped/kidnapper: an evil spirit trying to steal, kill or destroy (*John 10:10*)

killer: an evil spirit that seeks your life or success (*1 Cor. 15:55*)

kiln: a place of waiting and gaining strength under heat (1 Pet. 4:12; Nah. 3:13–15)

king: person in supreme authority; can represent Jesus (Dan. 2:37)

kiss/kissing: intimacy (Song 1:1–2; Ps. 2:12)

kitchen: working hard to spiritually nourish others (Luke 10:40)

kite (flying on string): earthly prayer tethered to unseen answers in heaven (*Ps. 123:1*)

KKK: prejudice and racism (*Gal. 3:28–29*)

knees: symbolic of being on your knees in prayer (Eph. 3:14 NKJV; Dan. 6:10 NKJV)

knife: weapon (Prov. 23:2); cut spiritual meat into bite-size pieces for teaching; see meat

knight: a rescuer or deliverer, often representing Jesus (*Ps. 144:2*)

knocking: something or someone trying to gain entrance, maybe Jesus (Rev. 3:20)

labor: birthing something in life through intense strain (Jer. 6:24)

labyrinth/maze: being lost, confused and trapped (*Luke 19:10; 1 Cor. 14:33 NKJV*)

ladder: occupational or spiritual promotion (Gen. 28:12)

lamb: Christ (John 1:29); young children or baby Christians (John 21:15)

lamp/lanterns: revelation and the Word of God (Ps. 119:105)

Las Vegas: a seat of sin; "Sin City," Sodom and Gomorrah (*Gen. 19:24–25*)

laughing: the joy of the Lord (Prov. 17:22; Job 8:21; Neh. 8:10)

laundry: airing sin—"dirty laundry" (*Rom. 13:12*); secrets of the heart (1 Cor. 14:25)

lawn mowers: stewardship or maintenance of one's fields (*Isa. 61:5; Dan. 4:15*)

lava: slow destruction and judgment (*Rev. 8:8*)

La-Z-Boy recliner: sluggardness and laziness (*Eccles. 10:18*)

leaking: loss; draining situations and problems (Nah. 2:8 NLT)

leash: restrictions or limitations (*1 Cor. 7:35;* Job 41:5 NIV)

leaven: hypocrisy or a Pharisee influence (Matt. 16:11)

left turn: the opposite of a right turn is a "wrong" turn or decision in life (Eccles. 10:2)

leopard: may represent a sudden, evil ambush (Hos. 13:7 NKJV; Jer. 5:6 NKJV)

leprosy: rejection or being outcast (Lev. 13:45)

letter: if to you, regard the message; if to others, things you wanted to say (2 Cor. 10:9)

Leviathan: a large, destructive force or spirit (Job 41:1)

library: a desire for knowledge of God's will (*Eccles. 12:12*)

licking dust: enemies of God eventually lick the dust (Ps. 72:9)

lie detector test: the presence of deceit or the need for truthfulness (*Col. 3:9*)

light: God's first creation (Gen. 1:3); God's Word (Ps. 27:1; Prov. 6:23)

lightbulb: a bright or creative idea; revelation or wisdom (*Luke 2:32* NKJV)

lighthouse: hope when searching (*Job 17:15* NKJV)

lightning: revelation or supernatural power (Ezek. 1:14)

limp-handed: weak and without influence or power (Jer. 50:43 NASB)

limping: having wrestled with God and been humbled (Gen. 32:25)

lion: Jesus—the Lion of the Tribe of Judah (Ps. 17:12); prowling enemy (1 Pet. 5:8)

lions' den: a very public and dangerous place of testing (Nahum 2:11)

lips: unclean speech (Isa. 6:5); with honey is seduction (Prov. 5:3)

lipstick: decorative, rich lips and speech (1 Cor. 1:5)

liver: a filter for the Body of Christ, namely discernment (*Ps. 119:125* NLT)

livestock: may mean dealing with live stocks in the stock market; plenty (Ps. 50:10)

lock: a situation requiring a key of wisdom to gain entry (Matt. 16:19; Neh. 7:3 ISV)

locker rooms: coaching or preparing for an event in one's life (*Eph. 6:15* NKJV)

locusts: devouring pestilence symbolizing a swarming evil army (Joel 2:25)

lottery: sudden financial gain (*Prov. 13:11; Heb. 13:5*); blessing (*Phil. 4:19*)

love: pure affection, the opposite of lust (1 Cor. 13)

luggage: baggage from one's past (*Matt. 11:28*); prepared to move on (*Luke 10:4*)

lukewarm water: spiritual compromise, lethargy or passivity (Rev. 3:15)

lungs: life and breath and praise (Gen. 2:7; Ps. 150:6)

lust: lustful dreams are not from God; may reveal lust in your heart (1 John 2:16; Col. 3:5)

lying: a liar in a dream is a lying spirit; notice if you lie in your dreams (Prov. 26:28)

maggot: defeat and death (Isa. 14:11)

magic/magician: witchcraft, divination, deceiving spirits and fraud (Acts 13:10)

magnifying glass: intent examination (2 Cor. 13:5)

maid: servanthood; someone who cleans up others' messes in prayer; see janitor

mailbox: prophetic ministry; where prophetic messages are delivered (Mark 6:11)

mailman: a messenger or prophet (2 Kings 19:14)

makeup: covering one's flaws (2 Kings 9:30)

mall: may mean "maladies" (since the root *mal* occurs in many illnesses) and may divulge that the dream is about your health (*Matt. 10:1* YLT)

manger: humble beginnings; the birth of Christ (Luke 2:7)

manna: supernatural provision from an unknown source, "what is it?" (Exod. 16:35)

mansion: a heavenly residence in eternity (Ps. 49:14–15)

mantle: authority, office, position, ranking (1 Kings 19:19 NASB)

manure: filth where placed or seen; however, promotes growth (Ezek. 4:12)

map: direction for one's life or a literal location (Ezek. 5:2 NLT)

marathon: see race

marching: a coming army (Joel 2:7); in unison or unity (Josh. 6:7)

marriage: dreaming of marriage may mean working together (3 John 1:8 NIV; Heb. 13:4)

mascara: anything to do with eyes suggests improving vision or creative perspective; see eyes

mask: disguise or deceit (2 Cor. 11:14)

mattress: sleep and the need to rest more (Ps. 127:2)

measuring stick/tape: see ruler

meat: spiritual nourishment for the mature; important spiritual truths (1 Cor. 3:2)

medal: reward, honor and recognition (Rev. 22:12 NIV)

medical exam: the need for spiritual or emotional introspection (Mark 2:17; Jer. 33:6)

medicine: God's remedy for a situation or problem (Jer. 8:22)

melting: resignation and the loss of one's firm beliefs (Isa. 13:7)

menorah: the nation of Israel or God's chosen people (Exod. 25:31–40)

menstruation: purification (2 Sam. 11:4); may be literal message of timing (Gen. 31:35)

mental hospital: internal conflict with overwhelming emotional confusion (Isa. 26:3)

menu: one's options or choices in life (Ps. 25:12; Est. 2:9 NLT)

meteor: the end of days or last day disasters (Matt. 24:29; Rev. 8:10)

microphone/megaphone: can symbolize having a voice to influence many (Ps. 130:2)

microscope: intense self-examination (Lam. 3:40)

midnight: a time to pray for others while they sleep, and to thank God (Ps. 119:62)

mildew/mold: a curse to be broken off (Amos 4:9)

military uniforms: a call to prepare for battle (Eph. 6:11; 2 Tim. 2:3–4)

milk: God's Word (1 Pet. 2:2)

millstone: being weighed down with either sin or grief (Heb. 12:1 NLT)

minefield: concealed dangers and obstacles (Job 28:10–13)

mining: digging for God's wisdom and truths (*Eccles. 7:25*)

mire: sinking in trials and appearing trapped by one's enemy (Ps. 69:2)

mirror: self-appraisal or evaluation (James 1:23)

miscarriage/abortion: a canceled or terminated goal or project (*Isa. 66:9*)

missiles: spiritual warfare bombardment (Eph. 6:16)

missionary: literal or symbolic of ministry travels or financial investment (Acts 15:36)

mockingbird: mockery or scorn from relationships (*Luke 22:63*)

moldy bread: a call to find fresh teaching (Josh. 9:12; *John 6:51*)

money: financial blessing and prosperity; see riches

monkey: oppressive spirit taking one captive—"monkey on his back" (*Hab. 1:9* NASB)

monk/nun: hiding from others (*Matt. 5:15–16*); pray without ceasing (1 *Thess. 5:17*)

monster: a demonic oppressor using intimidation to defeat (Isa. 51:9 NIV; 2 *Tim. 1:7*)

moon: night, but also the end of a journey or a season (Ps. 104:19)

mop: needing to clean one's path and walk with God (Eph. 4:1 NASB)

mortgage: large debt (*Rom. 13:8* NIV)

moth: a devourer of one's possessions (Ps. 39:11)

motorcycle: small and efficient, fast-moving ministry (*Acts 17:28a*)

mountain: troubles to be overcome and cast away with faith and speech (Mark 11:23)

mourning/mourners: spirits of grief; death (Matt. 5:4)

mouse: unclean choices (Lev. 11:29)

mouth: a symbol of your words and speech, and thus, your world; see tongue

movie: used in dreams to show something literal; note titles, actors' names (*Col. 1:26*)

moving van/truck: transitioning in ministry or relocating literally in life (*Acts 17:28a*)

mud/dirt: can symbolize being stained by sin (Isa. 57:20; Ps. 1:18)

muddy water: "muddying the water"— to make things less clear or pure (Prov. 25:26)

mule: an unbridled, stubborn person (Ps. 32:9–10)

murder/murderer: an evil spirit seeking to destroy one's life (*John 10:10*)

muscles: spiritual strength (Matt. 12:29)

music notes: the flow of life; living in harmony with others (Rom. 12:16 NIV)

musical instruments: unity with diversity (Ps. 98:6; 150; Eph. 5:19)

mustard or mustard seed: represent small faith (Matt. 13:31–32)

mute: presence of a deaf and dumb spirit; cannot speak for self (Matt. 9:33; Mark 9:17–29)

muzzle: being forbidden to speak; guarding one's mouth from sin (Ps. 39:1)

nagging: a harassing spirit; torment (Judg. 16:16 NIV)

nail polish: preparing the hands for battle or a big job ahead; see fingers (*Ps. 144:1*)

naked: pure (Gen. 2:25; Job 1:21); shame (Isa. 47:3); vulnerable, uncovered (Gen. 9:21)

names: pray for those seen in dreams; research name meaning for a message to yourself

nearsighted: shortsighted; need to think futuristically, "see down the road" (2 Pet. 1:9)

neck: that which supports the head or the one in authority (Prov. 6:21)

necklace: a yoke around the neck; a bondage (Ps. 73:6 NIV; Isa. 10:27)

needle (eye of): impossible odds when praying for the wealthy to be saved (Matt. 19:24)

neighbor: often a literal call to pray for them; symbolically means God's family (Matt. 19:19)

nest: one's home (Prov. 27:8; Job 29:18 NASB)

nets: tools for winning the lost (Luke 5:2–4); a trap laid by spiritual enemies (Ps. 141:10)

new year: a new beginning; a fresh start (2 Cor. 5:17; Exod. 40:2)

newspaper: spreading the word about something to many (Isa. 33:13 KJV)

nightclub: foolish or sinful conduct (Eccles. 7:4 NASB); see bar

noon: noonday brightness represents God's blessings and healing (Job 11:17; Isa. 58:10)

noose: impending judgment; death by hanging (Job 18:10; Est. 7:10)

nose: may represent scent, or abstractly, discernment; if bloody, strife (Prov. 30:33)

nudity: see naked

numbness: desensitized by life (Ps. 38:8 NASB); see paralyzed

nurse: an aid who brings you health in Christ (Num. 11:12 NIV); see doctor

nursing/breastfeed: a call to breastfeed (Isa. 66:11; 1 Thess. 2:7); feed a desire (Ps. 37:4)

nuts and bolts: taking care of the details (Luke 10:41 NLT; 1 Chron. 28:19 NIV)

oak: great strength (Amos 2:9; Ps. 29:9 NIV)

oar: without one in a boat, it means no progress (Acts 17:28; Ezek. 27:29; Hab. 3:10 NLT)

oasis: a place of refreshment in a desert season of life; see desert (Exod. 15:23)

obesity: struggling with great, well-fed fleshly desires (Gal. 5:16)

ocean: God's deep truths/judgments (Ps. 36:6 NLT); if tossed at sea, immature (Eph. 4:14)

occult: may mean literal curses or spells being cast at you; pray protection (Prov. 26:2)

office: may symbolize co-workers or administrative details of a project (2 Tim. 2:15 NIV)

oil: invites anointing (Exod. 29:7); Holy Spirit (1 Sam. 16:13); used for healing (James 5:14)

oil (crude): abundant finances and gushing provision (Phil. 4:19)

ointment: soothing, healing balm (Jer. 8:22)

old friends: see ex

old homes: usually a time line drawing attention to a healing season (1 Chron. 17:27 NIV)

old pets: usually a time line pointing to emotions you had while with a pet (Prov. 12:10)

olive/olive oil: the oil of peace is coming; used in peace offerings (Lev. 7:12 NLT)

olive branch: global symbol of peace; grafted-in Gentile Christians (Rom. 11:17)

Olympics: competition; needing endurance and stamina (1 Cor. 9:24; 1 Tim. 6:12 NET)

onions: crying or tears (Rev. 21:4)

orchestra/symphony: see musical instruments

orgy: dark sexual deviancy (1 Cor. 6:9; 1 Pet. 4:3 NIV; Gal. 5:21 NIV)

orphan: emotionally or spiritually abandoned (Ps. 10:14 NASB; James 1:27)

ostrich: poor common sense and heartlessness (Lam. 4:3)

Ouija Board: playing around with demonic entities (Lev. 19:31)

oven: incubating new ideas or goals that require time (Ps. 27:14)

owl: demonic spirits disguised as spirit guides; abomination (Lev. 11:13–18)

ox: strength; increase (Prov. 14:4)

oyster: a producer and home to hidden, sacred treasure (Matt. 7:6)

paddling: discipline; see spanking

pain: literal or emotional pain to your body or to the Body of Jesus (Rev. 21:4)

paint: covering something up or a fresh coat that covers old stains (Jer. 22:14 NASB)

painting: see paint

pale horse: death (Rev. 6:8)

pallbearer: friend carrying you through seasons of death and hardship (Eccles. 12:5 NASB)

palm: when opened to you, an invitation and promise for care (Isa. 49:16)

palm reading: sorcery and divination (Lev. 20:6)

palm tree: flourishing; righteousness (Ps. 92:12)

panther: approaching evil (Prov. 26:13; Prov. 29:25)

pants: if without, symbolizes vulnerability; see naked

paparazzi: coming fame; may reveal idolatry, fame, respect of persons (Acts 10:34 KJV)

parachute: safety and rescue during crisis (Ps. 144:7 NIV)

parade: victory and success (Est. 6:9; 2 Cor. 2:14 NIV)

paralyzed: the enemy is trying to cripple you (John 5:8)

paramedic: an aid during a time of medical emergency; healing being near (Ps. 147:3)

parent: authority (Deut. 5:16); earthly father may = heavenly Father (Heb. 12:10–11)

park: a place to relax and enjoy creation (Eccles. 2:5; Gen. 24:63 NET)

parrot: a gossip, anyone who repeats what he or she hears (Prov. 17:9 NIV)

party: a celebration (Luke 15:24); if a wild or drunken party, ungodly (Gal. 5:21 NLT)

passenger (in a moving vehicle): partners in ministry or in a move of God; see cars

passport: international travel (Exod. 13:21 NASB)

pastries: may represent gossip (Prov. 18:8 NASB)

pasture: peaceful life (Ps. 95:7; Ps. 23)

path: one's journey through life; if level, represents walking in God's ways (Ps. 27:11)

pawnshop: the path of poverty (Ps. 109:11 NASB)

paycheck: the wages of one's lifestyle (Rom. 6:23); financial reward (Matt. 10:10b)

peace: proof of a God-centered thought life (Isa. 26:3)

peacock: pride or showiness (1 Kings 10:22 NASB)

pearl: the Gospel of Christ (Matt. 7:6); something valuable (Matt. 13:45)

pen/pencil: the writing gift and the ability to communicate (Ps. 45:1)

penny: perhaps a symbol of poverty (Mark 12:42)

pentagram: satanic worship or occult practices (Mic. 5:12)

perfume: gladness of heart (Prov. 27:9); aroma of Christ (2 Cor. 2:14–15; Eph. 5:2 NASB)

peroxide: healing of wounds, emotional, spiritual or physical (Job 5:18)

pestilence: God's judgment on wickedness (Ps. 91:6 NIV; Hab. 3:5 NIV)

Pharaoh: pride and hard-heartedness in authority (Exod. 8:19)

photographer: one who makes memories for others (1 Thess. 3:6)

pig: unclean living (2 Pet. 2:22; Matt. 7:6)

pig snout: if with a gold ring, represents a woman without discretion (Prov. 11:22)

pigeon: was an offering for sin in the Old Testament; a call to repentance (Lev. 1:14)

piggy bank: financial savings, bits at a time; faithful stewardship (Luke 12:42 NASB)

pimple/acne: a situation that needs to come to a head to find healing (Prov. 4:22)

pinions: see feathers

pioneers: leadership; trailblazers; the opposite of a settler (Num. 33:1)

pirate: a thieving spirit being sent to steal your finances (John 10:10)

pit: see hole

pit bull: fierceness and savagery in conversation (Prov. 26:17 NET)

plague: God's judgment upon wickedness (Ps. 106:29)

plane: see airplane

planting: sowing and reaping (Ps. 107:37–38; Mark 4); see farm

plants/vines: family and children (Ps. 128:3)

plate/platter: schedule—"a lot on my plate," especially servanthood (Luke 10:40)

platoon: a united group of praying believers in spiritual warfare (Rev. 19:19)

playground: a place for child's play, a call to maturity (1 Cor. 13:11)

plow: faithful, hard Christian work (1 Cor. 9:10)

plumb line: lining up with the truth (Amos 7:8)

plumbing (pipes): flow in production; if crooked, obstructions (Isa. 40:4; Luke 3:5 NLT)

poison: lying, wicked words (Ps. 140:3)

police/cop: spiritual authority (1 Pet. 2:13)

polishing: paying attention to excellence in one's work (Ezek. 21:11; Phil. 4:8)

pollution: a nation's wickedness (Ps. 106:38 NLT)

polygraph machine: see lie detector test

pomegranates: God's sweetness (Song 4:3; Exod. 28:34)

pond: a small place where people gather together, i.e., work, club, school (Joel 2:16)

porcupine: a prickly, worrisome situation (Isa. 14:23 ASV; Matt. 6:34)

pork: see pig

porn: spirit of perversion confronting you or that you have confronted in someone else (Ps. 101:3)

pot hole: being stuck or hitting a rocky path in your journey (Prov. 10:9)

potter's wheel/pottery: being molded or fashioned by God (Jer. 18:6)

prayer: while asleep or while waking, proves our spirit never sleeps (1 Thess. 5:17)

preacher/clergy: Jesus, Great Pastor/Shepherd (Heb. 13:20); literal pastor

pregnancy: conceiving an idea, waiting through its gestation and delivery (Isa. 66:9)

pressure cooker: the pressure cooker of life and stress (Job 33:7 NASB)

prince: could be a demonic principality (Dan. 10:13 NLT); or Satan (Eph. 2:2 NASB)

principal: a demonic principality or territorial spirit over a region or group; see prince

prison/dungeon: bondages/restrictions (Isa. 42:7)

prophet: God's voice to you; pay attention to precisely what is said! (Deut. 18:19)

prostitute: see harlot

pruning: a season of God removing things from you to promote growth (John 15:2)

psychics (mediums): an evil spirit trying to counsel you in a dream (1 Sam. 28:3–24)

pulpit: a call to preach or teach (Neh. 8:4–6 KJV)

puppet/marionette: a person controlled by a spirit (1 Kings 22:22–23)

purple: the color of royalty with humility (John 19:2)

purse: wealth or finances (Prov. 7:20 NIV)

python: large, crushing, evil spirit–like depression, anxiety (Isa. 59:4–5)

Q-tip: the need to clean out one's ears and listen to wisdom (Isa. 6:10)

quadruplets: double portion—a double double! (2 Kings 2:9; Job 42:10)

quail: God's creative provision in the desert (Ps. 105:40)

quarterback: leadership under pressure; great responsibility (Neh. 9:38)

quarters: represents ¼ of something, e.g., of a year or sum of money (Job 31:6)

queen: may mean "the Queen of Heaven," an evil focus of worship/idolatry (Jer. 7:18)

queen bee: a highly productive person or woman (Prov. 31)

question marks: the questions in your life (Matt. 22:46)

quicksand: emotional sinking that can kill you (Ps. 69:2)

quiver: the womb, with children as arrows (Ps. 127:3–5)

quiz: see test

race: endurance; running the race of life (1 Cor. 9:24)

radio: communication in the airwaves and prayer (1 Cor. 14:5–9; Eph. 2:2)

raft: safety on the troubled seas of life (Ps. 65:7)

rags: poverty or dead works (Isa. 64:6)

rain: if soft, flourishing prosperity (Ps. 72:6); if hard, the storms of life (Matt. 7:25)

rainbow: promises God has made to you (Gen. 9:13)

ram: God's provision when the time of testing has passed (Gen. 22:13)

rape: implies taking something without consent, by force (John 10:10; Gen. 34:27 DARBY)

rapids: an out-of-control set of circumstances (Ps. 46:2–4; Isa. 43:2)

rapture: Christ's Second Coming; a call to salvation or prayer for the lost (1 Thess. 4:17)

rat: see mouse

raw meat: laziness (Prov. 12:27)

razor: lies and destruction (Ps. 52:2)

rearview mirror: focusing on the past, not moving forward (Phil. 3:13; Luke 9:62)

red: modern meanings in context—love, passion, courage, heat; scriptural—blood (1 John 5:6)

Red Cross: salvation and Christ's sacrifice of His life (1 John 5:6)

red eyes: red-eyed entities in dreams/visions are demonic; can symbolize drinking alcohol (Prov. 23:29)

red horse: war (Rev. 6:4)

red tape: a tedious process in achieving a goal (Phil. 4:13)

referee: a mediator or advocate, possibly Christ or the literal person shown (John 15:26)

reflection: seeing self in mirror or water represents seeing into the heart (Prov. 27:19)

relatives: see family

relay race: teamwork (Eph. 4:16)

remote control: control over your life or another's (1 Thess. 4:4 NIV)

reptile: a demonic spirit; see snake

restaurant: where spiritual food is prepared, i.e., a church (1 Cor. 10:3)

resurrection: life where there was death, physically, spiritually and emotionally (John 11:25)

resuscitate: see resurrection

reunion: unity; a gathering for memories (Jer. 3:18)

rhinestones: artificiality, phoniness, insincerity or deceit (2 Cor. 13:8)

rib: woman from and by man's side (Gen. 2:22)

ribbons: praise, worship and celebration (Ps. 20:5)

riches: God's financial security (Phil. 4:19)

right turn: a turn toward wisdom (Eccles. 10:2)

ring: favor, authority and affirmation (Jer. 22:24; Hag. 2:23)

river: refreshing (Ps. 105:41); peace like a river (Isa. 48:18); clean, living water (John 7:38)

roads: direction for one's life path; see journey/trip

roadblock: in one's way on life's journey (Lam. 3:9; Isa. 40:4)

road signs: follow the sign's message: "slow," "stop" "yield" "watch for children," etc. (Jer. 31:21)

robe: modern—relaxation; scriptural—wealth and authority (Isa. 22:21)

rock: Christ, the Rock of Ages (1 Cor. 10:4)

roller coaster: thrilling fun; see amusement park/fair

roof: covering for your household, protection in life's storms (Ps. 5:11)

rooster: a wake-up call (Mark 13:35); denial of Jesus (Matt. 14:72)

roots: the history of a thing or people (Ps. 80:9; Ps. 1:3)

rope: bound in sin (Prov. 5:22 NLT); triple braid symbolizes power in unity (Eccles. 4:12)

roses: healing; Jesus, the Rose of Sharon (Song 2:1)

rotting fruit: a sign of bad choices in life (Luke 6:43)

rowing: hard manual labor under oppression (Mark 6:48)

rubies: of great value (Isa. 54:12)

ruler/tape measure: trying to measure up (1 Sam. 16:7)

running: the race of life and your journey (Phil. 2:16)

rust: old, tarnished or needing practice; earthly riches (Matt. 6:19)

sackcloth: fasting, repentance and prayer (Ps. 35:13)

safe: a place of safety, being safe (Prov. 18:10)

salmon: having to swim upstream, go against the flow (Phil. 4:13)

salt: "salt of the earth" (Matt. 5:13); graceful speech (Col. 4:6); healing water (2 Kings 2:21)

sandals: see shoe

sandstorm: a desert storm symbolizing great trial (Ps. 83:13–15)

Satan: rebuke him using Jesus' name if he is seen or heard in a dream (Acts 26:18; Luke 10:17–19)

saw: God's power to cut or tear down (Isa. 10:34)

scabs: indication that an emotional wound is healing but is not to be picked at (Ps. 147:3)

scars: past emotional wounds, hurts (John 20:27)

scarecrow: fear; putting one's faith in the wrong strength (Jer. 10:5; Ps. 28:8)

school: learning; grade level shows difficulty of tests (Matt. 11:29; Acts 19:9 NASB)

scissors: cutting or pruning (Isa. 18:5)

scorpion: mix of a snake and a spider, both of which represent demons (Luke 10:19)

scroll: a written command and a commission from God (Ezek. 3:1)

séance: could mean someone with occult ties is trying to influence your life (*Isa. 54:17*)

seat belt: protection, especially in ministry (*Ps. 5:11*); see car

secretary: a helper; assistants in dreams may be angels (*Dan. 10:13* NLT; Rom. 16:22)

security guard: possibly an angel; a protector in authority (*1 Chron. 9:27*)

seed: an investment to be tended (Mark 4:31–32)

sewer: a dirty environment (*James 1:21*)

sex: may reveal a spirit of lust; if dreaming of a past relationship, break soul ties in prayer (*1 John 3:3*)

shade: a reprieve from hard work; protection (Ps. 121:5)

shadow: covered by God (Ps. 91; 36:7); if dark, may be demonic/death (Ps. 44:19; 23:4)

shaking hands: two people shaking hands symbolizes agreement (Job 17:3 KJV)

shampoo/conditioner: a need for cleansing and conditioning/softening (*Ps. 51:2*)

shark: a hidden demonic predator; pray prayers of protection if seen in dream (*Isa. 27:1*)

sheep: Christians; children of the Great Shepherd (John 10:15, 27)

sheepdog: evangelistic; rounding up the sheep (*John 10:16*)

shelter: a place of protection from the elements of life (Ps. 61:4)

shepherd: Jesus, or a literal pastor to pray for (Ps. 23:1)

sheriff: an enforcer of the law; possibly a pastor or teacher (*Gal. 3:21; Matt. 5:17*)

shield: one's faith that extinguishes the enemy's arrows (Eph. 6:16)

ships: a group or organization with many on board (Acts 27:37)

shipwreck: the destruction or sinking of a ship (group) or one's own faith (*1 Tim. 1:19*)

shirt: one's personal covering; if giving shirt off your back, sacrifice (Matt. 5:40)

shoe: the gospel of peace, walking in peace (Eph. 6:11)

shopping: choices and selections to be made (Deut. 30:19)

shopping cart: what is in the cart is what to focus on; food = spiritual food, etc. (John 6:27)

shoulders: shouldering a burden (Gen. 49:15); also government (Isa. 9:6)

showers: see rain

sickle: for harvesting, symbolically for souls or evangelism (Joel 3:13; Mark 4:29)

silver: knowledge; insight, understanding (Prov. 2:3–4); testing, refining (Mal. 3:3)

sinking: disaster or emotional despair (Jer. 51:64; Ps. 69:15)

sinking ship: failure of a larger work (1 Tim. 1:19); see shipwreck

sirens: a warning that battle is coming; a call to pray and trust for victory (*Num. 10:9*)

sister: if not literal, a dear friend (Matt. 12:50)

skipping: being carefree (Job 21:11)

skull/crossbones: death, opposing Christ's message (*Luke 23:33; Prov. 8:36*)

skydiving: freedom with risks (*Gal. 5:13*)

sled: expedient prayers during wartime (*Job 38:22–23*); see snow

sleep/fatigue: a need for spiritual awakening (Prov. 6:9; Eph. 5:14)

sleeping bag: travel or emotional/spiritual homelessness (*Jer. 10:17* NASB)

smoking: addictive behavior (*Gal. 5:1*)

snake: Satan (Genesis 3:14a); alcohol/wine (Proverbs 23:32); evildoers (Ps. 140:3)

snow: a call to war/pray seen in a dream or awake; snow heralds war (Job 38:22–23)

soap: spiritual cleansing (Isa. 1:25 NASB)

soldiers: part of God's army (2 Tim. 2:3; 1 Cor. 9:7); used by Satan (Mark 6:27 NLT)

spanking: discipline or punishment (Prov. 13:24)

sparrow: the Father's watchful care (Matt. 10:29)

spear: may represent a weapon/strategy God is going to give you for a problem (Ps. 35:3)

spider: sin; deception; false doctrine; temptation (Job 8:14; Isa. 59:5)

spit: utter contempt (Job 17:6)

spoon: ability to feed self or others spiritually (Matt. 25:37); if baby spoon, see babies

spring: new beginnings and new life (Zech. 10:1)

staff: pastoral ministry, the tools of a shepherd (Ps. 23:4)

stairs/steps: stages that take you to a higher place in life or in prayer (Job 14:16)

stars: children (Neh. 9:23; Gen. 37:9–10)

Statue of Liberty: the USA; the Holy Spirit's liberty (2 Cor. 3:17 NASB)

steak: spiritual food for the mature (Heb. 5:12)

steering wheel: direction for the road of life (Ps. 32:8)

stillborn: a long-awaited dream symbolically carried to term, and then it dies (Isa. 66:9)

sting: see bees

stop sign: to literally stop, as in behavior, activity, etc.; see road signs

stork: a pregnancy; new baby; new experiences (Jer. 8:7; John 3:3)

storms: see rain

stove: projects in one's life, i.e., "it's on the back burner"; see oven

straitjacket: mental imprisonment (Isa. 26:3; 2 Cor. 3:11)

strangers: spirits, bad or good—watch their defining behaviors (Heb. 5:14)

strangulation: trying to choke out one's faith (Ps. 140:4)

straw: lesser works that will be burned up one day (1 Cor. 3:12–13)

street names: study all street name meanings and relevance to you; see names

strongman: a strong demonic spirit requiring binding in prayer (Mark 3:27)

student: see school

submarine: submission to authority; coming under (Rom. 13:1 NLT)

sugar: sweetness of life; too much means imbalanced spiritual diet (Rom. 14:17)

suicide: ruining one's own reputation by foolishness (Eccles. 7:17)

suitcase/bag: baggage from one's past (Matt. 11:28); prepared to move on (Luke 10:4)

summer: a season of making plans and working hard (Prov. 6:8 NASB)

sun: the Son, Jesus (Mal. 4:2)

sunburn: great time spent with the Son, Jesus (Matt. 17:2)

sunrise: the beginning of a thing, a life or a season (Eccles. 1:5)

sunset: the end of a thing, a life or a season (Ps. 113:3)

superheroes: supernatural abilities for spiritual warfare (2 Cor. 10:4–5)

surfboard: riding a coming wave of success (Ps. 118:25; 51:15)

surgery: the Great Physician repairing emotions with His skilled hand (Luke 5:31)

surgical instruments: show which surgery—e.g., "open heart surgery"; see surgery

surrounded: being slandered by others (Ps. 109:3)

swearing/cussing: an unclean spirit (Eph. 5:4)

sweeping: see broom

swimming: leisure; possibly trying to stay afloat; see drowning

sword: harsh words (Ps. 57:4); the sword of the Spirit, God's Word (Eph. 6:17)

tablet: the heart, ready to be inscribed upon (Prov. 7:3)

tailor: perhaps an angel or the Holy Spirit preparing you for a life event (*Luke 22:9*)

tambourine: praise and celebration (Ps. 81:2; Jer. 31:4)

tape measure: see measuring stick/tape

target: aiming for a goal, good or bad (Lam. 3:12)

tarot cards: demonic; fortune telling (*Acts 16:16*)

teacher: a pastor, teacher or Jesus Himself (Luke 6:40)

tears: see crying

teeth: needed for a mature spiritual diet (Heb. 5:14)

teeth falling out: losing one's ability to consume a healthy spiritual diet (Heb. 5:12)

telephone: communication—with others, but mainly with God (*Jer. 33:3*)

telescopes: the prophetic gift and looking into the future (*1 Cor. 13:2*)

television: media arts; may mean distraction (*Prov. 6:6–11; Ps. 101:3*)

tennis: Who begins the game? This is the one who is "serving" (*Matt. 23:11*)

tent: our temporary, earthly body (2 Cor. 5:1–6); see camp/ campgrounds

termites: small, spiritual attacks eating away at your faith's foundation (Ps. 11:3)

test: being tested by life's trials (2 Cor. 8:22 NASB); a lesson to learn (Ps. 119:71)

text messages: "receiving words," i.e., prophetic words (Eccles. 12:10 NIV; 1 Cor. 2:13)

theatre: living on "the stage of life" with others watching (*Matt. 5:16*)

thermometer/fever: spiritual infection in the Church Body, or in yours; see fever

thief: Satan, or one of his spirits sent to steal from you (John 10:10a; Prov. 29:24)

thigh: a covenant between two people in biblical times (Gen. 24:9)

thirst: spiritual thirst for Living Water, Jesus (Matt. 5:6; John 4:14)

thorns: trials (2 Cor. 12); life's cares choking our faith (Mark 4:18–19)

throne: the seat of God's authority (Isa. 66:1; Rev. 7:10)

thunder: like God's voice (Job 40:9; 1 Sam. 2:10); God's anger (Job 36:33 NLT)

tick: life itself is in the blood (*Lev. 17:11a*), so a tick denotes something draining it

ticket: a coming journey or entrance into a new place in life (Exod. 33:10)

tidal wave: overwhelming conflict (2 Sam. 22:5); see hurricane, floods

tiger: may represent a sudden, surprise attack (*Prov. 29:25*)

tightrope: having to watch one's steps to avoid danger (Ps. 119:133)

tin: the worthless dross and debris of one's life (Isa. 1:25 KJV)

tires: "where the rubber meets the road"; if flat, shows inconvenience (*Acts 17:28a*) toilet: the most vulnerable and suscepti-ble of all positions we can be in when it is in use (Job 36:7)

tongue: decides your future; holds the power of life and death (Prov. 18:21; James 3:4–5)

toothpaste: the need to clean one's mouth, speech, attitude (*Matt. 15:11*)

tornado: a warning of coming danger or attack and a call to pray (Ps. 55:8 NASB)

towel: service and humility (John 13:4)

track: a race you are in (1 Cor. 9:25); see running

tractor: brings greater and faster return for your spiritual sowing; see cars and farm

traffic light: life direction—red: stop / yellow: caution / green: go; see road signs

train: speed and connection

trap: could indicate a coming, hidden snare in life (Prov. 29:25)

treasure chest: hidden prizes, awards and spiritual jewels (*Matt. 13:52* ISV)

trees: nations (Ezek. 31:14); people (Dan. 4:20–22; Matt. 13:31–32; Ps. 52:8)

triplets: a coming triple blessing or a triple alliance of friends (*Eccles. 4:12*)

troops: see army, soldiers (Mic. 5:1)

trophy: may represent a coming award or convey God's recognition (*Rom. 2:6; 2 Tim. 4:8*)

truck: ministry or a corporate move of God, varying by size of truck; see car

trumpet: celebration or praise (Ps. 98:6); a call to war (Amos 3:6)

tug-of-war: a competition; pray for peace with person shown (*Eph. 6:12* NIV)

tulips: speech and your "two lips"; see mouth, tongue

tumor: may be a literal call to prayer; removal of a bad personal growth (*Eph. 4:16*)

turban: righteousness (Job 29:14)

turtle: slow, withdrawn; spirit of stu-por; cautious; protected; safe; steady (*James 1:19*)

twins: the double-portion anointing on your life (2 Kings 2:9; Job 42:10)

two cents: a worthless opinion; small acts of obedience seen by God (Mark 12:42; Luke 12:6)

umbilical cord: a connection to life and spiritual nourishment (*Col. 2:19*)

umbrella: personal covering or protec-tion in life's storms (*Ps. 27:5*)

umpire: advocate, moderator and ref-eree, maybe a leader or good friend (Job 16:19 NIV)

uniform: conformity or unity (2 Sam. 20:8 ISV)

universe: God's eternal creativity (Heb. 11:3; Eph. 4:10)

upstairs: the 2nd heaven where we do spiritual warfare prayer; see building levels

vacation: refreshment and rest (*Heb. 4:10*)

vacuum: while in use, shows the need to remove dirt from object or person shown (*Lev. 22:5*)

vampires: someone who sucks the life out of you (*Lev. 17:11a*); see tick

vault: see safe

vegetables: a healthy spiritual diet; see food

veil: something that is being hidden (Ps. 139:15)

vein: contains the blood, or the life (Lev. 17:11a); see vampire

vertigo: being out of balance or off-balance (2 Cor. 8:13 GW)

village: a community or group of people close to you (Eph. 2:19; Luke 9:56)

vine: Jesus is the vine, we are the branches, and in Him we bear fruit (John 15:5)

vineyard: the world is God's—the Vinedresser's—vineyard (Isa. 5:1; Matt. 21:28)

vitamins: a supplement to your spiritual diet, i.e., teaching, etc. (*3 John 2*)

voices: God's voice always brings peace; Satan's will bring fear or confusion (John 10:27)

vomit: ridding yourself of upsetting things; also, compared to foolishness (2 Pet. 2:22)

voodoo doll: a symbol of witchcraft and curses being spoken over you (pray Prov. 26:2)

vultures: unclean, impure and ravaged (Prov. 30:17)

wading: experimenting; testing the waters (Ezek. 47:4)

wagons: used by pioneers in trailblazing; a pioneering spirit (Ps. 65:11 ESV)

waiter: someone who serves spiritual food; may be a deacon (Acts 6:2–6)

waking: a need for spiritual awakening (Rom. 13:11)

wallet: wealth or finances (Prov. 7:20 NLT)

war: see battle

warehouse: a symbolic place where God stores up and then distributes to us (Job 38:22–23)

warlock: see psychics, witch

washing: if clothes, represents holiness or cleansing from sin (Ps. 51:7); see bathing

washing machine: where deep cleansing occurs in one's life (*Isa. 1:18*)

wasps: see bees

watch: God's timing for you individually (*2 Pet. 3:9*)

watchdog: symbolizes God's guardianship for you or the person in the dream (*Exod. 28:14*)

water: precedes birth, brings cleansing, implies baptism (Ezek. 16:4; John 3:5; Num. 19:21)

waterfall: overwhelming refreshment after a long climb (Ps. 42:7; Rev. 14:2)

waves: grief (2 Sam. 22:5); or billows of blessings and love (Ps. 42:7–8 NLT)

weaving: the many lessons/experiences woven into the tapestry of your life (Ps. 139:15 NIV)

wedding/wedding cake: undying, sweet love (*Song 7:12*; *Ps. 100:5 DARBY*)

weeds: sins and hindrances to your spiritual sowing and reaping; see gardening

well: generational blessing and legacy (Gen. 26:17–35; John 4:12)

whale: chastisement that turns out to be our salvation (Jonah 1:7)

wheat: the godly; Christians (Matt. 13:24–30)

wheelchair: a handicapped position in a situation (*Acts 3:6*)

wheels: see tires

whirlwind: sudden calamity (Prov. 1:27); God's mode of operation (Job 38:1; 2 Kings 1:11)

whispering: secrecy (Ezek. 33:30 NLT; Isa. 45:19 NLT); gossip (Lam. 3:62 NIV)

white: Christ's glory (Mark 9:3 NIV; Rev. 20:11); purity (Rev. 3:4; 19:8)

white horse: the return of Christ (Rev. 6:2)

wilderness: see desert

wig: a cover-up; an untruth (*John 16:13*)

wind: change; God's messenger of change, "the winds of change" (Ps. 104:4 NIV; Eph. 4:14)

window: may be God revealing a "window of opportunity" (Gen. 8:6; 2 Cor. 11:33)

wine: likened to a snakebite or viper's poison (Prov. 23:32–33)

wings: the protection of angels (Ps. 91)

winter: dormancy or the last part of someone's life (Ps. 74:17; Song 2:11)

witch: witchcraft; an evil spirit attempting to frighten/curse you (1 Chron. 10:13; Prov. 26:2)

withering: no longer thriving; seeing one's circumstances diminish (Ezek. 17:10; Prov. 11:10)

wizard: see psychics

wolves: spirits (through people) that come to attack God's flock (Acts 20:29; Matt. 10:16)

woods: see trees

workshop: God's process of building your life (*Heb. 11:10*)

wound: an area of emotional hurt (Jer. 8:22)

wreath: may be a holiday timeline clue; on the head it symbolizes wisdom (Prov. 4:7–9)

wrestling: wrestling with a stranger means struggling against an evil spirit (Eph. 6:12)

writing: pay attention to message, whether on a wall or on paper! (Dan. 5:5)

Xerox machine: repetition or endless cycles of a situation (*Job 33:29*)

X-ray: having intense perception and spiritual discernment (*Ps. 119:125 NLT*)

yawning: see waking, sleep/fatigue

yeast: religious behaviors that puff you up, e.g., hypocrisy (Matt. 16:6)

yelling: irritating, annoying situations or people (Prov. 27:14)

yellow: cowardliness (Josh. 1:7)

yield: a call to submission; see road signs

yin-yang: someone influenced by incorrect Asian philosophy (*Ps. 119:3*)

yoga: influences of Hinduism, Buddhism, Jainism or Sikhism (Ezek. 11:12)

yoke: a picture of slavery; see necklace

yo-yo: indecisiveness (Ps. 20:8)

zebra: a black or white situation that calls for an unequivocal decision (1 Kings 3:9)

zipper on lips: see buttons on mouth; a sign that you are to keep quiet (*Lam. 3:28*)

zodiac signs/horoscopes: symbols of magic and sorcery to be avoided (Deut. 4:19)

zombies: the lost who are dead in sin; the walking dead (*Eph. 2:1–5*)

Symbolic Numbers in Scripture

Never engage in numerology, which is the study of the occult significance of numbers. But when 12 and 3 and 40 appear in the Bible with such frequency, and when the Bible contains a whole book called Numbers, I think it is okay to ask God what certain numbers mean. Is it a coincidence that God chose 12 men to birth Israel's tribes and Jesus chose 12 men to birth His disciples? (See Genesis 42:13; 49:28; Matthew 10:1–4.) And is it a coincidence that Jonah was in the belly of a whale for 3 days and that Jesus was in the grave for 3 days, or does one foreshadow the other symbolically? Jesus answers that Himself in

Matthew 12:40: "For as Jonah was three days and three nights in the belly of the great fish, so will the Son of Man be three days and three nights in the heart of the earth."

Note: Remember that numbers in your dreams or visions are sometimes literal dates, amounts of money and the like, and they may be interpreted as straightforward messages unique to you and not found in Scripture.

1 unity (John 17:22–23; Phil. 2:1–2; Ps. 133:1)

2 agreement (Matt. 18:19); double portion (Isa. 61:7)

3 resurrection (Luke 24:6–7)

4 sun, moon and stars created on the fourth day to mark seasons (Gen. 1:19–20)

5 five-fold ministry (Eph. 4:11); multiplication miracles (John 6:9–10); grace (Luke 7:41–42)

6 number of the Beast (Rev. 13:18); in 6 days do your work (Exod. 20:9); the hour of darkness (Matt. 27:45)

7 finality, perfection, completion and rest (Exod. 20:10); victory through obedience (Josh. 6:4)

8 new beginnings (1 Pet. 3:20); covenant, circumcision (Gen. 21:4); consecration (Exod. 22:30)

9 fruit of the Spirit (Gal. 5:22–23); gifts of the Spirit (1 Cor. 12:8–10), fruit of the womb (full term)

10 law and order (Exod. 20); tithe (Mal. 3:8–10); testing and responsibility (Matt. 25:1–13, 28)

11 incompletion, disorganization—need for apostolic/governmental order (Acts 1:26)

12 government rule/authority—12 tribes and 12 apostles (Luke 6:12–13); illumination (John 11:9)

13 rebellion (Gen. 14:4; 17:25); war (Est. 9:16)

14 celebration, joy and feasting (Est. 9:17–22)

15 restoration (Isa. 38:5)

16 proper foundations (Exod. 36:30)

17 the flooding and washing away of sin (Gen. 7:11); the end and the beginning (Gen. 8:4)

18 bondages (Luke 13:11, 16); oppressions (Judg. 10:8)

19 enemy schemes and destruction (2 Kings 25:8–9; 2 Sam. 2:30)

20 responsibility, readiness for service (Num. 1:3)

21 resistance (Dan. 10:13)

22 urgent need for battle strategy (Judg. 7:3; 20:21)

23 the deafness of God's people (Jer. 25:2–4); the complete goodness of God, our Shepherd (Ps. 23)

24 perfection of worship (Rev. 11:16)

25 visitation in times of distress (Ezek. 40:1–2)
30 maturity and ministry release (Luke 3:23)
40 testing (Matt. 4:2; 1 Kings 19:8); observation (Num. 13:25); wandering (Num. 14:33); cleansing (Gen. 7:12, 17)
50 Jubilee! (Lev. 25:10–11); Pentecost! (Acts 2:1–4); refuge and deliverance (1 Kings 18:4); retirement (Num. 8:25)
60 a call to go higher and meet your full potential without compromise (Mark 4:8)
70 visitation with God (Exod. 24:9); commissioning

(Luke 10:1 NASB); legacy (Gen. 46:27)
80 widespread peace (Judg. 3:30)
90 miraculous fruitfulness— Sarah was 90 at Isaac's birth (Gen. 17:17)
100 fulfillment—Abraham was 100 at Isaac's birth (Gen. 21:5); multiplication (2 Sam. 24:3); 100-fold return (Mark 4:8)
500 the distinction between what is holy and what is common (Exod. 42:20)
666 the number of evil, the mark of the Beast (Rev. 13:18)
1000 the Millennial Reign with Christ (Rev. 20:1–3; 20:7–9; 21:1–3)

The Interpreter Within

The Holy Spirit within you is the best interpreter of your dream or vision. While it is true that God often gives one person the dream or vision and another person the interpretation to keep us needing one another, there are times when no friend, pastor or dream dictionary can help you. And on the occasions when you look up a symbol here and it does not "click" in your heart, my advice is to keep seeking and praying. God has concealed it in this manner to draw you unto Himself, so go to Him. Listen to Proverbs 25:2: "It is the glory of God to conceal a matter, but the glory of kings is to search out a matter."

The teacher of my first class on the prophetic taught me that verse back in 1994. He used to advise us to ask ourselves after a dream, "What am I left with?" He taught us to examine the emotions we awake with and use them as signposts in our journey toward interpretation. So I ask you the same. Do you feel peace? Or are you left with fear? Any dream where you awake in fear is not of God. If you or your child suffers from nightmares, pray each night before bed and declare that your bed is a peaceful place where only the Holy Spirit is allowed to speak to you.

Finally, journal. Prophet James Goll says that journaling is stewarding revelation. In his new book *Exploring Your Dreams and Visions: Receive and Understand Your Dreams, Visions, and Supernatural Experiences—Your Personal Revelatory Journal* (Destiny Image, 2012), he says, "Journaling is a tried and tested spiritual tool that will help you retain revelation and grow in your capacity to discern the voice of the Holy Spirit. I have tried it, and it works!"[2]

I suggest that you start a log—what I call a Lookbook—for all of your seeing experiences, both dreams and visions. Keep it by your bedside and carry it with you to church. But be careful not to let it replace your emphasis on God's Word. Goll warns,

> Some believers express concern that journaling is an attempt to put subjective revelation on the same level of authority as Scripture. This is not the case at all. The Bible *alone* is the infallible Word of God. Journaling is just another tool to help us retain and be more faithful with what He speaks to us.[3]

As for sharing your dreams with others, I will leave you with this hard-and-fast rule that I set for myself years ago and have taught others along the way: "Revelation without interpretation hinders application." Nothing is worse for your reputation than telling someone about your "blue pig on a pink fence" dream and expecting them to be edified when you yourself are clueless as to its meaning. Pray about what you see. Journal what you interpret. If the dream or vision is for someone else, pray for his or her heart to be prepared before you ever come to the person. Remember, timing is everything.

Cryptic Does Not Mean Crazy

You gotta love Ezekiel. The visions he saw were nothing short of hallucinogenic, yet his nation would not have survived without them. And he still feeds us today. Wheels full of eyes? Creatures with four faces? Seriously? I sometimes think he was seeing sky images he had no contextual words for at that time, like airplanes and helicopters.

What if Ezekiel had dismissed all of that important information as a pizza dream? Impossible, since pizza was not even invented for another fifteen hundred years, but I guess this is a prophet we are talking about. Thank goodness he did not dismiss what he saw. He chose to "perceive" it as the voice of his Lord. Ezekiel saw the voice of God.

My brain is pretty concrete, so Ezekiel-type dreams require divine wisdom for me to interpret for someone. I say "for someone" because I rarely have them myself. Oh, I dream in plenty of symbols almost nightly, but not creatures with multiple faces and eyes. And I cannot take credit for wondering if Ezekiel's creatures were airplanes, because years ago someone planted the thought in my head, and many commentaries later, I decided to mention it here so that I could persuade you to do as Ezekiel did—"perceive" when God is speaking to you and do not dismiss something because it seems incoherent. Cryptic does not always mean crazy.

Cryptic does not always mean crazy.

Ezekiel's contemporaries were the prophets Jeremiah and Isaiah, but while Jeremiah's book is all doom and Isaiah's book is all consolation, Ezekiel's provides a beautiful mixture of both, beginning with doom and ending with comfort. I believe "Ezekiel seers" have this same mode of operation. They often see visions that contain stipulations and conditions: "If you will do this, then God can do this for you." So while the front end of the message (or "advice," if this seer is just your friend) may seem a little negative, a positive outcome is on its heels. If you cannot see that, then who is really the one being negative?

If you yourself are an Ezekiel, be very careful of what you put before your eyes in terms of movies and images, especially at night if you are a dreamer. And do not be discouraged when you are misunderstood, isolating yourself from the people whom God wants to grace you to serve. They need you! Some pastor somewhere needs you! It is vital that prophetic people respect the office of pastor in the local church. If there is ever an incident where they feel they cannot respect the man himself, they must maintain a reverence for the office he holds. To disrespect that office will clog your visionary filter, because I am telling you, God loves His shepherds and *will* stop the prophetic flow to you if you do not respect them. Never leave where you are to move to the "wounded seer's island." Before you know it, all pastors are traitors and organized religion is evil.

> I am telling you, God loves His shepherds and will stop the prophetic flow to you if you do not respect them.

Whenever I see one of these loud-mouthed, organized religion haters—and now I am speaking of those who are not Christians at all—I see through the roughness and mourn the calling the person has missed. God gifted such people with the nature of a prophet, but either some religious fool put a bad taste in their mouths when it comes to Christianity, or they got offended at the concept of needing grace and denied it. But I personally love these types. The Church needs more tenacious revolutionaries to lead us, but if, in asking them to unite in a common faith, we ask them to conform to a cookie-cutter personality, we will lose them. We have lost so many. These types usually wind up shipwrecked and alone. Do not be among them, especially if you are a seer.

If Counsel be your cousin
And Prayer, your trusted twin
Then Wisdom is your brother
And Discernment, your close kin

© Laura Harris Smith,
February 2013

PRAYER

Let's pray out loud together:

> *God, interpretations belong to You, as do the dreams and visions You send. In the interpretations are the messages You want me to pray with and live by, so I thank You that as I seek You diligently in prayer, I will find You. In Jesus' name, Amen.*

IMPARTATION

Right now, I release and impart to you the ability to discern God's will with what you see in your dreams and visions. I also call forth godly counsel for you to turn to as you process what is revealed. Finally, I pray that faith is ignited in your heart as you trust God with what you see and let it find its way into your life. (Now open your hands, shut your eyes and receive it.)

8

20/20 Hearing

So far we have spent about 40,000 words discussing your eyes (I guess you could say that is about 20,000 per eye), and now it is time for us to turn our full attention to your ears. We have discussed how God can bypass deaf spiritual ears with vivid dreams and visions, but I would be a bad friend if I did not investigate the reasons why you are not hearing His voice, or are not hearing it as clearly as you would like.

Have you ever wondered what clogs your spiritual ears? You will remember we learned in chapter 1 that God is not a silent, muted God, so even in seasons when His voice is inaudible, that does not mean He is not speaking. He is just on a different frequency, and you have somehow gotten on the wrong channel. Becoming aware of how you got there is the first step toward getting back on the same wavelength with God's voice.

S-T-A-T-I-C

Static is one of those irritating nuisances that impede communication. If you have ever owned a phone, a television or a radio, you know it is true, even in today's digital age. The transmitter may be in perfect working condition, along with the reception device itself, but if there is static or any other kind of interference in between them, the signal will be lost. What is the static that comes in between you and God? In between His voice and your ears? Here is how I define *static*:

Sin

Time

Ambivalence

Trials

Illiteracy (not reading the Word)

Competing voices

Sin

Appropriately, this comes first because not only is it the most vicious hindrance, but it is the hindrance that must be dealt with first if you want to hear God's voice (or see it). You could rid yourself of all the other static, but if you disregard this one, you will see no change. So let me pull out all my big guns and devote some seriously blunt attention to this one, more than to any of the others.

Sin will keep you from hearing God because it keeps you *from* God. It produces disfellowship, and if left unconfessed and unchanged, it mass-produces it. God is holy and cannot dwell where there is sin, so it stands to reason that if you are too far from God, you are out of earshot. But the real dilemma is that humankind is sinful by nature; how do we ever have a fair shot at a relationship with God, period? That is why He sent His Son in human form, so that by having walked in the same shoes as we do in this fallen world, He is immediately compassionate about the temptations we weather.

But God did not just send His Son to be compassionate. He sent Him to take your place at death's door so that when you get there one day, you can cross that threshold into an eternity in God's presence without having your debt of sinful humanity be an issue. But that does not happen if you get to the door and He does not know you. If you did not invite Jesus to be a part of your life, then why would He be a part of your death? He is a gentleman and will never force Himself on you or anyone.

God also did not just send Jesus to be a moral teacher. Consider this example: You are sinking in the ocean and a boat comes by. As you flail around, you wait for someone to save you. You do not need compassion because compassion alone will not rescue you. And you do not need a teacher to tell you how to tread water faster, or even a coach to encourage you to hang in there. What you need is a savior. That is what Jesus is—or what He wants to be for you.

> If you did not invite Jesus to be a part of your life, then why would He be a part of your death?

So first, you need to make sure that you have truly been saved. Can you name the date when you received Christ into your heart? Not when you were baptized, your parents baptized you or you joined a church, but when you prayed for salvation and saw a sweeping life change.

If you cannot name a date, make sure that you did not just begin living a lifestyle without the new life inside of you. We must fully repent of our wrong living and be born again. Only after that birth can God truly be your Father and can you know His voice. "Whoever belongs to God hears what God says. The reason you do not hear is that you do not belong to God" (John 8:47 NIV). Wow. "You do not belong to God"? The New King James Version says, "You are not of God," and *of* is the Greek word *ek*, which also means "by." In essence, this verse is saying you do not hear God because you are not "by" Him. Again, you are out of earshot.

Once you are saved, there is no substitute for holiness in your life. Unless you say yes to walking wholeheartedly in the Holy Spirit, you will never activate holiness. Romans 8:5–6 says,

"For those who live according to the flesh set their minds on the things of the flesh, but those who live according to the Spirit, the things of the Spirit. For to be carnally minded is death, but to be spiritually minded is life and peace." *Holiness* is the Hebrew word *qodesh*, meaning "set-apartness," and in the Greek it is *hagiosyne*, which among other things means "moral purity."

Some people counter, "I can do this-or-that and still be a Christian," and that is true. But come on, we are all smart enough to see from the previous biblical definitions that true holiness means that your conduct is set apart from the way the world lives and that you possess a moral purity the lost do not. Your life should look very different from the lives of your lost friends and family members. So should your refrigerator's contents, the media that enters your home and the language you use. So different that the lost all would be highly uncomfortable around you if it were not for your limitless love and irresistible laugh. A dinner invitation to your home should generate in your unsaved friends an internal confrontation between wanting to elude you and being utterly unable to live without you—a clashing of conviction and curiosity. (And curiosity always wins.)

Moral impurity will not necessarily keep you out of heaven, but it will keep you from hearing God's voice clearly before you get there. True, sin is sin is sin, but later in this chapter we will check out a passage that lists specific sins that are red flags you are not walking in God's Spirit, but in your flesh. Remember, without walking in God's Holy Spirit, you will never be holy, and without being holy, you will never be "by" God, and without being by God, you cannot hear Him.

You can sense the pleading in the apostle Peter's voice in 1 Peter 2:11 (KJV): "I beseech you as strangers and pilgrims, abstain from fleshly lusts, which war against the soul." Same for the apostle Paul when he wrote, "Because we have these promises, dear friends, let us cleanse ourselves from everything that can defile our body or spirit. And let us work toward complete holiness because we fear God" (2 Corinthians 7:1 NLT). Now let me ask you, what would you say are the things you do that defile your body or spirit?

I am confident that the moment you read that question, the Holy Spirit whispered something to you. If not, He will. You need to give that very thing to God and not take it back. Is it really worth it? Do not mess around with sin. Delayed obedience is disobedience. And do not dismiss what you heard as not being God's voice, because Scripture is very clear that the more you dismiss it, the less you will hear His voice. Hebrews 3:13–15 says,

> But exhort one another daily, while it is called "Today," lest any of you be hardened through the deceitfulness of sin. For we have become partakers of Christ if we hold the beginning of our confidence steadfast to the end, while it is said:
>
> > "Today, if you will hear His voice,
> > Do not harden your hearts as in the rebellion. . . ."

A hard heart breeds clogged ears. Do not mess around with sin or with ignoring God's voice today. You might not hear Him tomorrow.

Time

Another reason you might not hear God is due to the distractions of your busy schedule. Work meetings, school deadlines, children's needs, parents' needs and even relationships can eat up our time and leave none for God. And let's not forget all ministers suffering from STLS ("Serving-The-Lord-Syndrome"), who never stop to sit at His feet to listen. We spend so much time ministering to Jesus' Body that we never look up just a few inches to gaze into His face. He is the head. We cannot only love Him from the neck down.

But let's face it—we cannot blame work or ministry. The truth is that we even go on vacation and still struggle to find 30 minutes to sit alone with God. With 1,440 minutes each day, you would think we could give Him a puny 30. Why not 60? But

Jesus knew that friendship with us would be challenging. You could hear it in His voice when He asked Peter, "Could you not watch with me one hour?" (Matthew 26:40–41).

If STLS is truly a disease, then I had a fatal case. A home-schooling mother of six, a grandmother of then four, an ordained minister, Creative Arts Conservatory director, teacher, author, wife, daughter and more. And I was not like Martha, who got mad at doing other people's jobs for them. I *loved* doing other people's jobs. But coupled with the sleep debt I confessed to you in previous chapters, I was headed for trouble, in utter oblivion. But boy, did God get my attention.

Imagine you come home one day to an email from a stranger who lives ten thousand miles away, does not even speak your language, and claims in very broken English that God showed her your face in a vision, gave her your foreign name and sent her to tell you to slow down and spend more time with Him. Hello! Maydi, a Spirit-filled Indonesian college student half my age, had never heard my name before, but while she was in deep worship one day, God showed her in a vision my face, my name and my city on a map. She googled her way to my website, where all three finally aligned.

God supernaturally led Maydi to me because He was jealous for me. He missed me. But despite feeling happy about being so loved and cherished, I breezed right past lovestruck and landed in sobriety, making drastic changes to my priorities. For a year, Maydi continued to prophesy from the other side of the world with visions God gave her of me, one of which directly led to the writing of this book. But even then, with me ready to begin, God still wanted me to Himself for a while before releasing me to another project. Soon after, I preached a sermon at church on this very topic—"Trading Distractions for Prayer"—and as I packed up my MacBook Pro laptop to take it home after church that day, it crashed to the ground. It felt as if someone had literally grabbed it out of my hands. "Macbeth" was a goner. Maydi said it was "an attack by Satan allowed by God." I wondered.

Immediately, I bought another one, and it, too, mysteriously broke. Then in one week, my nice, large screen HD TV broke, my cell phone died and my car went kaput. Finally, I got the hint. I was going to have to practice what I preached that Sunday, confess my distractedness and get focused in prayer. "Listening prayer" I began calling it. I could not go anywhere, do anything, call anybody or write anything. I was entirely hidden. I was entirely undistracted.

With no computer to use to write creatively, edit videos, email people or even do church correspondence, I unplugged from life. For one whole year God kept my finances tied up in other worthwhile family needs, which prevented me from getting the laptop I needed. All I had was time and Zinnia seeds, so I invited my three grandsons over and planted a big Zinnia patch. Avery and Ezra (twins then five) and brother, Trevor (then four), helped me find my way back to center that summer. All I did was plant flowers, cut flowers, make lemonade and pray. I had to borrow one of my children's computers to post pictures on Facebook just so people would know I was not dead.

For a year, Maydi continued to prophesy from the other side of the world with visions God gave her of me, one of which directly led to the writing of this book.

The next year, some dear friends offered to buy me the exact laptop I needed (all $4,500 of it), and it was custom-made and had to be built overseas by Apple. Lo and behold, it arrived at my house one year to the day from when I had preached that sermon on prayer that led to my computer crash. Only God could orchestrate that timing. It was His way of saying He had given me a full year off to test my obedience, help me rest and heal, focus in prayer and prepare to write.

The computer came, the book outline was produced and pitched to an editor and I had a book deal—all before the book was even written, which is another thing only God could orchestrate. Next came the sleep doctor interview that made me realize God had saved my life by forcing me to rest that summer, and it put me on a mission to convince others. Hopefully, you were one of them. Take time to rest and be still to hear God's voice. Deal with your distractions before God does, because trust me, *He will.*

Ambivalence

There is nothing like ambivalence to quench faith fast and interfere with your spiritual hearing (and sight). To be ambivalent means to be uncertain, unsure, doubtful, indecisive, inconclusive, double-minded, undecided, torn, on the fence, hesitating, wavering or vacillating. Let's say you pray to hear God's voice better, but then waver and doubt if you ever really will. Then He speaks, but you do not perceive it because you were on the fence, still torn about whether or not hearing God's voice is even possible. He tries again. You think you hear it this time, but you are uncertain if it was for real, so you tell no one. What a cycle! You asked, He answered, but you do not believe. It is as if you cannot take yes for an answer.

Also, wrong teaching can leave us ambivalent about hearing God's voice. Perhaps we have not heard what the Bible really says about it because our leaders did not want to get our hopes up. Maybe they themselves were ambivalent, so we never heard. But if we do not hear, how can we believe? Consider Romans 10:14, 17:

> How then shall they call on Him in whom they have not believed? And how shall they believe in Him of whom they have not heard? And how shall they hear without a preacher? . . . So then faith comes by hearing, and hearing by the word of God.

Submerge yourself in Scriptures that remind you God wants to talk to you. Memorize Jeremiah 33:3 (NIV), "Call to me and I will answer you and tell you great and unsearchable things you do not know." Remind yourself that God's first item of business after creating mankind in Genesis 1:27 was to speak to them in verse 28, establishing His voice with them so there could be relationship. And even before that, in the opening verses of Genesis 1, God used His voice to create the world itself: "Then God said, 'Let there be light'; and there was light" (Genesis 1:3). He did not wave a wand or "think" it all into existence; He used His voice. God has a voice. So do you. They were predestined to recognize each other.

> God has a voice. So do you. They were predestined to recognize each other.

Trials

Sometimes we get so overwhelmed with personal drama that our prayer sessions begin with an immediate grocery list. We have set aside 300 seconds to sit with God, and all of them are meticulously choreographed to ensure He remembers our bills, health and relationships. I tell my children all the time that they will get more out of Mama if they enter the kitchen and greet me each morning with love and gratitude, not a list of today's to-dos. Same with God. "Enter into His gates with thanksgiving, and into His courts with praise. Be thankful to Him, and bless His name" (Psalm 100:4).

Because we treat prayer more like a Dictaphone and less like a telephone, we do all the talking and no listening. Ecclesiastes 5:2 says, "Do not be rash with your mouth, and let not your heart utter anything hastily before God. For God is in heaven, and you on earth; therefore let your words be few." Laura Harris Smith translation: "Shut up and listen."

If only we could learn to wait on the Lord. If only we could sit there and not feel awkward about the silence (and could even hunger for it). Imagine the answers that await us there, anticipating that we will come find them. The cures to modern illnesses. The creative scripts that could be written. The simple solutions to unravel ailing marriages. If only we could be still and listen. Instead, we jump up and run. We rob ourselves of the best part.

I am reminded of mother's milk and of how doctors say the longer an infant nurses, the sweeter the milk becomes. They call it hindmilk, and it is the richest and best. Most of us settle for the foremilk—if we come to feed at all. This brings to mind one of the most tender names of God, El Shaddai, which is taken from the Hebrew word *shad* or *shadayim*, meaning "breast." The name implies that God *is* nourishment. It is not something He does; it is who He is.

Illiteracy

The Church has become illiterate. She does not know how to read the Word of God. Christians everywhere admit that finding time to study Scripture is as hard as finding time to pray—maybe harder. You have undoubtedly experienced it, too. You open your Bible, but nothing is illuminated to you. You read a few verses. Nothing. You flip randomly to another book and do the same. Nothing still. You take a deep breath, figure God sees that you tried, and you close your Bible and leave. You never got to the hindmilk at all, and had very little foremilk, either.

A good Christian devotional is a great way to linger in the Word. I have heard from people who say they will not read the Bible without one, and I have talked to others who treat devotionals like cop-outs. I go through seasons. At the time of this writing, I am using a devotional that has the dates marked out for me, because when I am writing a book and am in Scripture all day digging, I want to be spoon-fed. I want something simple that I can sit and breathe in. A truth. And as I wait there contemplating that one nugget of truth, I always hear God's voice. "Everyone who is of the truth hears My voice" (Jesus to Pilate in John 18:37).

Overall, though, if you feel that nothing you do makes the Word of God come alive, then you have a bigger issue. You may either need to be baptized in His Holy Spirit (something we will discuss further in chapter 10), or you may be battling demonic opposition. I have heard people say they can be lying in bed and reading any other book and not feel tired, but when they open their Bible, it is as though a daze comes over them and they fall asleep. That is a spiritual force at work. The enemy does not want you to read God's Word. In it are the answers to your fears and the keys to your living. Satan would love nothing more than for you never to know what is inside. After all, how can you stand on God's promises if you do not know what they are?

In our quest to see and hear the voice of God, we must read God's Word to authenticate that what we are seeing and hearing is even from Him. If anything we dream or hear contradicts the Bible, we must abandon it immediately. The Holy Spirit would never rebut Scripture. Think about it: Jesus *is* the Living Word. John 1:14 (NIV) says, "The Word became flesh and made his dwelling among us," and for that matter, John 1:1 says, "In the beginning was the Word, and the Word was with God, and the Word was God." So there is no way that the Living Word is ever going to contradict the written Word. That is your litmus test.

Competing Voices

The final form of static actually comes in *many* forms that are the voices of people all around you—your influencers. You have one friend who seems to speak negativity constantly when around you, putting a pessimistic slant on your faith. You have a family member whom you love but dread contact with because his or her counsel crowds your head with doubt. You might be able to shake off these people's words when they speak, but like seeds, their words are planted within your spirit. Then when trouble comes, out of nowhere you suddenly experience an uncontrollable pull toward doubt or fear. You hesitate, and your faith freezes. It is too late to make

> The only thing in between God's mouth and your ears is air, but Satan is the "prince of the power of the air" (Ephesians 2:2).

the connection to where it all originated, but it often originated with unwise counsel from a voice competing with God's.

It is not that you cannot hear God's voice when you are in this place; it is that so many other voices are competing with His that you cannot decipher whose is whose. And what about the enemy's voice? Heaven knows he tries to meddle and make static, too. In fact, the only thing in between God's mouth and your ears is air, but Satan is the "prince of the power of the air" (Ephesians 2:2). His influence there is great. You can learn to recognize the difference between God's voice and his. More on that in a second.

How to Hear God

God speaks in many ways. Through the sermons at your local church. Through dreams and visions. Through a prophet. Through a whisper or audibly. Even through billboards, television and secular music. Think of that special person in your life who tells you he or she loves you. Sometimes it is through a phone call, sometimes a card, sometimes with a special song you share or even through a whisper in your ear. It is the same with God if you will live with your eyes wide open.

When most people ask how to hear God, what they really mean is, "How do I know if a voice I hear in my head is God or is just my own thoughts?" We have already discussed in the section just above that in prayer you have to drown out the external voices of those who wrongly influence your faith. But now we need to identify the internal voices.

You have thoughts all day long out of the blue. Sometimes they seem divine, other times immoral and other times downright harebrained. Are those all just your own voice? No, they are not. In fact, I believe five different opinions run through a person's head on any given day. Five different voices—all bold and determined—and none of them have a problem expressing themselves. Here they are:

1. *Your conscience's voice*

This voice has been in our heads since we were children. It is the moral voice of right and wrong. Everybody has one, but not always a good one. According to Scripture, there are five kinds of consciences, too:

- A pure conscience (1 Timothy 3:9)
- A good conscience (Hebrews 13:18)
- A weak conscience (1 Corinthians 8:7)
- A seared conscience (1 Timothy 4:2)
- An evil, defiled conscience (Titus 1:15)

"Let us draw near with a true heart in full assurance of faith, having our hearts sprinkled from an evil conscience and our bodies washed with pure water" (Hebrews 10:22).

2. *Your reasoning's voice*

Consider Mark 2:6–8:

> And some of the scribes were sitting there and reasoning in their hearts, "Why does this Man speak blasphemies like this? Who can forgive sins but God alone?"
>
> But immediately, when Jesus perceived in His spirit that they reasoned thus within themselves, He said to them, "Why do you reason about these things in your hearts?"

These verses perfectly reveal the reasoning voice. The Temple teachers and Pharisees were so busy using their minds to rationalize who Jesus was that their hearts entirely missed their Messiah. Someone who relies too heavily on the voice of reason will immediately begin weighing facts and data without first stopping everything (and I do mean everything) and asking God for His view.

This reasoning voice causes you to painstakingly plan and gather facts and then make decisions, a process that is not without merit, but only after you first have earnestly sought God. If this is the strongest voice in your head, when you are met with an opportunity that involves faith or risk, you will often say, "Well, but we must exercise wisdom," when in truth, the wisdom you come up with is not from God at all. If you become offended when challenged that this voice ought not be the primary voice in your decision-making processes, just remember that the Pharisees made it their primary concern and missed marvelous opportunities for blessing.

3. Your flesh's voice

This voice is often the most opinionated of the bunch. In fact, many people blame things on the devil that are entirely the fault of their undisciplined, sinful flesh. Many Christians abuse grace, stating that their sins are no worse than someone else's, when in fact the Bible seems to give us some clear-cut transgressions that God singles out, perhaps because He knows they affect others and not just ourselves. "The Seven Deadly Sins" is a list King Solomon wrote in Proverbs to convey seven things that God "detests": (1) a proud look, (2) a lying tongue, (3) hands that shed innocent blood, (4) a heart that devises wicked plots, (5) feet that are swift to run into mischief, (6) a deceitful witness that uttereth lies, (7) him that soweth discord among brethren. (See Proverbs 6:16–19.)

But since we are talking about the flesh's voice, we must visit Galatians 5:16–21, which lists seventeen sins that are red flags to you. These indicate that you are acting upon your flesh's counsel. Verse 21 ends with "those who practice such things will not inherit the kingdom of God." Here they are: (1) adultery—unlawful sexual relations, (2) fornication—pornography, prostitution, incest, (3) uncleanness—lust, sexual perversions, homosexuality, lesbianism, pedophilia, (4) lewdness—overeater, lazy, undisciplined, (5) idolatry—worship anything (possessions, money) or even people (sports stars, celebrities, preachers, one's own children . . .), (6) sorcery—horoscopes, witchcraft, spells, luck charms, zodiac signs, (7) hatred—bitterness, grudges, anger, (8) contentions—starting debates, stirring up division, quarreling, (9) jealousies—a rivalry, covetousness, (10) outburst of wrath—creating public or private turmoil, domestic abuse, (11) selfish ambition—vengeances, overly competitive spirit, (12) dissensions—creating strife in personal and corporate relationships, (13) heresies—atheism, agnosticism, rebellious nonconformity, (14) envy—discontentment that stops at nothing, (15) murder—to kill, destroy, (16) drunkenness—alcoholic, public or private intoxication, drug addictions, (17) revelings—wild parties, obscene media, bars or clubs, house parties and the like.

4. Satan's voice

Sure, Satan's voice can cause you to fulfill all seventeen sins of the flesh we just read about, but here I want to describe that voice that is less overtly evil and tries to trick you into thinking it is God. It usually mixes in a little bit of accuracy, tempting you to follow it. For instance, it will tell you, "Your past is sinful, so you shouldn't even bother pursuing a relationship with this godly person." Perhaps you did have a history of bad choices, but to keep you from pursuing better relationships, the enemy will mix that truth in with his bad counsel to get you to believe it is God's voice. Do not be fooled.

Do you know the voice of your spouse or parents or best friend? Do you think you could be tricked by an imposter into thinking it is one of them on the phone? No, because you intimately know them, their inflections and their dispositions. I know God's personality when He speaks to me. It is never condemning, although occasionally very assertive. But He knows I respond well to it and that my crowded mind often necessitates it. God leads His people. Satan pushes his. God is a Shepherd leading trusting sheep, while Satan spends his time rounding up stubborn goats. Which are you?

You can always—without fail—know it is Satan's voice when the words you hear make you rationalize sin (Isaiah 5:20), feel unforgiving (Matthew 6:15), feel fearful (Mark 4:40), feel bitter (Colossians 3:19), seek revenge (Ezekiel 25:15), feel rage and anger (Ephesians 4:31), doubt Scripture (Hebrews 3:12), feel discouraged (Numbers 32:6–10), feel hopeless (Job 7:1–15), experience confusion (Acts 19:32), want to lie (1 John 2:4), be ashamed of the Gospel (Mark 8:38), want to curse God (Job 2:9), want to disobey God's Word (Joshua 5:6), be blinded (2 Corinthians 4:4), feel tormented (Matthew 8:6), feel oppressed (Acts 10:38), be deaf to God's voice, (John 10:5), be deceived (Revelation 20:7–8) and be tempted to stir up divisions in your personal and business relationships (Mark 3:25).

God leads His people.

Satan pushes his.

What a list! Take a few minutes and read each of those powerful Scriptures so that the living Word can help you discern the enemy's voice when it whispers.

5. God's voice

Now that you know what God's voice *does not* sound like, what *does* it sound like? I wish I could tell you that I hear God's voice audibly every day of my life, but the truth is, it has happened to me very few times. Many other people I know have heard His audible voice, but even if they had not, many in Scripture did. We have the Ten Commandments because God dictated them to Moses audibly in Exodus 20. At the Mount of Transfiguration in Matthew 17:5, God affirmed Jesus audibly. He did the same at Jesus' baptism in Matthew 3:17. Second Peter 1:16–18 confirms this voice from heaven. God "is the same yesterday, today and forever" (Hebrews 13:8), so He is still speaking audibly today.

I love Psalm 29:3–5 (NASB):

> The voice of the LORD is upon the waters;
> The God of glory thunders,
> The LORD is over many waters.
> The voice of the LORD is powerful,

The voice of the LORD is majestic.
The voice of the LORD breaks the cedars;
Yes, the LORD breaks in pieces the cedars of Lebanon.

Wouldn't it be wonderful if we experienced God's voice this mightily every day? But most of the time, what we get is the small, still voice. Why so? Because it requires relationship. God can zap anybody into obedience with a dish-rattling encounter (as can any heavy-handed parent), but the still, small voice requires that you know God really, really well, which is what He is after. First Kings 19:12 (NIV) describes God's voice coming to Elijah as a "gentle whisper." But I am here to testify that this voice is often stronger than something audible, and it rattles you to your core. There have been times in prayer when it felt like my heart had ears, my kidneys had ears, my arms, my legs and *all of me*. Hearing only with the actual ears in that type of encounter pales in comparison.

I once heard an interview with a famous television psychic who was asked, "How do you know what's your voice and the voice of your spirit guide?" The answer was, "It sounds sort of like the voice you hear when you're reading a book silently to yourself."

How telling! That is because it *is* either your voice, or that of the enemy trying to mimic your voice so what you hear will sound less disreputable to you. He cannot mimic God's voice, and he is not going to come in an obviously evil voice or you would dismiss it immediately. So steer clear of this counsel. I am not saying you will hear a deep, grandfatherly voice per se, but God's voice never sounds like "my" voice to me.

As I said earlier, God can also speak by getting your attention through billboards, license plates, secular music, church marquees, sermons at your local church or through a myriad of other creative means. Master salesman, marketer and entertainment management guru Ken Kragen (who worked with the Bee Gees, Olivia Newton John, Burt Reynolds and more) always lectured on doing things in "threes," meaning that in today's busy marketplace you have to get people's attention three times before they remember you. I find it is often the same for God.

Let me give you one example: Our family is part of a talent agency that gets us work in television and more. When we first signed in 2001, the last four digits of the owner's phone number started showing up everywhere in my path. Let's say they were 1639. One day, I was taking a walk and stopped to rest. Looking up, I noticed that the mailbox in front of me read 1639. Days later, my check came to the table at a restaurant, and the bill was $16.39. A few days later, while homeschooling, my child answered a math problem with the total 1,639.

"Okay, Lord, loud and clear!" I knew it was a call to pray for my agent, but I did not know her well enough at the time to ask if there was anything specifically I could pray for, or even if she believed in prayer.

When I heard a voice telling me, "You can't tell her you're praying for her. She'll think you're a religious freak and never hire you to do anything," I knew that was not God's voice. Why would God tell me not to let people know He had them in mind? Telling them shows His great love for them. I emailed her, and the response was wonderful. She said that she believed in prayer and thanked me. But the real thanks came just days later, when she called me from home. Steph said, "Laura, I was standing in my shower picking the glass out of my body and realized I needed to call you. I was just in a horrible wreck this morning, and the side of the car that was demolished was the side my infant son usually sits on. He was not with me today, as he normally is. I know it was because of your prayers." Our hearts were knit together from that day. It has resulted in more blessings than I can recount, including financial ones.

The voice of God will never contradict Scripture. It will always do one of these twelve things:

- Comfort you (Psalm 23:4; John 14:16)
- Warn you (Acts 21:4, 10–14; Ephesians 6:4)
- Edify you (Ephesians 4:12)

- Convict you of sin, but never condemn you (Romans 6)
- Rebuke and reprove you (Titus 1:13; 2 Timothy 4:2)
- Bring Scripture to memory (John 14:26)
- Guide you into truth (John 16:13)
- Exhort you (Romans 12:1; Jude 1:3)   .
- Remind you of God's love (Jeremiah 31:31; John 3:1)
- Increase your faith (Romans 10:17)
- Instruct you in righteousness/right standing with God (2 Timothy 3:16)
- Bring salvation and healing (Romans 10:9–10; 2 Timothy 3:15)

We come to God by faith, but we grow in Him experientially. You can learn to discern with utmost certainty the differences between God's voice, yours, other people's and the enemy's. Hebrews 5:14 says the spiritually mature "have their senses exercised to discern both good and evil." But with that maturity of discerning good and evil comes an awakening, an awareness of heavenly activity both light and dark. Once that switch is flipped, you will never be the same.

Loud and Clear

I implore you to rid your life of the static we have learned about in this chapter and to come to God expectant to hear His voice. Fifteen times in the New Testament you see the following phrase: "Let he who has an ear to hear, hear!" Matthew, Mark, Luke and John all recorded Jesus saying it. Imagine the positive outcome on your life if you will always hear God's voice and obey it. You will be a better parent. You will be a better friend. You will be a better spouse. You will be a better leader. You will be a better daughter or son. You will be a better businessman or businesswoman. You will be a better financier. You will be a better . . . you.

I often find that people who have a hard time communicating with their heavenly Father may have had difficulty communicating with their earthly father. In fact, I find the two relationships can mirror each other, period. If you had a father who was heavy-handed, you may view God as the same. Coming to Him is hard. If you had a dad who did not care how terribly you misbehaved and set no boundaries for you, then you grow up thinking you can get by with anything with God, without consequence. And if you grew up away from your father, only speaking to him rarely, you may have a hard time remembering to talk to your heavenly Father at all. It is not that you do not love God, but you became accustomed to your father relationship being maintained at a distance. Be healed today from all father wounds and ask God to renew your mind to receive Him and His Father voice.

You can learn to discern with utmost certainty the differences between God's voice, yours, other people's and the enemy's.

Maybe you used to hear His voice clearly, but do not now. Maybe you have rid your mind of all the static (sin, time, ambivalence, trials, illiteracy and competing voices), but still feel deaf. Perhaps all you need is a dose of childlike faith. Let me close this chapter with a story. My daughter Jessica and her husband, Kyle, bought a new home last year and moved in with their five children (all under the age of five). The house sits up on a beautiful hill on a wide piece of property, at the top of which the city train runs closely, right behind the house. When they first moved in, my grandsons talked about this train nonstop. They were big fans of Thomas the Tank Engine, so they loved it every time the train passed by. It is so close to their house that it would even wake them up if it passed by at night. But in the short year they have lived there, they have gotten used to the sound of the train, and it has lost its "wow" factor. They still love the train, and they still include it in their outdoor play, but somehow it has lost its ability to drown out everything else when it passes by. Sometimes they do not even hear or acknowledge the train at all.

Maybe it is the same with you and God's voice. At some time in your life, hearing God's voice was of vital importance to you. Then over time, the new wore off and it got fainter and fainter. Eventually, you doubted if you were hearing it at all. Perhaps it even used to wake you up at night, but after you kept refusing to get up and pray, it quit coming. It was not that God quit speaking. You quit listening. You quit trusting it was His voice. But it does not matter how far away you have gotten from God's voice; it is only one step back to get within earshot again. Are you ready to make that happen?

A prayer of dedication:

Today, oh God, I vow to put my heart into Your hands
And humbly plead for You to knead until it understands

That words alone cannot fulfill the duties that are mine
But virtue too, toward man and You, is what I must combine

So give me eyes and ears of faith that make Your chosen choice
That I might be found pure in heart and hear Your still small voice

© Laura Harris Smith, 2002

PRAYER

Let's pray out loud together:

Father . . . You are my Father, and I know You want to talk to me. May I be attentive always! Forgive me of sins that have come between us, Lord, and forgive me for the time constraints I have put on You when I am in prayer. Help me wait on You there. Deliver me from all doubts and ambivalence, and help me drown out the trials and competing voices that speak louder to me than You do when we are together. I want to hear Your voice, Lord. Speak. I'll be listening. In Jesus' name, Amen.

IMPARTATION

Right now, I release and impart to you the *hunger* for holiness, the *hatred* for sin and compromise, and the *yearning* to hear God's voice internally and externally. Remember Revelation 3:20 (KJV), "Behold, I stand at the door, and knock: if any man hear my voice, and open the door, I will come in to him, and will sup with him, and he with me." (Now open your hands, shut your eyes and receive it.)

9

Deaf and Dumb, but Not Blind!

The Voice of America is the United States government's official broadcast institution that provides broadcasts for radio, television and Internet in more than 43 countries. For years, it was transmitted into Europe through the Iron Curtain to communist captives in need of hope for democracy. But often, local communist leaders would highjack the channel's frequency with gibberish so that incoming messages of optimism would be confused. As a result, the captives would lose all hope and expectancy.

Satan does the same thing with Christians. If he can weasel his way in between you and God on your normal communication lines, he can intercept incoming messages and scramble them up, leaving you feeling orphaned, hopeless and ignored by God. While the previous chapter covered tips to get the static caused by personal wrongs out of our spiritual ears, this one will deal with what to do when the static is not your fault at all, and in fact is demonically devised, perhaps even by a high-ranking territorial principality like the one Daniel battled in prayer in

Daniel 10. If it is a whole region of people that Satan wants to disorganize and confuse, he will assign these territorial spirits to do his bidding, the same way in which God sends His angels to do His. It is spiritual warfare 101.

Remember that Satan is the "prince of the power of the air," according to Ephesians 2:2, so we can say that the air is his playground, office desk and townhome. He is poised there, just waiting to speak gibberish to the frequency on which he knows God and His people communicate. This is my exact story, and I would like to tell it to you. It is very personal, and I have never chronicled it before in full. I ask that you read it prayerfully, without doctrinal bias or fear. I believe that by the end of it, you will see a bigger picture and join me in the crusade to help others overcome their spiritual deafness. Region by region, we can do it.

Cheer Up

It begins not in the spirit at all, but with a thirteen-year-old girl who had just made cheerleader. I had been a Christian for three years and was already teaching kids' Bible studies and leading them to Jesus on my school bus and in my front yard. I obviously was not any kind of scholar, but I just looked for unhappy people and told them I could help them be happier. And it was working. I guess you could say I was cheerleading people to Jesus. I was voted by my classmates as having "Most School Spirit" at the end of the year, but I think that had less to do with cheering a team than it did cheering individuals toward their God-given purposes. Life was good. School was good. Church was good. I had no way of knowing that a "Wanted" poster had gone up in hell with my face on it.

And then I got the diagnosis. In the middle of all this triumph came what felt like tragedy. Epilepsy. They called it "petit mal," which involves small absence seizures called staring spells. But mine were so quick (2–3 seconds each) that no one ever knew

about them until I told them. Even my own dear mother and
stepfather did not know. I did not understand what was happening.
Finally, one day I told Mama and she took me for testing.
I came from a wonderful Christian family, but we never really
discussed healing and had not experienced any major infirmities
that caused us to talk about it. I vividly remember Mama cried
at the diagnosis and said she wished it could be her and not me.

I continued to act, cheer and write and
took my medicine for the next dozen years.
I even married Chris and had my first two
children, Jessica and Julian. I was teaching
at church, acting on local TV, starting a
Christian dinner theatre and writing plays
for publication. But while my will and faith
were strong, my body was still sick. Sadly,
I had pie-sectioned off my life into the categories of body, soul and spirit, and it never
dawned on me that they could influence each
other. Grace and sheer determination had kicked in. Life was
good. Family was good. Church was good. Once again, I did
not understand how something as simple as happiness could
anger the enemy. I guess it does because he has never known it.

> I did not understand
> how something as
> simple as happiness
> could anger the enemy.
> I guess it does because
> he has never known it.

Then in 1990, after moving into a new home and having my
third child, Jhason, I had my first convulsion. For twelve years
I had been used to the smaller 2–3 second petit mal absence
seizures, but this was a grand mal convulsion in which I was
unconscious or reemerging from unconsciousness for more than
an hour. It happened soon after I had allowed some friends at
our Friday night Bible study to pray over my newborn son for
healing from a blood disorder caused by a two-month case of
life-threatening jaundice. Jhason was miraculously healed just
before the scheduled hospital interventions (which would have
included a total body blood transfusion), leaving the doctors
scratching their heads. But what left me scratching my head was
that these same friends on the same night had also prayed for

my healing. I was not healed. In fact, the convulsion came the same weekend they prayed.

It was long and ugly and violent. I was rushed to the hospital by ambulance, and after regaining consciousness, I was released. Medication was increased. And then the cycle happened again: Grace kicked in, I found happiness and the enemy got angry and pushed even harder. But instead of pushing back, I just stuck to grace and happiness. Except for this brief brush with healing at our Friday night Bible study, no one in my family, neighborhood or church ever talked about divine healing, and I had no idea that it was my birthright and I could fight for it. I also had never really heard about spiritual warfare or that I had authority over this vicious cycle of thievery the enemy had me in as he tried to own my happiness.

Think about it—why does a thief steal? So that he can take something you have and use it as his own. No thief breaks into your home and steals your TV so he can throw it in a trash can. Likewise, Satan does not steal your happiness so he can move on to committing his next crime. I believe he steals your happiness in an attempt to use it and experience this foreign emotion himself. I think he is jealous for it, so he sees it, wants it and takes it. It is an impossible sequence as he goes through person after person, trying to make it work. It never does, and he is never satisfied. But like a homeless person looking for someplace to lay his head, the enemy cannot give up. First Peter 5:8 says it best: "Be sober, be vigilant; because your adversary the devil walks about like a roaring lion, seeking whom he may devour."

The next two arduous years brought more grand mal convulsions and another baby, Jeorgi. And while I would love to tell you that my pregnancy with her was uneventful, it was not. I spent the first trimester in bed in a drug-induced stupor due to a medication change for all my various seizures, only to find out months later that I was on a barbiturate, at which point I switched again. But in those dark ninety days with a muddy mind, my spirit finally had revelation of what the enemy was doing. He had overplayed his hand. My desperation *forced* me to fight for healing. Not just to ask and sit back and see what God would do, but to partner with Him and *fight*. This time, I would not use grace and happiness as crutches that could only help me hobble through to the next trial.

When I came out of that three-month stupor, I came out fighting. With my pen and my prayers. I dug into the Word of God and memorized the healing Scriptures, and my prayer life doubled. Because of that time in Scripture and prayer, my creativity multiplied, too, and somehow I became twice as productive. I wrote my first book during those last trimesters, turning in the manuscript just 48 hours before Jeorgi's healthy debut. I also wrote another dinner theatre play during the last trimester and directed its production.

Over the next year, it was obvious that this combination of time in God's Word and prayer had turned me into a spiritual triathlete. But the enemy, nipping at my heels, struck even harder. I began having regular convulsions, and the smaller seizures were coming every day, sometimes over a hundred a day. While you could hide a few at 2–3 seconds each, you could not hide a hundred. Doctors did not know what to do with me, and no amount of medicine was helping.

The King and I

Then, just before midnight on January 26, 1993, while I was on my knees reading my Bible, as I had done thousands of times before, God decided to do something He had never done any of those thousands of times. One minute I was in study mode, and the next minute God's Spirit overcame mine and I could no longer read a word on the page. As if something started at the top of my head and moved down my whole being while I was still kneeling, the weighted glory of God bent me over until I found myself on my face, totally unable to move.

I had never been "slain in the Spirit," experienced the presence of God or been baptized in the Holy Spirit (and honestly,

I did not even know such biblical experiences existed). But as I hunched there, doubled over on my face, it was as if the atmosphere was altered and someone entered the room. Sort of like how, even with your eyes closed, you can tell when someone approaches by how the air between you changes. It instantaneously affected the molecular structure of my whole being—body, mind and spirit—and suddenly, every moment got big.

Daniel 10 described my frailty exactly, when Daniel said, "I bowed with my face toward the ground and was speechless. . . . 'How can I, your servant, talk with you, my lord? My strength is gone and I can hardly breathe'" (verses 15, 17 NIV). John described it, too, in Revelation 1:17 (NIV), when he was on the island of Patmos: "When I saw him, I fell at his feet as though dead." But Ezekiel said it best: "And behold, the glory of the LORD filled the house of the LORD, and I fell on my face" (Ezekiel 44:4).

The glory of the Lord did fill my house when this King stepped in, and an intense rush of majesty overwhelmed me, leaving my entire body with no sensation. Trust me, I had no idea this kind of stuff still happened today. I think maybe I pictured it only happening to people in robes and sandals. I could see the carpet an inch below my eyes, but I remember distinctly, to this day, the feeling that if I lifted my head to see His face, my flesh would melt off my bones.

Somehow, I *knew* the King had come just so I could ask Him the question I desperately needed answered: "Are You going to heal me, God?" So I asked, never looking up.

"Yes, daughter. In fact, I have already begun to heal you, but it will be by process."

He answered with seventeen words that have defined the last two decades of my life: "Yes, daughter. In fact, I have already begun to heal you, but it will be by process." I wish He had stressed those last two words with a little more inflection in His voice, but I was too elated over the first two words to care. I had a word from God Himself that healing was in my future.

I was baptized in the Holy Spirit later that fall (something we will explore in chapter 10), we joined a Spirit-filled church and I began to have my first regular visions. However, they were not angel wings and crosses, as I had requested, but were images that were very difficult to discern. Sure, years before, I had seen a demonic creature behind me in a mirror, but these visions were actually stranger. Demons were in the Bible, at least, but I was seeing Indians in full headdress running toward me with bloody tomahawks—while I was sitting in my bedroom, minding my own business.

Then I found out I lived on the Trail of Tears, and that my house was on what had been President Andrew Jackson's plantation. To confirm it all, I was finding Indian artifacts in my yard. Turns out that Andy Jackson signed the Indian Removal Act in 1830, which gave birth to one of the darkest chapters in America's history. But I was clueless about all that at the time. I was too busy changing diapers, writing plays and trying to figure out how to get rid of these angry Indians.

The more I prayed for myself and for God to cleanse the land I lived on and forgive the atrocities that had occurred there, the worse my health got. With grace and happiness as weapons (no longer crutches), I fought off discouragement, but on the hard days, when the multiple absence seizures crowded my mind, I would grieve. It was as if my faith was constantly interrupted with them multiple times each day—sometimes each hour. But after each one, I would "come to" and remind myself, *Oh yeah. You are Laura Harris Smith. You are a woman of faith. Healing is yours.*

Although the two- to three-second absence seizures and the visions both took my concentration to another place, they were very different. One bolstered my faith and left me with information I could pray with, and the other left me fighting horrible headaches and defeat. I saw the increase of the seizures as the enemy's way of vying for my concentration so that the visions would not come, or as harming my memory so that I would not remember them. I had experienced seizures for fifteen years without having visions, so I knew one did not cause the other or it would have shown up years before. The visions did not come until I had been filled with the Holy Spirit. The increase in the petit mal absence seizures and the introduction of the grand mal convulsions did not come until I had experienced this filling, either, so I see now that they were the enemy's way of trying to interrupt my life and calling as a communicator about visionary gifts.

It seemed the only thing I could do without interruption was pray in the Spirit, so I did. A lot. Then one day in 1993, I was walking from my bedroom to my kitchen, and as I looked toward my front door, there in my foyer stood a dark, foreboding creature. He was in the form of a man, dressed in all black. Black cape, black hat with a big, black feather plume and big, black strapping boots that came up over his knees.

He looked like a general from another era. Hands on hips, he was staring me down proudly. Cockily is more like it. But totally at peace, I never broke my stride. He stood perfectly erect, with head held high, and watched me my whole way to the kitchen. When I got there and turned around, he was gone. It was just feet away from where I had had my majestic visitation from Jesus earlier that year. This one was a visitation of another kind.

A few days later, I asked my new pastors what on earth this creature could be. They introduced me to the biblical topic of demonic principalities and territorial spirits, and they suggested that perhaps this entity was a general in Satan's army who had been assigned to this region. I was familiar with the Daniel 10 story of Daniel battling territorial principalities, but on that day I saw Ephesians 6:12 with new eyes: "For we do not wrestle against flesh and blood, but against principalities, against powers, against the rulers of the darkness of this age, against spiritual hosts of wickedness in the heavenly places."

I heard every word my pastors said that day, but I had no idea what any of it had to do with me. My stepmother, Janice, would go on to say that this creature had shown up to see who was causing him so much trouble in prayer and to check her out. I did not know for sure. I just wanted to be healed, write plays and change diapers. I filed the whole experience away under "P" for principality.

The Deaf and Dumb Spirit

A few weeks later, as I was finishing up my first-ever class on prophetic ministry, I missed the final exam because I had a very violent convulsion. The teacher had not known until then that I had this condition, but was scheduled to speak at our church soon after. He prophesied over me: "That which hinders you hinders the city."

I was utterly baffled. What did God think "hindered" me? Another piece of this word included, " . . . and when he falls, many under him will fall and widespread healing will be released." All put together, it linked my health struggle with something greater. Perhaps it was a prophetic embodiment, meaning that something hindering *my* body was symbolic of something hindering Jesus' Body in my city. It was then that I discovered Mark 9, the only passage in Scripture where Jesus gave a spirit a precise name. It was the story of the little epileptic boy and the "deaf and dumb spirit." Please take a moment and read this carefully with me:

> Then one of the crowd answered and said, "Teacher, I brought You my son, who has a mute spirit. And wherever it seizes him, it throws him down; he foams at the mouth, gnashes his teeth, and becomes rigid. So I spoke to Your disciples, that they should cast it out, but they could not."
>
> He answered him and said, "O faithless generation, how long shall I be with you? How long shall I bear with you? Bring him to Me." Then they brought him to Him. And when he saw Him, immediately the spirit convulsed him, and he fell on the ground and wallowed, foaming at the mouth.
>
> So He asked his father, "How long has this been happening to him?"

And he said, "From childhood. And often he has thrown him both into the fire and into the water to destroy him. But if You can do anything, have compassion on us and help us."

Jesus said to him, "If you can believe, all things are possible to him who believes."

Immediately the father of the child cried out and said with tears, "Lord, I believe; help my unbelief!"

When Jesus saw that the people came running together, He rebuked the unclean spirit, saying to it: "Deaf and dumb spirit, I command you, come out of him and enter him no more!" Then the spirit cried out, convulsed him greatly, and came out of him. And he became as one dead, so that many said, "He is dead." But Jesus took him by the hand and lifted him up, and he arose.

And when He had come into the house, His disciples asked Him privately, "Why could we not cast it out?"

So He said to them, "This kind can come out by nothing but prayer and fasting."

Mark 9:17–29

My entire focus changed that fall. How could a spirit affect a city? How could a deaf and dumb spirit affect a population of people? Was that the general who had come to check me out that day in my foyer? I began praying prayers I had no previous vocabulary for—using Matthew 12:29 and 18:18, *binding* spiritual deafness and muteness and *loosing* freedom over people in my city to pray, praise, prophesy and evangelize like never before. Nashville is known as the Protestant Vatican, with more churches per capita than any other city, and so I could not imagine why God would think such a spirit plagued our town. Nonetheless, I threw all of my faith and obedience into these prayers.

The convulsions increased even more, and doctors were dumbfounded. Nobody could help me, not even the best doctors or medicines. The convulsions became cruelly violent; I lived with constant bruises, my tongue was constantly torn and bleeding, and I was beginning to suffer memory loss. I would go on to have more than eighty convulsions. One doctor said

I should be dead. I would be unconscious for hours after each episode, unable to hear or speak. Thus, Jesus' Mark 9 title: the "deaf and dumb spirit."

Simultaneously, I saw the Body of Jesus in my city taking a beating. Such denominational competition. So much religiosity and stale tradition. Church splits seemed as rampant as church plants in our city, creating an atmosphere of spiritual strife. Of course, everybody was happy between 9:00 and 12:00 on Sunday mornings.

Then in 1998, I read a copy of *Possessing the Gates of the Enemy* by Cindy Jacobs (Chosen, 2009), and it fueled my soul. As I researched more about Cindy and Generals of Intercession, I discovered that she oversaw the USSWN, or the United States Spiritual Warfare Network (later changed to USSPN, or United States Strategic Prayer Network, and overseen by Chuck Pierce).

> One doctor said I should be dead. I would be unconscious for hours after each episode, unable to hear or speak. Thus, Jesus' Mark 9 title: the "deaf and dumb spirit."

Wanting to participate, I went to their website to see who the Tennessee state coordinator was and discovered there was not one. After talking it over with Chris, I sent a brave fax to the Generals of Intercession headquarters and volunteered for the post. After submitting my bio and talking with Cindy, I was invited on board.

Even though I was a published author, had spoken regularly and had done some TV, my health struggle had left me with a keen understanding of how small I was and of how dependent on God I had to stay, so in short, I could not believe Cindy received me. Oh, did those years with Cindy and her husband, Mike, change my life. At their feet I learned so much about spiritual mapping, territorial strongholds and how to change regions and nations without ever leaving my closet. It was on certain prayer coordinator trips with them that I first worked with James and Michal Ann Goll, who eventually moved to Nashville, to my great delight. I kept plugging away, with Nashville's deliverance always at the forefront of my mind, speaking about it when invited and writing about it, too.

Somehow, I knew Nashville's liberation would coincide with mine—*not* that God was "allowing" me to keep having seizures or was denying me healing. In fact, I already saw myself as healed. God's Word offers His children healing without strings. It is just that I began to interpret the seizures creatively. I began studying the discernment of spirits gift (see 1 Corinthians 12:7–10; Hebrews 5:14; 1 John 4:1–6) and came to the conclusion that I was just very sensitive to the presence of that deaf and dumb spirit and seemed to be affected in my body when it was operational nearby. Some people smell things when they discern evil spirits (like sulfur) or see things (like demons) or even hear things (like hissing), but perhaps this was my version of the discernment of spirits gift with this evil spirit. It also explained why doctors could not help me medically.

Let me use the analogy of allergies. People cannot see the invisible allergens that affect their bodies, but they see the reactions that occur at the allergens' presence. The pollen and dander are invisible, but the hives and watery eyes blow their cover and give them away. People then take medicine, and the allergic reaction subsides. I began noticing that this was happening to me, spiritually speaking. The deaf and dumb spirit was my pollen, the seizures were the reaction and my only medicine was intercessory prayer for the Body of Christ in my region.

I could walk into an event, a conference or even just someone's home and tell if that spirit was present. And not just because I would have a small absence seizure, but because I began to notice patterns of behavior in people in the room, which I will discuss momentarily. But also, when I traveled, I noticed that in some cities I would not have the small seizures. Coincidence? Maybe. But the seizures would return in the air as our airplane approached the Nashville airport. I could have a four-hour, seizure-free flight, but the seizures often would return when I hit the air above Nashville (and they did not when I landed in other cities). It was not a reaction to something in Nashville's city air, because keep in mind that I was still enclosed in an environmentally controlled airplane. My body was reacting physically to what hindered my city spiritually.

I began to make mental notes—and eventually written ones— of what was happening contextually whenever I had these seizures and suspected this spirit's presence. For instance, my husband and I would be sitting in a counseling session with a couple whose marriage was ailing, and they would find themselves in the middle of a calm he-said, she-said exchange. No one would be yelling, but no one would be listening to anyone else, either. The conversation would almost seem comical because Chris and I could hear the trap in which this couple was caught, but they could not:

Husband: "You told me to take out the trash."

Wife: "No, I didn't. I told you to take out the trash."

Husband: "That's what I said. You told me to take out the trash."

Wife: "No, I didn't. I told you to take out the trash!"

Chris and I would snicker, but then it would happen. I would have an absence seizure. No one knew it and I would never tell, but I would stop the whole conversation and ask that we pray for the removal of the deaf and dumb influence. We would continue the conversation afterward, and it was as if their ears had been unclogged.

That is one of many examples. I would like to share the list of others I have made over the years:

Emotional manifestations of the deaf and dumb spirit: communication breaches (cannot hear each other), accusations, concentration issues, manic-depressive and bipolar issues, depression, phobias, grief, extreme fatigue, dullness, escapism, emotional bruising, extreme fatigue, cutting and the like.

Physical manifestations of the deaf and dumb spirit: autism, epilepsy, seizures, deafness, muteness, fainting spells, learning disabilities, ADD, ADHD, narcolepsy, comas, inner-ear problems and equilibrium issues, vertigo, Alzheimer's and all memory conditions, mental retardations, dyslexia, stuttering and many neurological disorders.

Spiritual manifestations of the deaf and dumb spirit: spiritual deafness, unbelief, religiosity and rigidity, skepticism, doubt, the inability to concentrate on God's Word and receive revelation, the inability to hear God, spiritual muteness including the inability to receive one's prayer language, the inability to pray out loud, the inability to worship freely, the inability to prophesy and the inability to share one's faith.

Some things from that last category, spiritual manifestations, actually come from the Mark 9 text itself, things such as unbelief. The father of the epileptic boy says, "Lord, I believe; help my unbelief!" (verse 24). We see that when that spirit is present, it is very easy to lose faith. Even Jesus exclaimed, "O faithless generation, how long shall I be with you?" when He heard that the disciples could not cast the spirit out (verse 19). Also, notice that the boy was described as being rigid when this spirit came upon him (verse 18). Likewise, I have noticed a rigid religiosity in people who are spiritually influenced by this spirit.

Five Rankings of Satan's Army

Whenever I discuss the deaf and dumb spirit—the only spirit in Scripture that Jesus names Himself—I notice that it is easy to lose the listener unless I give scriptural support (which is wise and easily done, so that is fine). You would be hard-pressed to find someone who does not believe in God's army of angels, but ask a person if the devil has an army and you might get some strange looks. Truth is, Satan's forts are full of one-third of the angels, those who fell from heaven with him—namely, now demons (see Revelation 12:4–9). Several key verses in the New Testament clearly outline the enemy's armed forces and their rankings. I have italicized these soldiers' key titles as revealed in the verses that follow, so please resist the urge to speed-read. Study these attentively:

Finally, my brethren, be strong in the Lord and in the power of His might. Put on the whole armor of God, that you may be able to stand against the wiles of the devil. For we do not wrestle against flesh and blood, but against *principalities*, against *powers*, against the *rulers* of the darkness of this age, against spiritual hosts of wickedness in the heavenly places.

Ephesians 6:10–12

The New Living Translation of this passage says in verse 12, "For we are not fighting against flesh-and-blood enemies, but against evil *rulers* and *authorities* of the unseen world, against mighty *powers* in this dark world, and against evil *spirits* in the heavenly places." Here are more verses:

For by Him all things were created that are in heaven and that are on earth, visible and invisible, whether *thrones* or *dominions* or *principalities* or *powers*. All things were created through Him and for Him.

Colossians 1:16

He raised Him from the dead and seated Him at His right hand in the heavenly places, far above all *principality* and *power* and might and *dominion*, and every name that is named, not only in this age but also in that which is to come.

Ephesians 1:20–21

Now the manifold wisdom of God might be made known by the church to the *principalities* and *powers* in the heavenly places.

Ephesians 3:10

Let's now step inside the enemy's garrisons and see who is there.

1. Principalities

Greek *arche*—the first; the active cause; magistrate; of angels and demons, Greek root *archomai*—to be chief, leader, ruler.[1]

213

Romans 8:38 refers to these,

For I am persuaded that neither death nor life, nor angels nor principalities nor powers, nor things present nor things to come nor height nor depth, nor any other created thing, shall be able to separate us from the love of God which is in Christ Jesus our Lord.

(Other verses that use this term are Luke 12:11; John 1:1; Ephesians 3:10; 6:12; Colossians 2:10, 15.)

2. Authorities

Greek *exousia*—one who possesses authority; a thing subject to authority; the power of him whose will and command must be submitted to by others and obeyed.

First Corinthians 15:24 says, "Then comes the end, when He delivers the kingdom to God the Father, when He puts an end to all rule and all *authority* and power" (emphasis added). (See also Luke 20:20; Ephesians 1:21; Colossians 1:16; 2:10; 1 Peter 3:22.)

3. Spirits

Greek *pneuma*—a simple essence, devoid of all or at least all grosser matter, and possessing the power of knowing, desiring, deciding, and acting/used of demons or evil spirits who inhabit the bodies of men.

Mark 6:7 says, "And He called the twelve to Himself, and began to send them out two by two, and gave them power over unclean spirits." Ephesians 6:12 (NLT) says, "For we are not fighting against flesh-and-blood enemies, but against evil rulers and authorities of the unseen world, against mighty powers in this dark world, and against evil spirits in the heavenly places." (See also Matthew 10:1; 12:45; Mark 1:27; 3:11; Luke 4:36; 8:2.)

4. Demons

Greek *daimonion*—evil spirits or the messengers and ministers of devil; a spirit being inferior to God but superior to men.

Luke 4:41 says, "And demons also came out of many, crying out and saying, 'You are the Christ, the Son of God!'" Mark 16:17 says, "And these signs will follow those who believe: In My name they will cast out demons; they will speak with new tongues." (See also Luke 8:2; James 2:19; Revelation 9:20.)

5. Dominions

Greek *kyriotes*—one who possesses dominion, Greek root *kyrios*—the possessor or influencer of a thing; one who has control of the person. French root *mignonne*—minion: a follower or underling of a powerful person; henchman, brown-noser, suck-up, boot-licker.

Colossians 1:16 says, "For by Him all things were created that are in heaven and that are on earth, visible and invisible, whether thrones or *dominions* or principalities or powers. All things were created through Him and for Him" (emphasis added).

These are the five rankings of Satan's army, but there are other useful battle terms that also reveal demonic jurisdictions. Let's look at three more.

Rulers (including all of the above)

Greek *kosmokrator*—the devil and his demons. Greek root *kosmos*—the ungodly multitude; the whole mass of men alienated from God and therefore hostile to the cause of Christ.

Look at Ephesians 6:12 one more time: "For we do not wrestle against flesh and blood, but against principalities, against powers, against the rulers of the darkness of this age, against spiritual hosts of wickedness in the heavenly places."

Thrones

Greek *thronos*—a throne seat; a chair of state having a footstool.
Luke 1:52 says, "He has put down the mighty from their thrones, and exalted the lowly." (See also Colossians 1:16; Hebrews 12:2.)

Powers

Greek *exousia*—jurisdiction; physical and mental power over mankind; lawful.

First Peter 3:22 says, "[Christ] has gone into heaven and is at the right hand of God, angels and authorities and powers having been made subject to Him."

"By Process"

So I am saying that, based on these biblical definitions, I believe the deaf and dumb spirit is a demonic *arche* (principality) who exercises spiritual influence in geographical territories where he has been assigned by Satan to oppress the hearing and communication of that region's inhabitants, lost or saved. I believe this spirit has physical, emotional and spiritual manifestations that will vary from place to place, but in the end, it is just the same spirit with different hairdos.

I shared with you how this principality appeared uninvited in my foyer in 1993 as an intimidating, cocky war general, but I am pleased to tell you that I have seen him since in dreams, as have other people, and he is no longer intimidating and cocky. In one dream, he was a disabled war veteran stripped of rank, dressed shabbily and standing near the same spot near my front door, this time hobbling on a cane. In the most recent dream, he was on a deathbed, wheezing, with his days numbered. Stride for stride with his defeat has been my victory in the war against the seizures. I have not had a single convulsion in ten years, and the smaller episodes are fading, as well. I am taking less medication than I ever have before during this life journey, which has now spanned 35 years since that little cheerleader first received her diagnosis.

And if you are still asking, after all of this, why I believe my illness is more than an illness and is somehow connected to this spirit in Scripture, then my answer to you is, *If Jesus Himself looked at this same set of symptoms and called it a spirit in*

Scripture, then who am I to call it anything less? It is the same for you if you display any of these symptoms, too, emotionally, physically or spiritually. I do not believe in the demonic *possession* of Christians (the Holy Spirit resides within you, therefore no demonic presence can coexist there), but I do see evidence of the demonic *oppression* of many of God's people. The enemy will try anything to keep us down.

As I said before, I have this hunch that I am already healed, but as long as that spirit is even remotely operational here in Nashville and is plaguing the Body of Christ, the "allergic reactions" of the now-infrequent smaller seizures remind me to pray. I also surround myself with like-minded intercessors, including one who shares the same physical struggle I have had against the deaf and dumb spirit. That is my good friend Tonya. I also receive excellent medical care to sustain me during this time from a wonderful neurologist and a nutritionist who understand the timetable I am on in the fight against this principality. She plays a key role in keeping my entire body whole as I fight. Never look at medicine as God's competitor. When war comes, you use all your big guns.

> Based on these biblical definitions, I believe the deaf and dumb spirit is a demonic arche (principality) who exercises spiritual influence in geographical territories where he has been assigned by Satan to oppress the hearing and communication of that region's inhabitants, lost or saved.

I have spent the last twenty years of my life—since my visitation during the same year by this demonic general and by King Jesus—shamelessly telling anyone who would listen these three things: 1) God is healing me "by process." 2) God is healing my city "by process." 3) I believe my city is called to heal the nation—and *nations*—because of her unique platform. Nashville houses more Christian denominational headquarters than any city in the world, more Christian colleges, more Christian publishing companies, and is even home to Gideons International and to Thomas Nelson, the world's largest publisher of Bibles.

Nashville is home to multiple Christian radio headquarters, which host multiple programs on Nashville's airwaves, and let's not forget that not only is she home to the Christian music industry, but also to country music itself, which has its roots in Gospel music. The Sunday school literature printed in this city goes all over the world.

Truly, what happens in Nashville does *not* stay in Nashville. So when revival hits this city, a media revival will be imminent. Our teachers, DJs, music artists, preachers, publishers, denominational leaders and writers will speak, broadcast, sing, preach, publish, endorse and write media that will change the world. God will prove once again how wise He is by investing revival in Nashville. Keep your eye on her.

But my deliverance and Nashville's aside, I am convinced that there is a need for deliverance from this spiritual force in *the* Body, which includes you, whatever city you are in. As I said in chapter 1, books on what to do when God is silent still line the shelves of national bookstores. *Seeing the Voice of God* helps you use your eyes in the middle of a hearing war, but this chapter is specifically written to ask you to fight with me in the battle against the deaf and dumb spirit. What started out as my hindrance became my city's hindrance, and then my nation's. It is many of yours, too. As you have read this chapter, many of you have found within it symptoms of this spirit's meddlings in your life. Together, we can end his deafening influence by exposing him and it. You cannot be a doer unless you are a hearer (James 1:22).

Along the way, I also was able to make the connection between the angry Indians I had seen and this deaf and dumb spirit. On one desperate night, I asked God to reveal how this spirit had gained legal right to the skies over our city. There has to be an open door for this to happen—a corporate sin and/or a governmental toleration of it—and God reminded me of the atrocities committed against the Native Americans at the pen of Andrew Jackson, the original owner of the property where I still live. Soon after, I was contacted out of the blue by an Indian named Riverwind, a Tennessean and Christian minister, who shared with me his forefather's account of the Trail of Tears.

Riverwind said it was actually called "The Trail Where They Cried," and that it referred not to crying Indians, but to the white men who cried as the Indians marched. Evidently, by the time they were forced out of this area, the Cherokee nation and many other Indian tribes had been proselytized and converted to Christianity, so many of their white brothers and sisters mourned on both sides of the trail as they left. When Riverwind stated that the Indians had decided bravely not to cry and instead to hold their heads high—and that they *took a vow of silence*—I thought, *Silence, hmm.* . . . At that moment, the Holy Spirit revealed that this was the major entrance point for the deaf and dumb spirit.

Shortly after that, I was asking the Lord about the American Indians. "Lord, they were here first, but how did they get here? You didn't just plant them here when You put Adam in the Garden, did You? They came from somewhere. But where?" He whispered something that I began researching, and my research led to article after article on scholars who believe that the American Indians hail from the Ten Lost Tribes of Israel. It has been disputed many times, then revisited and then redisputed. But a Public Broadcasting Service (PBS) *NOVA* article in November 2000 titled "Where Are the Ten Lost Tribes?" strengthens this connection and seemingly confirms it.[2] If this is true, then the Indians' removal was not just racial genocide, and it was not only martyr-esque due to their Christian status, but it was also another Jewish holocaust. No wonder God was so concerned about this blood crying out from the ground. No wonder the skies over our city were so plagued with silence. No wonder I was seeing angry Indians!

I would also learn that Andrew Jackson's involvement with the Freemasons in our city involved two vows that opened doors to the deaf and dumb principality. In one vow for the Entered Apprentice Degree, initiates are warned about violating their oaths, and they "solemnly and sincerely promise and swear" to many things, including "having my throat cut across, my tongue torn out," both of which would leave one dumb and mute, I would say. Did this mean literally? Of course not. But when brotherhood secrets are revealed in confidence in some trivial, private conversation somewhere, the "symbolic" vow is a vow nonetheless and will come calling with its legal right for payment.

How? Remember, Proverbs 18:21 says the power of life and death is in the tongue. A vow or oath is binding in the spiritual realm, and therefore, while no literal repercussion may come, a spiritual one will. Especially since candidates in this case would seal the ritual oath with the words "So mote it be," a phrase used only in Freemasonry and witchcraft.[3] Instead of having one's tongue ripped out in the natural, perhaps this Freemason would find it difficult to share Christ or pray aloud, or even worship freely the Spirit. I have interviewed former Masons who left the brotherhood due to God's conviction. Many reference sources are available for Masons or the families of Masons who want to renounce vows and break off generational curses from themselves or their families.[4] Perhaps some individual lodges abstain from certain rituals and focus more on brotherhood, but that would be rare. I wish to offend no one here, and I have met many good men who were Freemasons. But its dark roots are not worthy of some of these good men I have known.

As for Jackson, he not only was a Nashvillian, but president of the United States. His actions, which at one point I thought only affected my city, actually affected our whole nation. According to the Masonic Digital Archives that I researched, Jackson was Most Worshipful Grand Master of the Grand Lodge in Tennessee from 1822–1824.[5]

Interestingly enough, when I researched the military uniform that I saw the principality general wearing in my foyer that day, it matched the time period when Nashville was founded. He has been here from the beginning, probably welcomed in by our founding government leaders' racial genocide and involvement with Freemasonry. These leaders had national influence.

Prayerfully examine your city and see if you recognize any of the spiritual manifestations of the deaf and dumb spirit, which I mentioned previously. If such symptoms plague your city, speak out, as I have. If you are experiencing the physical or emotional manifestations of it, stand up and take back your life. Even while seeking medical attention, try to look at your symptoms as having a spiritual root and pray accordingly. That turns it from an illness into an assignment. We will pray such a prayer together at the end of this chapter.

Many have taught on hearing the voice of God, but I have come face-to-face with the deaf and dumb principality and fought this hearing war with my very life. But even in the war I entered after seeing him that day in 1993, we still saw the miracle of two more babies, Jude in 1995 and Jenesis in 2000. Genesis 41:52 (NASB) says, "God has made me fruitful in the land of my affliction," and boy did He. Those six children were and are plunder in my arms upon exiting a multidecade war, and I am thankful we did not prevent them from coming due to fear.

But I once tallied up an average of all the unconscious minutes I have spent in my life between 35 years of petit mal seizures and 13 years of grand mals. It totaled almost 20 days of my life, unlived. What person would not want those back at the end of his or her life? This spirit has stolen much from me, but I have asked God to redeem those days and refund them back to me (with interest), in whatever way He sees fit.

I humbly submit to you that through this prayer and awareness, we have an opportunity here to unseat the deaf and dumb spirit worldwide.

So here is my elevator speech for you: This deaf and dumb influence has stolen much from God's people, but that is all about to change with your help. The timely publication of this book coincides with this principality's revealed decline, and I believe your prayers are all that is needed to send him back to the gates of hell with his tail between his legs, just as a territorial spirit was overcome in Daniel's day through prayer. I *humbly* submit to you that through this prayer and awareness, we have an opportunity here to unseat the deaf and dumb spirit worldwide. As was prophesied over me, "When he falls, many under him will fall and widespread healing will be released." Yes, I believe that even medical cures for physical infirmities I have mentioned here will soon follow. And spiritually, a hearing revival will follow. People will come to Jesus in record numbers. With tongues loosed and ears opened, people will prophesy, evangelize, worship, pray and praise God like never before. And your increased hearing will increase your faith, too, because Romans 10:17 says, "So then faith comes by hearing, and hearing by the word of God." Nothing will be impossible for you. Imagine it with me!

> Hear, you deaf
> and look, you blind, that you may see.
> Isaiah 42:18

WARprayer

Sign me up, I'm joining the ranks
In a war that is fought on the knees
And there I'll stay despite honor or thanks
'Til there is no more death or disease

Because I believe He has carried our griefs
Plus our sorrow, sickness and sin
And because up in Heaven there are no such thieves
Healing must be for us left herein

What if THIS day each knee hit its mark, made its plea
Would the whole of earth's voice death restrict?
In the peace we cry for, hands would cease from their
    war
And instead lay themselves on the sick

Enlisted or drafted, you're in, do not shrink!
Let petitions be plenty, not rare
In your eyes, as you rise, see yourself as the link
'Cause, my friend, we won't win 'cept through prayer

Let distractions lay halt at your feet
'Til today's underway, prayers complete . . .

© Laura Harris Smith, December 1999

PRAYER

Let's pray out loud together, starting with the words from Isaiah 50:4–5 (KJV):

The Lord GOD hath given me the tongue of the learned, that I should know how to speak a word in season to him that is weary: he wakeneth morning by morning, he wakeneth mine ear to hear as the learned.

The Lord GOD hath opened mine ear, and I was not rebellious, neither turned away back.

God, I receive that promise right now, that You will give me a new tongue and awaken my ears. Lord, please expose any influence of the deaf and dumb spirit in my life, my church, my school, my workplace, my community and my city, and let me use my new tongue and open ears to hear and speak Your thoughts to others about how they can find freedom from it physically, emotionally and spiritually. We declare over the deaf and dumb spirit—whether it be an individual war I am facing or a territorial one with it as a principality—that he is fully unseated from the heavens over my city and my country, and that there is no one else enthroned here except the Lord Jesus Himself. Remind me to pray daily about this until we see Your will done on earth as it is in heaven. In Jesus' name, Amen.

IMPARTATION

Right now, I release and impart to you hearing ears and a bold tongue. You will use them to speak to your friends about Christ, pray out loud with confidence, prophesy with clarity, praise God out loud during trials and worship Him freely in your home and at your church during your corporate worship services. I also speak healing over your body from any physical manifestation of the deaf and dumb spirit, and healing over you emotionally and in your relationship communications. "He who has an ear to hear, let him hear!" (Now open your hands, shut your eyes and receive it.)

10

Discernment of Spirits

My husband and I have a perpetual war over the thermostat in our home. His job is to set the thermostat responsibly, at a temperature that will result in financial peace at the end of the month. My job is to tell him that, yes, the children and I already have on socks and coats but are still freezing, and we need the heat turned up. He sets the necessary standard, and I tell him how that is working out for the masses.

I believe this is the perfect picture of what the pastor-prophet relationship should look like in every local church. The pastor sets the thermostat and asks the church to rise to it, whether it be a standard or a teaching emphasis or a churchwide budgetary need. The prophet is gifted to sense how the Body is responding (because of praying for them always), and then communicates to the pastor what the temperature of the house feels like. But where prophetic types often miss it is in regarding their discernment as higher than the pastoral standard, so they find fault with the pastor and start trying to change the thermostat themselves. It is often done out of concern and love, but if prophets really love their people, they will pass out coats and socks, if need be, until the pastor catches a cold and finally sees everyone shivering.

With that said, I believe the Old Testament prophets did have control of the thermostat—setting standards for whole nations, in fact. But the Old Testament office of prophet is different from the New Testament gift of prophecy today, and even different from today's office of prophet. Perhaps prophecy is a mystery to you. Perhaps you dream and see visions, but until you picked up this book, you had never thought of yourself as a seer, much less knew what that had to do with prophecy. Let's do a crash course and take care of that. Let's take prophecy from mystical to practical for a second and think of it as a pie. Take a look at its eight pieces with me, all of which fit together seamlessly and timelessly.

Prophecy's Eight Pieces

1. Scriptural Prophecy

The biblical canonization of Old and New Testament prophecies, both of which are infallible. Look at 2 Peter 1:20–21: "And so we have the prophetic word confirmed . . . knowing this first, that no prophecy of Scripture is of any private interpretation, for prophecy never came by the will of man, but holy men of God spoke as they were moved by the Holy Spirit."

2. Messianic Prophecy

Prophecies that foretold the coming of Christ. For example, Micah 5:2:

> But you, Bethlehem Ephrathah,
> Though you are little among the thousands of Judah,
> Yet out of you shall come forth to Me
> The One to be Ruler in Israel,

Whose goings forth are from of old,
From everlasting.

3. The Gift of Prophecy

An ongoing ability to speak on God's behalf. Paul tells us in 1 Corinthians 14:1 (ESV) to desire this gift especially out of all the other gifts when he says "earnestly desire the spiritual gifts, especially that you may prophesy." This gift can be for men or women. In Acts 21:9 (KJV) we hear about Philip's "four daughters, virgins, which did prophesy." Also, Paul told the women at Corinth what to wear when they prophesied (see 1 Corinthians 11:5). He also said, "Therefore, my brothers and sisters, be eager to prophesy" (1 Corinthians 14:39 NIV).

4. The Spirit of Prophecy

A temporary anointing for those who do not have the gift of prophecy, so that they speak under God's inspiration. First Samuel 10:10–11 gives an example:

> Then the Spirit of God came upon [Saul], and he prophesied among them. And it happened, when all who knew him formerly saw that he indeed prophesied among the prophets, that the people said to one another, "What is this that has come upon the son of Kish? Is Saul also among the prophets?"

Balaam's donkey in Numbers 22:28–30 is another example.

5. The Office of Prophet

Paul states plainly that prophets are still alive and well in the Body of Christ: "And God has placed in the church first of all apostles, second prophets . . ." (1 Corinthians 12:28 NIV). In Ephesians 4:11 Paul says, "And He Himself [Jesus] gave some to be apostles, some prophets, some evangelists, and some pastors and teachers." Also, in Acts 21:10 (KJV) he mentions "a certain prophet, named Agabus."

6. Encouragement Prophecy

First Corinthians 14:3 indicates that prophecy is for "edification and exhortation and comfort." Encouragement prophecy beautifully "builds up, lifts up or cheers up," even if the exhortation involves a challenge or admonishment.

7. Eschatological Prophecy

Prophecy about the end times, the Rapture, Tribulation, Millennial Reign and the like. Jesus said in Mark 13:7–8 (NIV),

> When you hear of wars and rumors of wars, do not be alarmed. Such things must happen, but the end is still to come. Nation will rise against nation, and kingdom against kingdom. There will be earthquakes in various places, and famines. These are the beginning of birth pains.

8. Prophetic Song

Any of the above, manifested in song. Exodus 15:20–21 (NIV) says, "Then Miriam the prophet, Aaron's sister, took a timbrel in her hand, and all the women followed her, with timbrels and dancing. Miriam sang to them." And Elisha said in 2 Kings 3:15, "But now bring me a musician. Then it happened, when the musician played, that the hand of the LORD came upon him."

Spirit Gifts to Aid the Seer

I want you to think of this chapter as your roots. Everyone in prophetic ministry wants wings, and hopefully the first nine chapters gave you that, but I exhort you never to fly without first knowing where you will land. Every seer needs the landing pad of a local church, and we will discuss that vital need for connection here. Seers—and all of us—must also be fueled by the fullness of the Holy Spirit, so we will also discuss Spirit baptism here, as well as all the gifts of the Spirit. One of those gifts is discernment of spirits. With that gift operational, you will be fully equipped to discern not only the presence of angels and the Holy Spirit, but of unclean spirits, too, something that will be very useful as you see and interpret. This discernment gift also will keep you from receiving counterfeits for your prophetic gift. We will read two testimonies involving that, one of a former psychic and one of a former lucid dreamer, now both Spirit-filled prophetic vessels.

Let's look right now at spiritual gifts to aid the seer. "Now concerning spiritual gifts, brethren," Paul said, "I do not want you to be unaware" (1 Corinthians 12:1 NASB).

I remember that when I was in a more conservative church, I learned about the spiritual gifts in 1 Peter 4:9–12 (NASB): "As each one has received a special gift, employ it." Included in this passage's list were hospitality, speaking and serving.

And then when I began attending a non-denominational Bible study, I heard about more spiritual gifts in Romans 12: "And we have different gifts according to the grace given to us" (verse 6 NET). This passage then lists prophecy, serving, teaching, exhortation, contributing, leadership and mercy.

Then, when I joined a Spirit-filled church, I heard about even more spiritual gifts in 1 Corinthians 12:4: "There are diversities of gifts, but the same Spirit." The list here includes word of wisdom, word of knowledge, faith, gifts of healing, the working of miracles, prophecy, discernment of spirits, speaking in tongues and interpreting tongues. Also, a few verses later, 1 Corinthians 12:28 lists many of these again, but adds to them helping and administration.

As if those were not enough gifts, when I was ordained I learned about the "office gifts" from Ephesians 4:4–16: apostles, prophets, evangelists, pastors and teachers.

What a giving God we serve! That is more than twenty gifts, and I have never met a Christian who did not have a creative, multiple mix of them. I have arranged all the gifts into five gift groups that I think will tell you a little bit about yourself. And when all the groups are combined, they, and we, all represent God's mind, voice, hands, heart and arms in the earth.

- *Discernment Gifts:* word of knowledge, word of wisdom, distinguishing of spirits (God's mind).
- *Communication Gifts:* prophecy, exhortation, teaching, speaking, evangelism, tongues, interpretation of tongues (God's voice).
- *Sign Gifts:* workings of miracles, gifts of healings (God's hands).
- *Influencer Gifts:* faith, contributing, helping, administration, serving, mercy (God's heart).
- *Rallying Gifts:* pastoring, teaching, apostleship, prophecy, evangelism (God's arms).

For seers, you will need to pay close attention to the communication gifts. Remember, dreams and visions are not a gift of the Spirit; they are mere communication with God. Thus, the communication gifts in Scripture will help you with them. Add to it the influencer gift of faith, and you will make great impact. You will employ these communication gifts when God gives you a dream for someone (prophecy, exhortation, teaching), or perhaps when you communicate a vision or word to a crowd (speaking, evangelism) or when you are praying with something you have seen (tongues, interpretation of tongues). And do not forget your supernaturally natural five senses that we discussed in chapter 1.

> Speaking in tongues is just the prayer gift.

Even though Paul told the church at Corinth that tongues were a sign to unbelievers, I included them in the communication gifts category because at the end of the day, speaking in tongues is just the prayer gift. All intercessors need it in their arsenal as they try to communicate with God using their limited human minds.

"For God's gifts and His call can never be withdrawn" (Romans 11:29 NLT).

Seeing Angels and Demons

I never tire of stopping midconversation and telling someone when I have seen an angel near them. If the timing is appropriate, it serves as a blessing to them to know they are protected and safe. I always remind them of Psalm 34:7, "The angel of the LORD encamps all around those who fear Him, and delivers them."

I started seeing angels after I was baptized in the Holy Spirit in 1993. I did not ask to see angels, but the Lord knew I needed to. With my ailing health and the constant threat of seizures, the enemy started tormenting me that I was going to die, maybe by drowning in the bathtub or while walking down our long staircase. He also whispered that I would be holding the baby, therefore killing her, too. Suddenly, I started seeing these bright bursts of light in these exact places. It looked like those old cube camera flashes we had back in the '70s, only brighter. I did not connect it all until I was listening to a sermon tape given to me by a friend. In it, a visiting minister described what happened when he saw angels. He said, "You may see a small, intense burst of light. . . ."

Right then I looked up, and there one was. On the staircase. The only other place I had seen it was over my bathtub, so I knew immediately that God had opened my eyes to my protection. After that, I did have a convulsion once in the tub, but it was just as I was stepping out, so when I fell, it was into our glass shower beside it. It was as if someone had pushed me to safety, and I did not have a scratch on me, even though all the glass had to be replaced. Five seconds earlier and I would have drowned. I can only imagine the invisible battle going on over my head, but my guardian angel won.

Once again, I thought of the story from 2 Kings 6:8–17 when Elisha and his servant, Gehazi, were surrounded on all sides by the Syrian army. Elisha was unafraid, but Gehazi, who was younger in the faith, was terror-stricken. Elisha did not need to see the spiritual armies of angels, horses and chariots of fire to know they were there, and I would not either now, but once upon a time I was Gehazi and did need to see them. God was merciful, and the only thing that wound up dying was my fear.

And in 2000, while I was alone in a hotel room in Boston during a leader's meeting for the USSPN I attended with Cindy Jacobs, the archangel Michael visited me as I was crying uncontrollably. Again, it was about my promised healing. God was my only hope and I made sure He did not forget it, and this night, I was spent. I can describe the archangel to you with great detail: so very handsome, strong with broad shoulders, dark hair with dark, intense eyes. He said nothing, but I suddenly "knew" his name. He was Michael, the archangel, sent by God to fortify my faith the way he was sent by God to fortify Daniel's.

There was no spoken conversation, but the message was loud and clear. God was confirming that this health struggle was more than a personal need for healing and that I was warring against something bigger. Michael does not show up if you have stubbed your toe. Archangels show up when the battle is territorial.

> Never engage in angel worship. This is disgusting to angels, as they themselves only worship God.

Please let me end with a warning: If spirits or angels come bearing names other than angels already named or described in Scripture, or if you are asked to call upon angels with thematic names that draw attention to themselves and not to Christ's mission, do not receive them or the people who promote them. I have seen people get caught up in angelic counterfeits (2 Corinthians 11:14 says that Satan sometimes comes as an angel of light), and then their falls were imminent. And never engage in angel worship. This is disgusting to angels, as they themselves only worship God. Do not pray to them, either, for Psalm 103:20 (NASB, emphasis added) reveals that they only obey God's commands, not yours: "Bless the LORD, you His angels, mighty in strength, who perform *His* word, obeying the voice of *His* word!" It does no good for you to "commission angels," because they only heed God's commissioning. Focus on God. Ask Him to round up the angels, and He will.

The Psychic Realm: An Interview

Whether it involves angels or demons, the world is infatuated right now with the paranormal. Television programming is full of mediums, psychics, ghost hunters, house exorcists and more. People crave spiritual connection to a higher power, but without grounding in God's Word and without the discernment of spirits gift, they will wind up communicating with a diabolical lower power. They will not recognize counterfeits when they come. Psychics are counterfeits of prophets. They get their information from Satan, whereas prophets get their information from God.

You have seen the shows where psychics speak to the dead and tell people with great accuracy what their grandmother is saying to them from the "other side." What they do not do is clarify which "other side" they are on. These psychics are not communicating with the actual dead, but with very old demonic spirits who, through observation, can relay information about anyone from the past, godly or ungodly. But do not be fooled. When a psychic dies, there will be thousands of spirits fighting over his or her soul, to drag that person into a very dark eternity, whereas when a prophet dies, there will be one Spirit—the Holy Spirit—ushering him or her into eternity with God.

Charles, a former psychic who is now a Christian filled with the Holy Spirit, believes that the enemy recognized his prophetic gift before he did and sought to pervert it early on. While Charles was still in high school, two friends (both witches) gave him a book on casting spells, but what started out as love spells and life spells for wealth and happiness quickly turned from white magic to dark magic. He found himself in the dark world of blood rituals, witchcraft, channeling, Ouija boards, crystal balls, levitation and tarot card reading. But he discovered he did not need the tarot cards to read people's pasts and futures because somehow he just "knew" information about people. It was the enemy "borrowing" the prophetic gift Charles had and using it for evil. It would be another seventeen years before Charles figured that out. Years that instigated drug abuse, homosexuality, attempted suicide and separation from God.

When I asked Charles to give me an example of a successful spell he once cast, he paused and then looked away. When he looked back at me, his eyes were full of tears. "Maim and kill," he whispered. He described driving down the interstate one day and feeling rage over a co-worker's actions, so he called upon every evil power to "maim and kill." Days later, the co-worker had a massive heart attack. She did not die, but her dog did at the same time. In retrospect, the co-worker probably had someone praying for her and those prayers sustained her, but the spirit of death that he released would not stop until it had killed something, which in this case was her dog.

Another time he became angry at a man, allowed the hate to take over and cast a similar vengeance spell. Within days the man had a bad car wreck. Charles said that these successful spells were seducing because there was so much power, but that you were left feeling very empty afterward. He said sometimes he got scared because there was so much darkness, especially with the channeling, during which he said he would invite spirits in and just take a backseat and let them drive. He would remember nothing afterward. One time, he came to and had a friend up against a wall, trying to break his arm.

But just as Charles did not need tarot cards to read people's pasts and futures, he also quit relying on the spell books and just spoke what he was inspired to declare in the moment. He would speak out and put faith behind his words, not even necessarily knowing it was the devil. When he told me this, he quickly added, "But it doesn't matter if you even know; it's going out into the spiritual realm anyway."

Charles hopes this will be powerful revelation even for Christians, that their words are powerful in changing their own situations. Proverbs 18:21 says the power of life and death is in the tongue. "It's easier to speak death than life if you're broken and wounded because you believe it about yourself," Charles says, adding, "The energy behind it is easier to tap into." As for speaking death and curses over people, Charles did it for years, but now he speaks life. Describing the way God uses him to give others accurate prophetic words about their past and future brings tears to his eyes again as we speak. "It's always life changing for them and for me," he says. "I'm sure it's not perfect because we're not perfect, but God still uses it, and it gets all around the junk and muddiness in our brain and is still perfect for that person."

I then asked him to describe the difference between what it feels like to prophesy versus casting spells. He answered, "In both you feel a stirring and a moving, but the prophetic is way better." He described to me how fulfilling it is to speak to someone's heart and see it changed by God's love. He added, "Foreknowledge is sweet."

Charles shared about his eventual salvation in Florida and about a deliverance session that started at the church altar one night while he was merely worshiping and ended with it taking six men to hold him down during expulsion prayer. "Witchcraft is a very strong spirit, not stronger than the Holy Spirit, but very strong. It's control and rebellion. And pride. If it weren't for Jesus and the call on my life—and obviously somebody was praying for me before—and if God didn't rescue me, I'm sure I would be dead. You cannot stay in that much darkness and live."

Charles says he used to hate the Body of Christ, probably because of the intense rejection he faced from them, but now he loves them intensely. It is that love that fuels his prophetic ministry. Charles got to see his son come to the Lord two summers ago. At the time of our interview, he was on day eight of a forty-day fast. When I asked what God was doing in him

I then asked him to describe the difference between what it feels like to prophesy versus casting spells. He answered, "In both you feel a stirring and a moving, but the prophetic is way better."

during this fast, he said, "I love the beautiful Bride of Jesus even more now."

Just as Charles's witchcraft experiences began with friends giving him a book, he and I both hope you will recommend this book containing his testimony about the power of God to your friends and influence them to accept no counterfeits.

Lucid Dreaming: An Interview

Lucid dreaming—a dream in which you are aware you are dreaming—promotes the idea of controlling your own dreams, which I personally find a tediously boring concept in comparison to what I have experienced with God's dreams. Controlling my dreams means that my one limited mind holds the sum total of the plots available for a dream. With prophetic dreams, the Creator of my soul (not to mention of the universe) pulls from His creative playbook of endless images meant to prosper and protect my real life and then visits me with them. Afterward, I get to wake up and live them, not wake up and realize they are fake and fleeting. So once again, lucid dreaming is a counterfeit of prophetic dreams.

Michael is a young man whose story is similar to that of Charles' in that a friend influenced him to try lucid dreaming and gave him material to get him started. In lucid dreaming, you lie down and relax, using stereo headphones to listen to audio tracks that emit a series of pulses, tones and voices. Anywhere up to 90 minutes later, you will have successfully entered a dream state in which you "wake up" in a dream and have total control over what you dream. A narrator walks you through a process that quickens all of your senses, and as you engage in lucid dreaming, your body falls asleep, but your brain does not. Michael says, "It's as if you are completely asleep but 100 percent completely awake. It dumps you immediately into REM dream sleep, and I could feel the transition when I began lucid dreaming. I was physically asleep and trapped inside my own body. I could even hear myself snoring with 100 percent consciousness."

The downside of lucid dreaming is that it feels as though you are living the dream in real time. Time appears to pass like real life. And like the popular dream movie *Inception*, which depicts layers of dreaming, Michael said that once he was stabbed in a dream, he felt the knife stabbing him and he woke up in another dream that was three years later, only to wake up again and still be in yet another dream, so now he was three dreams deep. He says, "It was like waking up from a concussion or like you got out of prison after twenty years and the world had changed. A night felt like a month. I lived days in these dreams, and many of them weren't good."

But one night, Michael started the routine of tones, pulses and narrations and decided midway through that he was too tired, so he took off the headphones and went to sleep naturally. What happened next proved to him that he was playing with fire. He entered into a dream so hideous that in it, he was trying to kill himself to be freed from it. Finally, the "set" of the dream began to crumble in front of him (again, like *Inception*), and he fell into a black hole, waking up in his bed. But he was not alone. Standing at the foot of his bed was a dark silhouette. I asked him what he felt, and he said, "Terror. Utter, absolute horror as though you'd come face-to-face with a demon." He was done with lucid dreaming for good.

Michael described the draw of lucid dreaming. There was no end to what he could dream, he said, stating, "The concept was that I could do whatever I wanted." Unfortunately, a ten-year struggle with pornography had turned his dreams into a breeding ground for addiction. Interestingly enough, the Lord used a dream to deliver him of the pornography—a prophetic dream, not a lucid dream. He described having no control over it and not wanting to because it was so powerful. It involved a small girl (probably an angel) giving him some cleansing water to drink to rid his mouth of waste. He woke up gagging and spewing something tarlike and sticky from his mouth. Since that dream, he has not struggled with pornography again. "The urge has been gone entirely. The uncontrollable urge is gone. And the stain is still on my carpet to remind me."

We are highly impressionable while we sleep. This is because God created sleep so that we can be still and vulnerable toward Him. You will remember that we discussed brain waves in chapter 4. We learned that beta and alpha waves occur while awake, beta waves appearing during your normal daily stimuli (talking, listening, processing information), and alpha waves being present during times of relaxation and peacefulness, such as when in prayer.

> The enemy craves our creativity, for we are never more like our Creator than when we are being creative.

But we also learned that in stage 1 (N1) sleep, the brain enters theta waves, which is a state called hypnogagia. If that word looks like hypnosis to you, it is because of its close relation. Lucid dream narrations basically hypnotize you and put you in a trancelike state. Theta waves are the state of consciousness that enhances creativity. People often recount seeing the color blue when in this transitional state, which is where the phrase "it came to me out of the blue" originates. Hypnotists prey upon this vulnerable state, and it is no wonder. The enemy craves our creativity, for we are never more like our Creator than when we are being creative.

Michael's deliverance dream came after he took two very important steps. First, he began attending a Spirit-filled church that taught on healing and deliverance, and second, he asked God for Holy Spirit baptism. Seeing as how those are both key elements for victorious living—not to mention for life as a discerning seer—I would like to devote the closing pages of this book to their importance.

The Holy Spirit Baptism

Doesn't every believer have the Holy Spirit? Before I was baptized in the Holy Spirit, I would get so offended at the notion that I did not have all of the Holy Spirit I needed. Even when writing this book, each time I used the terms *Spirit-filled* or *Holy Spirit baptism*, I could hear the skeptics in my head. You need not worry that I think I have a monopoly on the Holy Spirit over you or anyone, but I would like to walk you through the Scriptures that convinced me there was more of Him to be had. Why wouldn't that be good news?

First, who is the Holy Spirit? He is eternal (Hebrews 9:14), omnipresent (Psalm 139:7) and omniscient (John 14:26). Second, what does He do? He enkindled the writing of Scripture (2 Peter 1:21), helped create the world (Genesis 1:2), convicts of sin (John 16:8), makes us new (John 3:5–6), seals all believers (Ephesians 1:13–14) and makes His home in our hearts (1 Corinthians 3:16–17).

Third (and most important), *how* does He come? If we study the three Greek words Scripture uses to describe His activity, we can see three ways that the Holy Spirit manifests. These three little words changed my life. The first word is *para*, which means "with" and describes the Spirit drawing a person. John 14:17 (NIV, emphasis added) says, "But you know Him, for He lives *with* you and will be in you." The second word is *en*, which means "in" and shows that the Spirit lives inside a believer. John 14:20 (NIV, emphasis added) says, "On that day you will realize that I am *in* my Father, and you are *in* me, and I am *in* you." But the third word, *epi*, means "upon" and signifies the Spirit "coming upon" the believer with power. Acts 1:8 (NLT, emphasis added) says, "But you will receive power when the Holy Spirit comes *upon* you."

For 10 years I lived with the Holy Spirit *para* (with) me, drawing me until I was saved at the age of 10. Then for 17 years I lived with Him *en* me (still do, and so do you if you are saved). But at 27, I first experienced the *epi*, which was when the Holy Spirit came upon me and I spoke in a heavenly language. The *epi* is not a one-time experience. It certainly was not one time for Peter and John (as shown in the book of Acts), and it was not one time for me, either.

Other spirits—evil spirits—can try to *epi*, or come upon you, too. Just look at this word you have seen dozens of times: *epi-lepsy*. Make more sense now? You have heard of Christians falling under the power of the Holy Spirit, and perhaps you have been skeptical, but I have both fallen down with an evil spirit's *epi* and with the Holy Spirit's *epi*, and I tell you, they are both real. As I said in chapter 9, I do not believe a Christian can be possessed of a demon because a demon cannot dwell in someone the Holy Spirit already occupies. But the *epi* factor explains why a person can be a Christian and still be "under" attack. Remember, *epi* means "to come upon."

But what really convinced me that there was more of the Holy Spirit to be had were Jesus' own words to His disciples. In John 20:22 (NIV), after His resurrection, we hear, "And with that he breathed on them and said, 'Receive the Holy Spirit.'" So they had the Holy Spirit, right? But then, He later tells them there is more Holy Spirit coming. In Luke 24:49 (NIV), as He is leaving the earth, He says, "I am going to send you what my Father has promised; but stay in the city until you have been clothed with power from on high." He added in Acts 1:8, "But you shall receive power when the Holy Spirit has come *upon* you; and you shall be witnesses to Me in Jerusalem, and in all Judea and Samaria, and to the end of the earth" (emphasis added). If the disciples did not resist receiving more of the Holy Spirit, then neither should we.

This clearly shows there is a difference between receiving the Holy Spirit and being baptized in the Holy Spirit. Between His coming *in* and His coming *upon*. Didn't John prophesy it at Jesus' baptism in Matthew 3:11? "I indeed baptize you with water unto repentance, but He who is coming after me is mightier than I, whose sandals I am not worthy to carry. He will *baptize you with the Holy Spirit* and fire" (emphasis added).

We also see where others received this baptism of the Holy Spirit in Scripture:

- Acts 2:1–13, with the disciples. "All of them were filled with the Holy Spirit and began to speak in other tongues" (verse 4 NIV).

- Acts 8:12–19, with the Samaritans. "[They] prayed for them that they might receive the Holy Spirit" (verse 15).

- Acts 9:17, with Paul. "Brother Saul, the Lord—Jesus, who appeared to you on the road as you were coming here—has sent me so that you may see again and be filled with the Holy Spirit" (NIV).

- Acts 10:45–46, with Cornelius. "The gift of the Holy Spirit had been poured out even on the Gentiles. For they heard them speaking in tongues and praising God" (NIV).

- Acts 19:6, with the Ephesians. "When Paul placed his hands on them, the Holy Spirit came on them, and they spoke in tongues and prophesied" (NIV).

I remember when I was still apprehensive about the baptism of the Holy Spirit because I was afraid that praying in tongues would open a door to the demonic. How silly! But my logical husband looked at me one day and said, "Laura, have you asked God for this gift in 1 Corinthians 14?" I answered yes. He said to me, "Well, then, if you asked your heavenly Father for bread, He would not give you a fish. If you asked Him for a fish, He would not give you a serpent." Jesus spoke these words in Matthew 7:9–11. Luke 11:13 (NIV) records them, too, and ends with this: "If you then, though you are evil, know how to give good gifts to your children, how much more will your Father in heaven give the Holy Spirit to those who ask him!" Did you catch that? It says "give the Holy Spirit to those who ask him!" We are to *ask* for the Holy Spirit. I am going to ask for anything and everything that Jesus says I can ask Him for. Will you ask for more of the Holy Spirit? *Para, en* and *epi*?

I can say sincerely that the baptism of the Holy Spirit changed me, and I was already head over heels in love with Jesus for seventeen years beforehand. But ask anyone who knew me before and after. I can also definitely testify that I really began my prophetic dreaming once the Holy Spirit came upon me in this way. There is a whole other book I could write on that, but it is not our topic at hand.

Please promise me, my seer friend, that you will get into a church that will teach you about these things. Seers are notorious for becoming disenfranchised due to rejection and offense, so let's take some time now to discuss the importance of congregational connection.

Eye-Yai-Yai

If you do a topical study on dreams and visions, your research will show you that one-third of the Bible is about dreams and visions or the result of a dream or vision. One third! Churches that steer clear of the topic are, in this author's opinion, existing on only two-thirds of a scriptural diet and in danger of Revelation 22's warning about "taking away" from Scripture.

But let's be honest. Plenty of so-called seers also add to and take away from God's Word with their so-called discernments, which is treacherous, too. It is no wonder pastors avoid visionary gifts like the plague. It is messy ministry. The Word of God is black-and-white, absolute and unable to be argued with (argued about, but not with). Visions and dreams, on the other hand, are unpredictable, often symbolic, require interpretation and with just a little bit of wounded fleshiness, can easily become a train wreck. I have lived through it. Do not forget, my husband and I also pastor a church.

> One-third of the Bible is about dreams and visions or the result of a dream or vision. One third!

But pretending that seers do not exist is not the answer. My husband and I made a decision when we started Eastgate Creative Christian Fellowship not to restrict the flow of God by excluding the seer gifts. In fact, we trained our congregants to expect them—but not before setting some hard-and-fast house rules. We held a weekend conference called "Prophetic Etiquette," at which we discussed the biblical dos and don'ts of prophetic ministry. We plainly stated the specifics of how all things would be "done decently and in order" (1 Corinthians 14:40).

Our methods worked so well at Eastgate that we are even able to have a fifteen-minute "open mic" time during each Sunday morning service, where people form a short line just as our thirty-minute worship time is coming to a close and briefly share any visions they have had while worshiping or any relevant, recent dreams. They can also release prophetic words or Scriptures they have heard while in worship. But the trick is that Chris and I act as a double-filtering process that first weeds out all the dross.

Here is how that works. First, as worship is ending but the band is still playing, Chris prays aloud, asking the Holy Spirit to speak to each person there. He then instructs the audience to wait upon the Lord and listen, sharing only that which would edify the Body. He instructs them to come to me on the front row and share privately what they have heard or seen. This is where it gets fun. Oh, how I love my job!

In this sweet atmosphere where music marries ministry and births boldness, people step out in faith to see if they can make a difference in someone's life (and when they do, it makes it easier to do out on the streets, too). They trust me to listen and discern if their word is for the whole Church or just for them, if it is too vague or too long, and so on. Like Goldilocks deciding if the porridge is "too hot, too cold or just right." As a shepherdess, if I do not think something will edify my sheep, I ask the person to pray more first. People are never offended by the assignment.

We stick by the three rules that Paul outlines for corporate prophecy in 1 Corinthians 14:3: "But he who prophesies speaks edification and exhortation and comfort to men." So we say that the message must do one of those three: "build up, lift up or cheer up." If it does, I send the people on up to Chris, who stands by their side in case they deviate and go off on a tangent (which has never happened). They know this is not the place for doomsday judgment, but he stays front and center with them because, of course, his obligation is to protect his sheep, even from another sheep if need be. But the Spirit of God is too thick by that point for anyone to steward His presence irresponsibly.

It is so powerful to hear half a dozen unscripted revelations that all have the same theme. And it is even more powerful when my husband admits, "You all just preached my sermon!" That is proof that God has one voice. Chris and I would much rather God's words flow through His entire Body than just through us. If there is ever a lull and no one steps forward, we wait. The worship team plays softly and instrumentally, and we simply wait. People need to learn to wait on the Lord anyway. It is in those instances that the shy emerge, having gained their nerve and realized that the bold, whom they usually allow to speak for them, are not going to do so. These "waiting" times produce the cream of the crop, in my opinion. Congregants are also free to come to us anytime during the week with a dream or vision.

Eastgate's spiritual papa, Don Finto, visited one Sunday and said he wished he could bottle what we do during this prophetic-flow time and distribute it to other churches. But it is not ours to bottle. It is just the Word of God in motion.

Seers sometimes do not fit in to churches because no place has been created for them to fit in. Ask your pastors if they would be willing to implement this at your church. It is risky, but worth the investment to offer a little bit of training and reap the results. What is a Body with no eyes? We have auditory services where people sit and listen to speakers, but we have denied the Body vision from the seers. It takes trusting the Holy Spirit during your services, but now more than ever, the world needs this gift.

Why? Because we live in a post-verbal society. Moving images are everywhere, and we get our information from Internet images. As you watch the evening news now (if you still do), underneath the anchorperson is a moving feed of more headlines, and behind him or her are moving images or changing hues. Even billboards at stoplights change images three times now as we sit and wait, because we officially have the attention span of gnats. A picture is worth a thousand words. We leaders and pastors need to remember that and not shun the seers in this visual age.

What Say You?

Whether you are a seer or a shepherd of seers, I hope this book has beautified the way you view communication with God. Hopefully, you have learned that He is never silent, that you have four eyes and four ears and that you can expect to hear from God regularly through various categories of prophetic dreams. And if you were not convinced that sleep was the mattress of dreams, hopefully you will now make the necessary investments to get more rest. I will be praying that God helps you implement the dream recall strategies I have outlined so that you can remember all the dreams you will have as a result. Also, prepare yourself to become a humble vessel of dream interpretations for your friends.

And while you are awake, I believe God will open your eyes in the spirit realm to see visions and also to hear His voice with utmost clarity, drowning out all the other voices in your head. May you find breakthrough in any personal battles with spiritual deafness and feel the prompting of the Holy Spirit to join me in praying that the influences of the deaf and dumb spirit would no longer plague the Body of Christ.

> Prepare yourself to become a humble vessel of dream interpretations for your friends.

You are now equipped to see, interpret, hear, prophesy and resist all counterfeits. You also now have a serious decision to make in finding a church that will embrace your desire for this endowment and temper you as you grow in it. Or if you are a pastor, to turn your church into a house with 20/20 hearing by making room for the visionary gifts to be served at your family table each Sunday.

I've sung the line a hundred times, "twas blind but now
    I see"
But now I know it's more than placement on God's
    family tree

With opened eyes and ears I'll seek Him even though
    I'm flawed
I'll read His Word to test what's heard and see the voice
    of God.

© Laura Harris Smith, March 13, 2013

PRAYER

Let's pray out loud together:

God, I confess that Jesus Christ is the sole focus of my spiritual commitment, and I ask You now to baptize me in Your Holy Spirit. I desire the "epi" encounter where You come upon me with power, the way You did with so many others in Scripture and so many others still today. I want all of You there is to have, and I ask Your forgiveness for when I've settled for less. Sync my heart to beat with Yours, out of which will come 20/20 hearing and the seer anointing. In Jesus' name, Amen.

IMPARTATION

I release and impart to you the biblical baptism of God's Holy Spirit to make you holy, fine-tune your heart to His and open your eyes and ears to His irresistible voice. (Now open your hands, shut your eyes and receive it.)

Top 10 Frequently Asked Questions

I n my many years of teaching on dreams and visions, I have noticed that a handful of questions come up in people's minds repeatedly, regardless of their age, gender or denominational preference. What follows are the Top 10 questions. Maybe you are asking some of these yourself. Daydreaming about how wonderful it would be to sit with you face-to-face and answer these questions conversationally, I have designed a webpage where I communicate through video v-casts. The page makes use of a place you are probably visiting anyway, Facebook. Just find your question below and discover the answer by noting the video title beside the question. Then visit www.facebook.com/LauraHarrisSmithPage. Make sure to "Like" my page so that you will be notified every time new video Q&A's are posted. And feel free to post more Q's.

Do you have a dream symbol you need help with that is not mentioned in chapter 7's dream dictionary? Post the symbol on my Facebook page (not the whole dream, please) with your city, and I may include it in an upcoming video.

I would also enjoy hearing how *Seeing the Voice of God* has affected the way you communicate with God or how this book has influenced you. Let me know on Facebook, and also check out all the v-casts available at www.YouTube.com/LauraHarrisSmith.

"How do I know if a dream is from God or just worry?"
View *Was That Dream God or Worry?*

"What does God's voice sound like?"
View *Hearing God's Voice.*

"How did people in the Bible interpret dreams without the Scriptures?"
View *How Did Biblical Characters Interpret Dreams without the Bible?*

"How can I be sure that my dream interpretation is right?"
View *Interpreting Your Own Dream.*

"How do I share a dream with someone else?"
View *Sharing Your Dreams with Others.*

"How do I know if it's a vision or just daydreaming?"
View *Visions 101.*

"How can I increase my dreams?"
View *Increasing Your Dreams and Visions.*

"How do I get rid of nightmares?"
View *Nightmares and Night Terrors.*

"Do animals, babies and the blind dream?"
View *Do Animals Dream?*

"My church won't receive prophecy—what do I do?"
View *My Church and My Prophetic Gift.*

Notes

Chapter 1: Is God Ever Silent?

1. Dr. Tycho von Rosenvinge, "Solar Wind," NASA's GSFC Astrophysics Science Division, May 11, 2012, http://helios.gsfc.nasa.gov/sw.html.

2. "Deafness and Hearing Loss," World Health Organization, February 2013, http://www.who.int/mediacentre/factsheets/fs300/en/.

3. *New Oxford American Dictionary*, 3rd ed., s.v. "Perceive."

4. James W. Goll, *The Seer: The Prophetic Power of Visions, Dreams, and Open Heavens* (Shippensburg, Penn.: Destiny Image, 2004), 18.

5. Ibid., 22.

6. *New Oxford American Dictionary*, 3rd ed., s.v. "Sixth sense."

Chapter 4: Sleep: The Mattress of Dreams

1. "Facts and Stats," National Sleep Foundation, 2013, http://drowsydriving.org/about/facts-and-stats/.

2. Steven Bedard, Anna Fort, Elaine Gottlieb, Michael Laker, Cynthia A. McKeown, Christopher Riegle, and Arthur R. Smith (content producers), "Sleep, Performance, and Public Safety," Division of Sleep Medicine at Harvard Medical School, December 18, 2007, http://healthysleep.med.harvard.edu/healthy/matters/consequences/sleep-performance-and-public-safety.

3. Ibid.

4. Ibid.

5. *Nightline*, "Tired Skies: Pilot Fatigue and 'Crash Pads' Threaten the Safety of Airline Passengers," ABC News, February 9, 2011, http://abcnews.go.com/Blotter/pilot-fatigue-crash-pads-threaten-safety-airline-passengers/story?id=12874949&page=3.

6. *New Oxford American Dictionary*, 3rd ed., s.v. "Circadian."

Chapter 5: Dream Recall

1. "People and Discoveries," Public Broadcasting Service (PBS), 1998, http://www.pbs.org/wgbh/aso/databank/entries/dh00fr.html.

2. Sigmund Freud, *The Interpretation of Dreams*, 3rd ed., Psych Web, "Why Dreams Are Forgotten After Waking," http://www.psywww.com/books/interp/chap01d.htm.

3. William C. Dement, *Some Must Watch While Some Must Sleep* (New York: W. W. Norton, 1978), 37.

4. ION Archives, "Optimum Nutrition," Institute for Optimum Nutrition, Autumn 1986, http://www.ion.ac.uk/information/onarchives/goodsleep.

5. Lesley Stahl, "Science of Sleep, Part 1," CBS News, *60 Minutes*, June 15, 2008, http://www.cbsnews.com/video/watch/?id=4181992n.

6. National Institutes of Health, National Sleep Foundation, "Coping with Excessive Sleepiness," *Web*MD, June 16, 2012, http://www.webmd.com/sleep-disorders/excessive-sleepiness-10/sleep-101?page=2.

7. National Institute of Health, "Brain Basics: Understanding Sleep," NINDS, May 21, 2007, http://www.ninds.nih.gov/disorders/brain_basics/understanding_sleep.htm.

8. John Pinel, *Biopsychology* (Old Tappan, New Jersey: Allyn & Bacon, 2007). See also John Pinel, "Lecture 12a: The Physiological and Behavioral Correlates of Sleep and Dreaming," http://academic.uprm.edu/~ephoebus/id87.htm.

9. Kevin Daus, M.D., "Not Getting Enough Rem Sleep," Health Tap Health Network, 2013, https://www.healthtap.com/#topics/not-getting-enough-rem-sleep.

10. Lesley Stahl, "Science of Sleep, Part 1," CBS News, *60 Minutes*, June 15, 2008, http://www.cbsnews.com/video/watch/?id=4181992n.

11. National Institute of Health, "Brain Basics: Understanding Sleep," NINDS, May 21, 2007, http://www.ninds.nih.gov/disorders/brain_basics/understanding_sleep.htm.

12. M. Ebben, A. Lequerica, and A. Spielman, "Effects of pyridoxine on dreaming: a preliminary study," PubMed, February 2002, http://www.ncbi.nlm.nih.gov/pubmed/11883552.

13. Jane Thomson, H. Rankin, G. W. Ashcroft, Celia M. Yates, Judith K. McQueen, and S. W. Cummings, "Psychological Medicine," November 1982, http://journals.cambridge.org/action/displayAbstract?fromPage=online&aid=5211960.

14. Kendall Lee, M.D., Ph.D., "Mayo Clinic Researchers Measure Serotonin Levels Using a Novel Device Called WINCS," Mayo Clinic, February 4, 2011, http://www.mayoclinic.org/news2011-rst/6165.html.

15. Kristeen Cherney, "Should I Avoid Taking B Vitamins at Night?" Livestrong.com, June 21, 2011, http://www.livestrong.com/article/475502-should-i-avoid-taking-b-vitamins-at-night.

16. Mayo Clinic, "Vitamin B6 (pyridoxine)," Mayo Clinic, Sept. 1, 2012, http://www.mayoclinic.com/health/vitamin-b6/NS_patient-b6/DSECTION=evidence.

17. Institute of Medicine, Food and Nutrition Board, "Health Guide," *The New York Times*, March 14, 2013, http://health.nytimes.com/health/guides/nutrition/vitamins/overview.html.

18. Jacqui Donnelly, "The Toxicity of Water Soluble Vitamins," July 12, 2011, http://www.livestrong.com/article/490542-the-toxicity-of-water-soluble-vitamins/#ixzz2JticxR5q.

19. The RDA of vitamin B6 for men and women 19–50 years old is 1.3 mg. One bowl of Cheerios contains 25 percent of the RDA of B6 (or 0.325 mg). 0.325mg X 32 bowls = roughly 104 mg of vitamin B6.

20. J. Vormann, C. Feillet-Coudray, C. Coudray, J. C. Tressol, D. Pepin, A. Mazur, and S. A. Abrams, "Magnesium," Office of Dietary Supplements, 2003, http://ods.od.nih.gov/factsheets/Magnesium-HealthProfessional/.

21. Larry Armstrong, "What Is Chelated Magnesium and What Does Chelated Mean?", Livestrong.com, December 17, 2010, http://www.livestrong.com/article/336697-what-is-chelated-magnesium-and-what-does-chelated-mean/#ixzz2KG68rRuB.

22. ION Archives, "Optimum Nutrition," Institute for Optimum Nutrition, Autumn 1986, http://www.ion.ac.uk/information/onarchives/goodsleep.

23. Charlene Gamaldo, "Which Vitamins and Minerals Can Help Me Sleep Better?", Johns Hopkins Medicine, http://www.sharecare.com/question/vitamins-minerals-help-me-sleep-better.

24. ION Archives, "Optimum Nutrition," Institute for Optimum Nutrition, Autumn 1986, http://www.ion.ac.uk/information/onarchives/goodsleep.

25. Harvard School of Public Health, "Vitamin D and Health," 2013, http://www.hsph.harvard.edu/nutritionsource/vitamin-d/.

26. Lars Foleide, "Do Substances Like Drugs, Herbs and Foods Affect Our Dreams?", November 1, 2012, http://stason.org/TULARC/mind/dreaming/1-5-Do-substances-like-drugs-herbs-and-foods-affect-our-dr.html#.UapEiUDrylg.

27. Sage Kalmus, "Herbs for Rapid Eye Movement," Livestrong.com, July 21, 2011, http://www.livestrong.com/article/497678-herbs-for-rapid-eye-movement/.

28. Ibid.

29. Kathryn Meininger, "Herbal Supplements to Restore Memory Loss," Livestrong.com, May 13, 2011, http://www.livestrong.com/article/441266-herbal-supplements-to-restore-memory-loss/.

30. Valerie Ann Worwood, *The Complete Book of Essential Oils & Aromatherapy* (Novato: Calif.: New World Library, 1991), 179.

Chapter 6: Visions

1. The definitions in this section can all be found through the Blue Letter Bible website's "Biblical Language Tools: Search the Strong's Lexicon" feature, http://www.blueletterbible.org/search/lexiconc.cfm.

2. "Lexicon Results: Strong's G1611—*ekstasis*," Blue Letter Bible online, 1996–2013, http://www.blueletterbible.org/lang/lexicon/Lexicon.cfm?strongs=G1611.

3. "Lexicon Results: Strong's G3346—*metatithemi*," Blue Letter Bible online, 1996–2013, http://www.blueletterbible.org/lang/lexicon/Lexicon.cfm?strongs=G3346.

Chapter 7: Interpretations and Dream Dictionary

1. Additional translations not listed on the copyright page are Darby Translation (DARBY), Easy-to-Read Version (ERV), GOD'S WORD Translation (GW), Holman Christian Standard Bible (HCSB), International Standard Version (ISV) and Young's Literal Translation (YLT).

2. James Goll, "Journaling as a Tool of Retaining Revelation," Encounters Network, 2013, http://www.encountersnetwork.com/articles/Journaling_2-2013.html.

3. Ibid.

Chapter 9: Deaf and Dumb, but Not Blind!

1. The definitions in this section can be found through the Blue Letter Bible website's "Biblical Language Tools: Search the Strong's Lexicon" feature, http://www.blueletterbible.org/search/lexiconc.cfm.

2. *NOVA* Online, "Where Are the Ten Lost Tribes?", PBS, November 2000, http://www.pbs.org/wgbh/nova/israel/losttribes2.html.

3. Ken Symington, "Freemasonry Databank: Initiation to the First Degree up to the End of the Obligation," Christian Restoration, http://www.christian-restoration.com/fmasonry/first%20degree.htm.

4. Selwyn Stevens, "Freemasonry Curse Breaking Prayers," Jubilee Ministries, 2011, http://atver-acis.lv/files/Freemasonry-Curse-Breaking-Prayer.pdf.

5. Actual historic Masonic Digital Archives, http://cdm16287.contentdm.oclc.org/cdm/search/searchterm/1822.

About the Author

"It's a rare day I don't have a conversation with someone about communicating with God," says Laura Harris Smith, Chosen author and founding co-pastor of Eastgate Creative Christian Fellowship with husband, Chris. "My life and career as a communicator have taken many twists and turns, but no matter what arena I've found myself in—secular or spiritual—there has never been anyone who could resist such a conversation because everyone wants to know and be known."

Laura's television career began at the age of 3 in commercials, and by the age of 21 she found herself at Hollywood International Studios, facing a life-defining crossroad. Realizing a call on her life to train as well as entertain, Laura returned home to Nashville, Tennessee, and launched a Christian dinner theatre, which gave birth to her professional writing career. Plays led to books and books led to speaking and speaking led to an ordination in 2001, which amazingly not only opened more doors ministerially, but also brought her full circle, back into secular television by God's design. By 2006, she had become a television host on the Shop At Home TV Network. Eastgate, where her husband, Chris, is senior pastor, was being birthed simultaneously and is home to creative artisans of every kind, including those in the administrative arts (those left-brainers whose "administry" creatively keeps the innovations resourced and organized).

Having always had one foot in ministry and one in media, Laura is a published poet and the author of multiple books. She speaks and ministers across denominational lines and is known for bringing a lighthearted look at the heaviest of biblical topics. Married for thirty years, Chris and Laura have six children: Jessica, Julian, Jhason, Jeorgi, Jude and Jenesis, all homeschooled and all creative artisans. With half of their children now grown and married, Laura and Chris also have a growing list of grandchildren who now outnumber the kids.

To find out more about Laura and her ministry or materials, or to invite Laura to speak at your church or event, visit www.lauraharrissmith.com, www.facebook.com/lauraharrissmith page, www.eastgateccf.com or www.campsmith.net. You can also contact her for bookings at churches or events of any size by emailing booking@lauraharrissmith.com.